The

Watchmakers' Lathe

Its Use and Abuse

A Study of the Lathe in Its Various Forms, Past and
Present, Its Construction and Proper Uses.
For the Student and Apprentice.

BY WARD L. GOODRICH

Copyright © 2013 Read Books Ltd.
This book is copyright and may not be
reproduced or copied in any way without
the express permission of the publisher in writing

British Library Cataloguing-in-Publication Data
A catalogue record for this book is available from the
British Library

A History of Clocks and Watches

Horology (from the Latin, Horologium) is the science of measuring time. Clocks, watches, clockwork, sundials, clepsydras, timers, time recorders, marine chronometers and atomic clocks are all examples of instruments used to measure time. In current usage, horology refers mainly to the study of mechanical time-keeping devices, whilst chronometry more broadly included electronic devices that have largely supplanted mechanical clocks for accuracy and precision in time-keeping. Horology itself has an incredibly long history and there are many museums and several specialised libraries devoted to the subject. Perhaps the most famous is the *Royal Greenwich Observatory*, also the source of the Prime Meridian (longitude 0° 0' 0"), and the home of the first marine timekeepers accurate enough to determine longitude.

The word 'clock' is derived from the Celtic words *clagan* and *clocca* meaning 'bell'. A silent instrument missing such a mechanism has traditionally been known as a timepiece, although today the words have become interchangeable. The clock is one of the oldest human interventions, meeting the need to consistently measure intervals of time shorter than the natural units: the day, the lunar month and the year. The current sexagesimal system of time measurement dates to approximately 2000 BC in Sumer. The Ancient Egyptians divided the day into two twelve-hour periods and used large obelisks to track the movement of the sun. They also developed water clocks, which had also been employed frequently by the Ancient Greeks, who called them 'clepsydrae'. The Shang Dynasty is also believed to have used the outflow water clock around the same time.

The first mechanical clocks, employing the verge escapement mechanism (the mechanism that controls the rate of a clock by advancing the gear train at regular intervals or 'ticks') with a foliot or balance wheel timekeeper (a weighted wheel that rotates back and forth, being returned toward its centre position by a spiral), were invented in Europe at around the start of the fourteenth century. They became the standard timekeeping device until the pendulum clock was invented in 1656. This remained the most accurate timekeeper until the 1930s, when quartz oscillators (where the mechanical **resonance** of a vibrating crystal is used to create an electrical signal with a very precise **frequency**) were invented, followed by atomic clocks after World War Two. Although initially limited to laboratories, the development of microelectronics in the 1960s made **quartz clocks** both compact and cheap to produce, and by the 1980s they became the world's dominant timekeeping technology in both clocks and **wristwatches**.

The concept of the wristwatch goes back to the production of the very earliest watches in the sixteenth century. Elizabeth I of England received a wristwatch from Robert Dudley in 1571, described as an arm watch. From the beginning, they were almost exclusively worn by women, while men used pocket-watches up until the early twentieth century. This was not just a matter of fashion or prejudice; watches of the time were notoriously prone to fouling from exposure to the elements, and could only reliably be kept safe from harm if carried securely in the pocket. Wristwatches were first worn by military men towards the end of the nineteenth century, when the importance of synchronizing manoeuvres during war without potentially revealing the plan to the enemy through signalling was increasingly recognized. It was clear that using pocket watches while in the heat of battle or while mounted on a horse was impractical, so officers began to strap the watches to their wrist.

The company H. Williamson Ltd., based in Coventry, England, was one of the first to capitalize on this opportunity. During the company's 1916 AGM it was noted that '...the public is buying the practical things of life. Nobody can truthfully contend that the watch is a luxury. It is said that one soldier in every four wears a wristlet watch, and the other three mean to get one as soon as they can.' By the end of the War, almost all enlisted men wore a wristwatch, and after they were demobilized, the fashion soon caught on - the British *Horological Journal* wrote in 1917 that '...the wristlet watch was little used by the sterner sex before the war, but now is seen on the wrist of nearly every man in uniform and of many men in civilian attire.' Within a decade, sales of wristwatches had outstripped those of pocket watches.

Now that clocks and watches had become 'common objects' there was a massively increased demand on clockmakers for maintenance and repair. Julien Le Roy, a clockmaker of Versailles, invented a face that could be opened to view the inside clockwork – a development which many subsequent artisans copied. He also invented special repeating mechanisms to improve the precision of clocks and supervised over 3,500 watches. The more complicated the device however, the more often it needed repairing. Today, since almost all clocks are now factory-made, most modern clockmakers *only* repair clocks. They are frequently employed by jewellers, antique shops or places devoted strictly to repairing clocks and watches.

The clockmakers of the present must be able to read blueprints and instructions for numerous types of clocks and time pieces that vary from antique clocks to modern time pieces in order to fix and make clocks or watches. The trade requires fine motor coordination as clockmakers must frequently work on devices with small gears and fine machinery, as well as an appreciation for the original art form. As is evident from this very short history of clocks and watches, over the centuries the items themselves have changed – almost out of recognition, but the importance of time-keeping has not. It is an area which provides a constant source of fascination and scientific discovery, still very much evolving today. We hope the reader enjoys this book.

INTRODUCTION.

The American lathe and its attachments is a subject so vast that anything like a complete work upon it would be sufficient material for a book larger by far, perhaps, than any workman not thoroughly acquainted with the subject would deem possible. In point of accuracy, variety of work, and ease and convenience of manipulation, the American watchmakers' lathe, with its several attachments, stands supreme; any piece of work, however delicate and intricate, may be executed upon it by an accomplished workman. But let us recall the various stages through which the lathe has passed before arriving at its present state of perfection, in order that those of to-day may the better appreciate the accuracy and convenience of the modern watchmakers' lathe, which stands alone in design and construction of this class of machinery, as it is the only one which has been evolved from the brains of skilled engineers, familiar with all the demands of automatic machinery, and who, having the whole range of modern mechanical attainments at their fingers' ends have devised a simple and effective machine which the skill and ingenuity of the American mechanic have made possible for any watchmaker, even of limited means, to possess.

The present state of perfection in watches is dependent, to a very great extent, upon the accuracy of the tools producing them, the most important one being the lathe, in its various forms, not only because of the comparative ease and rapidity of performance, but also from the wide range of work and variety of operations which may be performed upon it. An American watchmakers' lathe, with a complete set of attachments, such as may be bought of the various manufacturers, is capable of producing a complete and perfect watch of the highest order, when manipulated by a skillful hand.

From an artistic point of view, many of the watches made by "the old masters" are most meritorious and worthy, when we consider the means at their command; but as time-keeepers they would to-day be pronounced complete failures, and while the work of these men, from a mechanical point, is all that could be expected of them at that time, yet their rude work, and still more rude tools, if applied to the fine watches of to-day, would be their death knell.

In some localities, even now, the natural born watchmaker who can tinker a watch or clock "so it will go" is looked upon as a mechanical prodigy. The day of those watches which kept time with the sun is past and gone, never more to return. The modern business man demands a timepiece approaching very closely to perfection, and such fine and delicate machines in turn require for their repair tools of the highest possible accuracy and a skillful hand, such as is only acquired by long and tedious practice. Some workmen seem to think that all that is necessary to do good work is to get a set of tools, however cheap, and consequently worthless. There are very few persons who have achieved success except by persistent labor and study of their chosen vocation.

In mechanics, as in all else, there is no such thing as perfection, and the highest that man can attain with his best efforts is to approach the ideal perfection as closely as possible.

While the modern American watchmakers' lathe and its attachments will produce accurate work with more ease and certainty than can be done by the tools generally prevalent in Europe, they cannot be used carelessly, but must be guided by a trained mind and skilled hand, and it is our desire to so explain these tools, their capabilities and the limitations to which they are subject, that the young man who enters the trade to-day may understand fully, what he may with justice require of his tools, and also what, in their turn, his tools will require of him, in order that they may receive that intelligent treatment, which is indispensable to their accuracy and length of life.

In order to understand fully the immense improvements to be found in common use to-day, let us glance at the origin and successive forms of this useful tool during the centuries it has been in use.

CHAPTER I.

A BRIEF HISTORY OF THE LATHE.

The lathe dates long before the Christian era, and in one of its forms, the potters' lathe, is mentioned in the Bible. A well-known authority has stated that what he called the "prehistoric lathe" is undoubtedly the earliest type, but we are inclined to believe that the true home of the lathe is Egypt, and that the lathe used in that country

Fig. 1. Prehistoric Lathe.

and some parts of the far east to-day is not very dissimilar to those used before the advent of the Christian era.

The so-called "prehistoric lathe" is illustrated very clearly in Fig. 1. It will be observed that the bearings consist of the forks of the two trees, and that the tool-rest consists of a sapling driven into the ground. The piece to be turned is revolved by means of a crank fastened to one end.

Fig. 2 illustrates what is known as the Egyptian lathe, and the form, modified slightly in various cases, is used extensively throughout Egypt and the Asiatic countries to-day. The lathe shown in the illustration seems capable of turning work within certain limits only, and is not adjustable; but the regular type is so made as to admit work of any length and any diameter. In the illustration it will be seen that the workman revolves the work by means of a bow with one hand, while with the other he holds the chisel

Fig. 2. Egyptian Lathe.

or cutting device, and his toes are used as a tool rest. In other varieties the turner drives two posts into the ground, the proper distance apart, to receive the work, and the slot, being deeper, and a number of holes being provided for the reception of the stay-pins, articles of various lengths and diameters may be readily substituted. In India the turner carries his apparatus from house to house or place to place, and when his services are required he drives his uprights into the ground and is instantly ready for business. As a rule he does not use a bow, but wraps a cord around the work, and the boy who usually accompanies him takes one end of the cord in his right hand and the other in his left, and, by alternately pulling on the rope with each hand, he gives the piece the desired motion.

It will be observed that in the prehistoric lathe a continuous motion could be given to the work, while in the

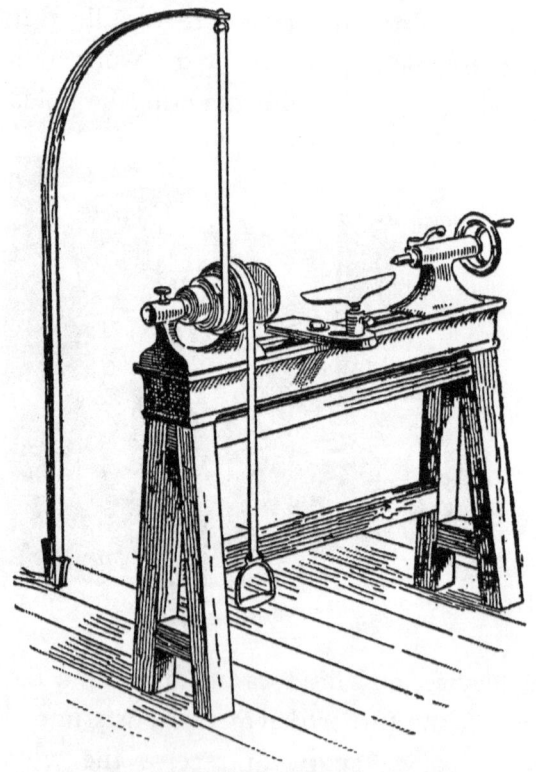

Fig. 3. Early English Lathe.

Egyptian pattern the motion is reciprocating or oscillating in its character.

Fig. 3 illustrates a later or more advanced type, with reciprocating motion. The pressure of the foot in the stirrup produces a forward motion of the head stock of the lathe, and when the pressure is released the spring of the bent wood causes the head to revolve in the opposite direction. Crude as this lathe may appear, it may still be found in use, or at least could a few years ago, in some places in England. A certain case-maker in England has still several such lathes on his premises. The proprietor being asked why he did not equip the lathes with steam-power, which he had in his shop, replied: "These good fellows would not then know how to use them; their grandfathers and fathers before them worked on this kind of lathe, and to try and change them would only result in loss to us."

The watchmaker's bow-lathe is exactly the same as the last two types mentioned, the only difference being in size. We are acquainted with several watchmakers, fine workmen, who still cling to the bow-lathe when they wish to do an exceptionally fine piece of work. They have, and understand pretty well, the use of the modern lathe, but such is the force of early education that they still believe that when accurate work is to be done the bow-lathe is the only thing to do it on.

It seems strange that, with all the boasted progress made in the nineteenth century, there should be still left among us people, and even nations, that, so far as modern tools and appliances are concerned, seem to still belong to the eighteenth and even the seventeenth centuries—people who, through prejudice or want of education, or something inexplicable, still prefer to use the turns or implements of a like nature rather than the modern American lathe for watchmakers, with its substantial base, its live spindle and its excellent slide-rest and adjuncts.

When we say this we do not wish to be construed as criticising the workmanship on the part of watchmakers of other nations, nor do we mean to say that the average American watchmaker is the superior or even the peer of the European. We have our full share of botches. We admire the workmanship of the European watchmaker, which, as a rule, is excellent, but we only regret that the men who have so much inherent genius should continue to employ methods so out of all keeping with their evident talents and skill.

The earliest form of lathe used by the watchmaking fraternity was undoubtedly what is known as the dead-

Fig. 4. Fiddle-Bow Lathe.

center. These lathes are known as "fiddle-bow lathes," because motion was imparted to them by means of a bow made of steel, wood, whalebone or other substances, and having a cord of catgut string, and they resembled the bow used by performers on the fiddle or violin.

Fig. 4 illustrates a watchmaker of the eighteenth century at work upon a lathe of this type. It is a portrait of A. L. Perelet, a noted French watchmaker, working at the bench at the advanced age of ninety-three years. In the dead-center lathe the object to be operated upon was held between two male or female centers which did not revolve, and were known as dead centers. While the dead-center type of lathe is not to be compared with the live spindle in point of utility, yet it possessed, no matter how poorly made, one vital point which many modern live spindle lathes do not possess—the element of truth; and unless the operator was a bungler, this point could never be eliminated. As stated above, this form of lathe still has its admirers

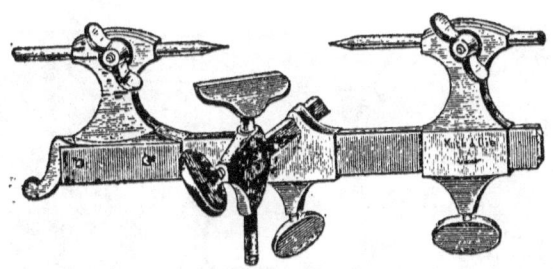

Fig. 5. Steel Turns.

among artisans who readily recognize the great capacity of the American lathe for the greater part of all watch repairing. With all its good points in regard to truth, the dead spindle lathe was relegated to the background in America when the live-spindle form made its appearance, for it was only possible to perform operations upon the surface of objects held in it; and again, the object had, under all conditions, to be first centered before the work began, and here half the true value of the lathe was lost owing to the great loss of time in this preliminary operation. It was impossible, except in a few cases, to work upon the inside of an article, and when the live spindle made its appearance the American watchmaker readily recognized its superiority in this regard.

The verge lathe, the turns, the Jacot tool, and the centering and drilling tool, are all examples of the dead-center lathe. Fig. 5 illustrates the steel turns as used by many English, French and German watchmakers to-day. The Jacot tool is illustrated in Fig. 6, and it, too, is extensively used in the above named countries. The earliest form of live-spindle lathe was known as the Swiss lathe. This lathe, although of the live-spindle type, had a solid and not a hollow spindle, and although an excellent tool in its day, it, too, had to succumb to the advancement of science in

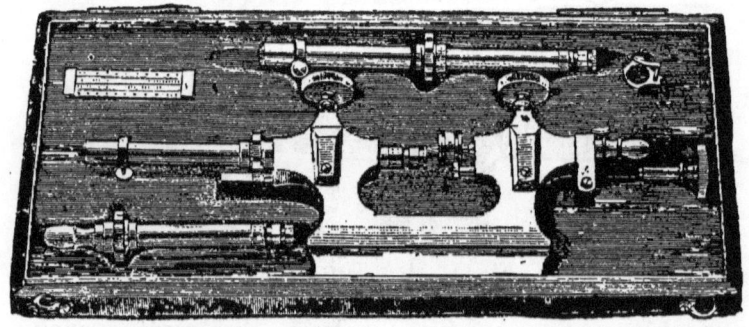

Fig. 6. The Jacot Lathe.

machine building. In one of the forms of this lathe it was so made that the front bearing for the arbor could be made to swing back on a joint, and the workman was thus enabled to take the arbor out with the least amount of trouble without removing the work which had been cemented upon the spindle, and substitute another spindle, if work upon the other had to be temporarily interrupted. It was, however, very weak and shaky, and under a heavy cut would be liable to tremble. The lathe had a clumsy T-rest which was held on the bar, that answered for a bed for the lathe in such a manner that the center of the T-rest could not be passed beyond the center of the lathe. The slide-rest which accompanied it was as much too small as the T-rest was too large, and it was absolutely valueless to the watchmaker.

Our remarks above were applied to the Swiss bench lathe and this type should not be confounded with the Swiss universal lathe, for in its day, and for the purpose intended, it was a very superior tool. It had a face plate which usually not only ran true, but presented a perfect plane at right angles to the arbor of the lathe. While the slide rest could not be compared to those used on modern American lathes of to-day, yet it was vastly superior to the ones that accom-

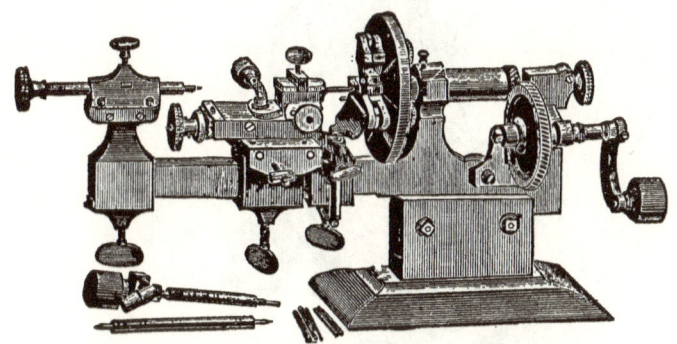

Fig. 7. Swiss Universal Lathe.

panied the Swiss bench lathe. ' Fig. 7 illustrates a form of Swiss universal lathe or mandrel which is still to be found on the English, French and German markets and which still retain the faults of the original lathes of nearly fifty years ago. It will be noted that while the universal head is strong and massive, the square bed on which all the resistance comes is weak and does not present surface enough to give a good, solid foundation to the slide rest.

Again the tool is limited in its application to watchmakers' work as the face plate is stationary on its arbor and cannot be removed and chucks substituted. Even when using it to face off work you cannot get at the work to the extreme edge, as the clamps prevent this. The watchmaker who buys such a machine has at his command a special tool which can only be used for a limited range of work. Again it is a hand tool and the right hand is constantly employed in turning the handle, leaving only the left hand to work with, and the modern watchmaker finds that very often two hands are not enough for some classes of work.

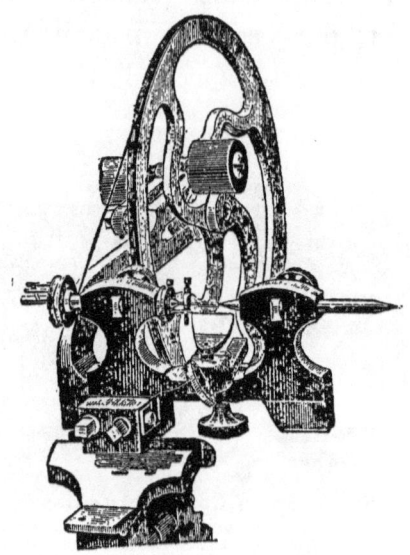

Fig. 8. The Dracip Lathe.

Next in order comes the Bottom lathe, which is doubtless still remembered by the older members of the craft. While this tool was considered a great improvement on the lathes on the market before it, being well made and substantial, yet it, too, faded from view, like snow before a summer sun, when the hollow spindle lathe put in its appearance.

As an example of the tools and methods that are out of date, let us call the attention of the reader to the Dracip lathe, which is a very popular tool among English watchmakers to-day and one which a modern English writer of horological literature extols in the highest terms. Fig. 8 illustrates this lathe ready for work. Like the turns, it is held in the vise, but, unlike it, motion is imparted to the work by means of a hand wheel and catgut cord. The right hand runner is precisely the same as used in the turns but the left hand one is pierced through its entire length to receive runners of less diameter. The inner spindle is a dead one and on its outer end runs a loose pulley from the face of which project two driving pins. This pulley is revolved by

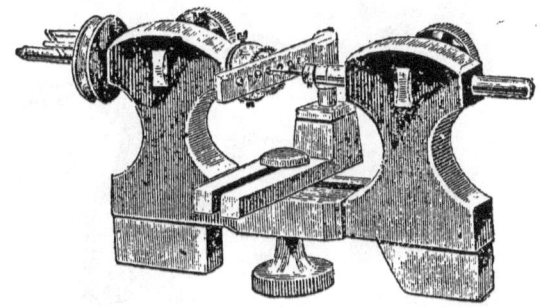

Fig. 9. Dracip Lathe Ready for Drilling.

means of a cord. Now as this loose pulley is rotated, it also rotates the smaller runner by means of the pin, which, sticking out of the body of the latter, projects between the two driving pins and this runner imparts motion to the work by means of the dog and driving pin on the other end, the dog being fastened to the work. Does the reader wonder that we cry out for reform and urge modern methods after this? The dog and the pin on the inner end of the runner may be seen in Fig. 8, while the two driving pins and the runner pin are more clearly shown in Fig. 9, which shows the lathe ready for drilling. Fig. 10 shows the lathe in position for drilling a pinion by means of a rotating drill, this pinion remaining stationary, and it also shows the reason for leaving the central slot in the base with its binding screw. The operator selects a suitable cone on the plate held in the T rest holder and centering it from the back he fixes the pinion in its place. The pin which runs from the left hand runner through the wheel is used to prevent the work from rotating while being drilled. He now inserts the drill in the tube and presses against the pinion by means of the rotating thumb-piece at the left. We believe this short description will be sufficient to convey an adequate idea of the Dracip lathe.

Fig. 10. Dracip Lathe Ready to Drill Pinion.

Mr. Charles S. Moseley, inventor of the split-chuck, as used to-day, originated that useful device in 1857 or 1858, to be used upon a solid spindle lathe by substituting a hollow lathe spindle and using a solid rod as the draw-in spindle. These lathes were used in the old Boston Watch Company's factory at Roxbury, Mass., at the time Mr. Moseley was in their employ. Prior to the time of his invention of the split-chuck, wax was used to hold the work in place. Mr. Moseley bored and tapped the end of the solid draw-in spindle for the reception of the chuck, but soon found that this was very unsatisfactory, and he set to work to devise some better form of lathe. The result of his patient toil and thought was the hollow live spindle lathe, with a taper mouth and draw-in spindle, practically as used by American watchmakers to-day. The watchmaking fraternity should be very grateful to Mr. Moseley for his contribution to watchmaking machinery, and yet so modest is he that no man has ever heard him boast of his achievements in this line, although this is but one of many of his inventions, all of which were patentable and none of which were ever patented and hence the low price at which lathes and attachments of various kinds may now be purchased. But to return to our subject.

In 1859, Charles S. Moseley designed for use in the factory of the American Watch Company a small lathe which he conceived would be a useful tool to the watch repairer, and which is the type of all the American watchmakers' lathes. It consists of a round bed secured to a round pedestal by a bolt, the same bolt passing through, and securing the lathe to the bench, headstock and tailstock secured to the bed by screws and nuts, and the headstock taking the split wire chuck.

This lathe only differed from the regular factory lathe by the manner of making the bed and pedestal. One of these lathes was made in the buildings of the American Watch Company, and shown in this country and in England, and then the subject was allowed to lapse, owing to Mr. Moseley becoming connected with the Nashua Watch Company.

While, as before stated, Mr. Moseley's hollow spindle lathe was practically the same as the lathe on the market to-day, yet there were a few points of minor difference, as the shape of the bed, the angles employed, the bearings, etc., and for this reason a diagram of his original lathe may not be devoid of all interest at this point. Fig. 11 illustrates the bed of the lathe, Fig. 12 the draw-in spindle, Fig. 13

the chuck and Fig. 14 the hollow spindle. It will be noted that this was not a center guide lathe, although the Moseley Lathe Company now employ that form. It will also be noted that the bed was flat on the under side instead of circular as now made. The dotted lines AA in Fig. 14 represent the interior of the arbor; BB the journal bushings.

In 1859, owing to dullness of times, A. Webster, then in charge of the machine shop of the American Watch Company, received orders from Mr. Robbins to reduce the force of machinists. Mr. Webster suggested to Mr. Robbins

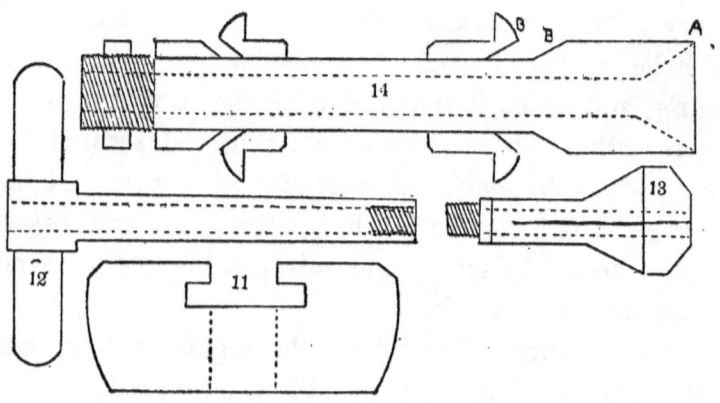

Sectional View Original Moseley Lathe.

that a business might be built up of building lathes for watch repairers, and received permission to design such a lathe, and taking the features of the Moseley lathe, changing the proportions and enlarging it, he designed a lathe, to which he added the universal head and the slide rest. A number of these lathes were started, but before completion business revived, so that the full force of machinists were again put upon the factory machinery, and only two of the lathes were sold, the others being put into use in the factory.

Two of the watch company's machinists—Messrs. Kidder and Adams—seeing the work stopped, concluded that it might be a business in which they might safely embark, and they left the factory, started a shop at Stony Brook and, taking the design of Mr. Webster, brought out a lathe, but before many had been sold, the business changed hands several times, until it was finally purchased in 1862 by John Stark, who for a number of years manufactured the lathe.

Fig. 15 illustrates one of the earliest lathes placed on the

Fig. 15. Earliest Form of Commercial Lathe.

market, with universal head and jeweling caliper in position. The head stock is extremely weak compared with lathes of to-day.

In 1862 great improvements had been made in the details of manufacture of lathes for factory use, by the introduction of hardened spindles and bearings, and the designing of grinding attachments for the purpose of doing that work, and John E. Whitcomb, thinking that these improved lathes would find a ready sale, left the watch factory and started in business in Boston with George F. Ballou, under the firm name of Ballou, Whitcomb & Co. About the same time Mr. Moseley designed another lathe, and started in the manufacture of the Moseley lathe in Elgin, and for a long time the Whitcomb, the Moseley and the Stark lathes were the only accurately made lathes in the country. In 1876 Mr. Webster connected himself with Mr. Whitcomb, forming the American Watch Tool Co.

In the meantime the Hopkins Watch Tool Company, the Mansfield Watch Tool Company, and the Ohio Watch Tool Company, and two or three other parties in Chicago brought out lathes of various qualities.

In 1889 Mr. Webster designed a lathe known as the Webster-Whitcomb, which shows a decided improvement over the one designed by him some thirty years previous. In the designing of this lathe, Mr. Webster brought the experience of thirty-three years in watch factory work, and in watch tool making. In this lathe the proper proportions of the spindle, its size, length, thickness and shape, received the most careful attention. The proportion of the bearings, the relative sizes of the chucks and the spindles, the form of the tailstock, and a hundred things that tend to make perfection in a lathe, were looked after with great care. The spindle should not be long enough to spring; it should be thick enough to retain its form under the strain that is put upon it, but not so heavy as to make its diameter excessive, and it should run with a minimum amount of friction, i. e., there should not be a hard and an easy place in its revolution.

The length and thickness of the chucks must be such as to give the best possible results, and they should be absolutely true. The threads should be smoothly cut, and the chucks should fit perfectly in the headstock.

While this chapter on the history of the lathe may be

devoid of value from a practical standpoint, yet we feel that the modern watchmaker should know something of the evolution of the little machine which occupies the left hand side of his bench and it may have a tendency to instill into him a more wholesome regard for that most useful machine and make him thankful for the devices which the patient application and deep thought of generations of watchmakers have brought forth for his benefit.

24 THE AMERICAN LATHE.

Fig. 16. A Standard American Watchmaker's Lathe. Length of bed (5) 10 to 14 inches. swing 3½ to 4¾ inches; distance between centers, 2½ to 5½ inches, according to size of lathe; bed to center 1¾ to 2⅜ inches. 5, Bed. 6, Head stock. 7, Tail stock. 8, Shoe of T-rest standard. 9, T-rest standard. 10, T-rest clamp. 11, T-rest. 12, Lathe spindle. 13, Front bearing dust cap. 14, Hard rubber cone pulley. 15, Split adjusting nut on lathe spindle. 16, Draw-in spindle for tightening chuck. 17, Hand wheel of draw-in spindle. 18, Index pin, working in index holes on pulley. 19, Headstock clamp. 20, T-rest clamp screw. 21, T-rest clamp washer. 22, Tail stock clamp. 23, Hard rubber button on tail stock spindle. 24, Tail stock spindle clamp. 25, Tail stock clamp. 26, Tail stock center.

CHAPTER II.

THE CONSTRUCTION OF THE WATCHMAKER'S LATHE.

Perhaps it may be well, in approaching our study of the American Lathe, to state concisely just what its points of merit are and in just what particulars it has, or claims to have, the advantage over the Swiss or Geneva lathe; and also in what respects some of the foreign imitations fail of equal attainments with the genuine. To anyone who has had experience with both, such a statement would be unnecessary; but as this is not written for such people, and as nearly everyone writing on the subject has contented himself with general expressions of praise for one and contempt for the other, it may be well to set them forth clearly for the benefit of the novice.

In the manufacture of lathes, the vital points are that the spindles of head and tail stocks shall be true, exactly in line with each other at all points of the lathe bed, wherever they may be placed, and that the parts bearing the strains shall be so proportioned mathematically that they will withstand working strains, without springing.

If we go into a machine shop and look at a machinist's, or engine lathe, we shall find a long bed of cast iron with the sides shaped like an I-beam, fastened at the ends and at intervals between them by webs of iron, to prevent the sides from springing. The whole construction exhibits careful thought to arrange the metal so as to best withstand the strains by having the greatest thickness of metal in the same direction as the greatest strain. For this reason the greatest thickness of metal is in a vertical direction; the flanges of the I-beam are wide and fully as thick as the wall of the I;

the angles where the wall and flange join are rounded, not, as so many suppose, to make a nice looking job, but in order to get more metal at that point and so provide against lateral as well as vertical strains. On the top of the upper flange are two projecting, inverted V-grooves, the inner one forming the guide for preserving the alignment of the head and tail stocks and the outer performing a like service for the slide rest. They are inverted so as to form a projection instead of a hole, because chips, dirt, etc., would soon fill the

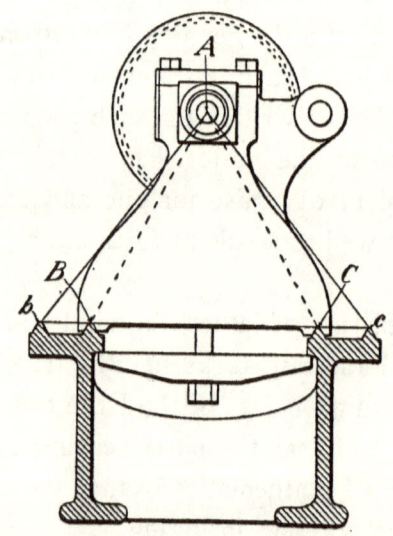

Fig. 17. Sectional View of Engine Lathe.

hole and necessitate cleaning whenever the head or tail stock had to be moved. The top edges of the V are chamfered off, so that tools, etc., falling on them will not bruise them and destroy their accuracy. You will notice in the accompanying sectional view of the head, Fig. 17, that the point forming the center of the spindle is marked A and the guides for the head and tail stocks B and C. Now our strains are so distributed that when work is done at A the strains will fall within the dotted triangle A, B, C, and the wider the base B, C of the triangle becomes in proportion to its height, the stronger the lathe will be, if the proper proportions of metal are placed in it. You can see at a glance that A, B, C, Fig. 18, is stronger than D, E, F, with the same pressure applied at A and at D.

If we add a slide rest and carry it upon the outer grooves

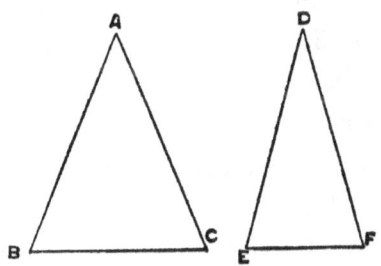

Fig. 1?. Comparative Strength of Wide and Narrow Triangles.

b and c, Fig. 17, we then have our triangle of forces as A, b, c, in which the base b, c, is still wider; and this is correct, because we take heavier cuts with the slide rest than we do when turning by hand, and consequently more force is exerted.

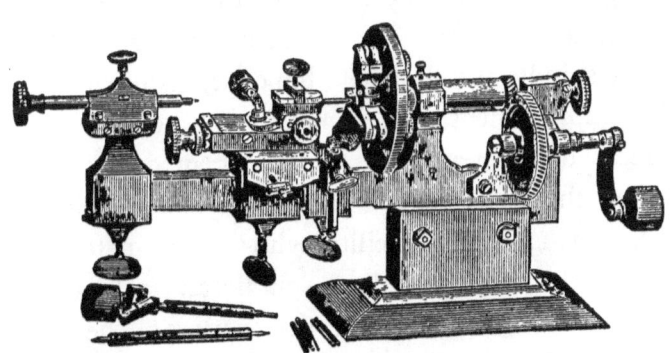

Fig. 19. English Mandrel.

Now that we understand the triangle of forces, let us examine the watchmakers' lathes. In the old type of lathe, called the mandrel, shown at Fig. 19, we have the earliest and worst form of bed, namely a rectangular bar, with square corners, and its narrowest dimensions forming the base of the triangle of support. In addition to this the necks of the head and tail stocks were cut away so much that not enough metal was left to form a rigid support for the spindles. The bed was square and the holes in the tail stock, slide rest and hand rest shoes had also to be squared to fit it. Anyone who has ever tried fitting square holes will easily see that the difficulties of fitting made uniformity of production of these lathes impossible and this, with the defects mentioned above, caused it to be superseded by the Swiss form of lathe, shown in Fig. 20. This was so much better adapted to unifomity of manufacture that it soon drove the other practically out of the market, although it had a solid spindle and the only way of working was by means of wax chucks and lathe dogs, such as the machinist uses today to revolve some kinds of work.

Then the Americans invented the split chuck, which necessitated a hollow spindle in the head stock; in order that the chuck might be fastened by screwing a rod on the end of the chuck with a collar on the rod, which bore against the rear end of the spindle and thus held the chuck in place. This was a great improvement, but it halted for some time, until the hollow draw-in spindle was substituted for the solid rod, when the two secured almost immediate adoption in America, owing to the facility with which material could be inserted through the hollow spindle and a large part of the work done before cutting the work off the rod; but the Europeans refused almost solidly to accept it. The trouble was that European manufacturers were still of the notion that it required delicate machinery to do delicate work and they made their head stock spindles too thin in the wall of the tube, so that they sprung in the bear-

THE AMERICAN LATHE.

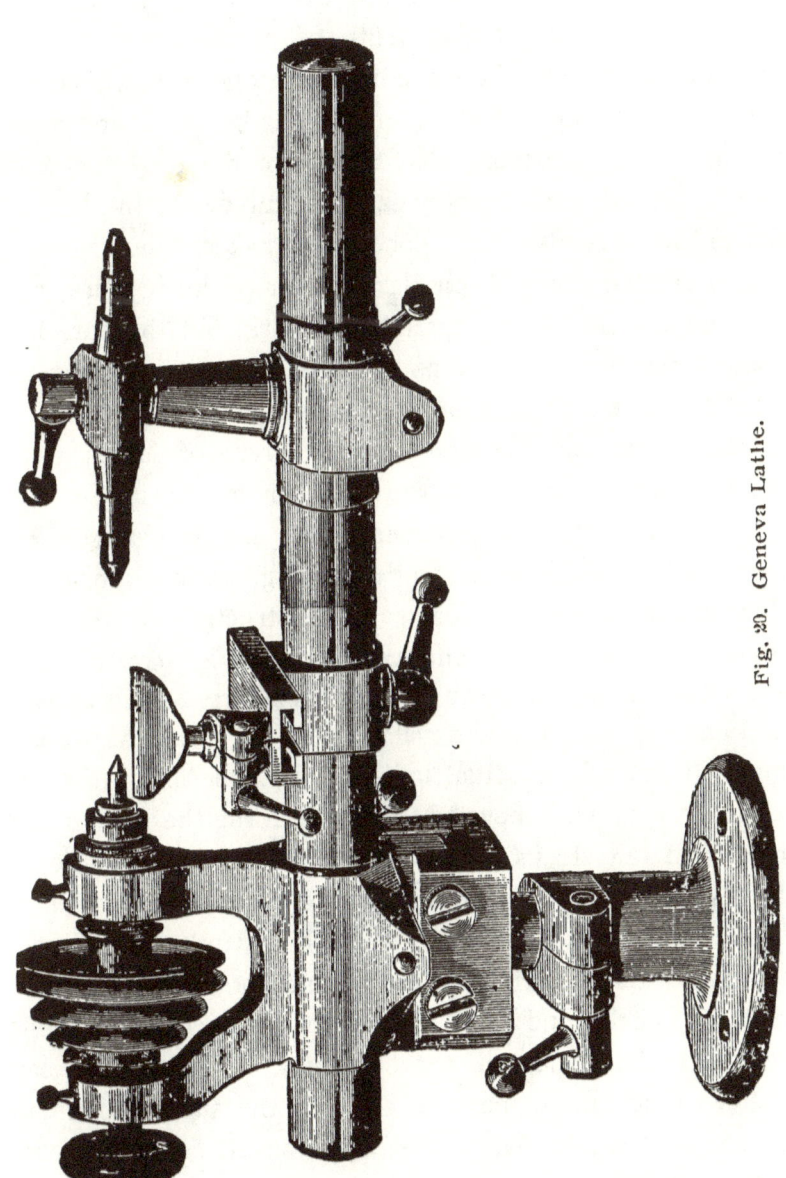

Fig. 20. Geneva Lathe.

ings and also sprung at the mouth, or chuck seat of the spindle, whenever the chuck was drawn down too tightly. Under these circumstances truth of revolution is impossible and even today there are many European watchmakers who cling to the old dead centers, lathe dogs and wax chucks, firmly believing that these are the only methods by which truth and accuracy can be secured. In the United States there are also many good watchmakers who are willing to use the draw-in spindle lathe for ordinary work, but still use cement chucks for all fine work, but they are becoming fewer in number as the vital points of the American lathe are becoming better understood in the trade.

The Swiss and German manufacturers of lathes were quick to adopt the hollow draw-in spindle and split chuck for the lathes exported to America, but did not change their patterns in other respects, and this brings us to a consideration of the respective forms of construction of the two lathes. In Figs. 16, 21 and 22 we have side, sectional and end views of the American lathe, and in Figs. 20 and 23 side and end views of the Geneva pattern. Both end views are one-half size of the actual lathes. The American lathe has a wider bed, with beveled edges to form the guides for head and tail stocks and a wide base for the triangle of forces, as explained at length in regard to the machinist's lathe. The Geneva lathe has a much narrower, round bed, which is cut away at the back to form the guides for head and tail stocks and thus still further reduces dimensions that were insufficient in the beginning. In the American pattern much more metal is evident; the surfaces coming in contact are all planes, and so arranged as to be accurately produced in large numbers. In the Geneva pattern the base of the triangle is altogether too narrow; the guides are close together, instead of being widely separated as in

THE AMERICAN LATHE. 31

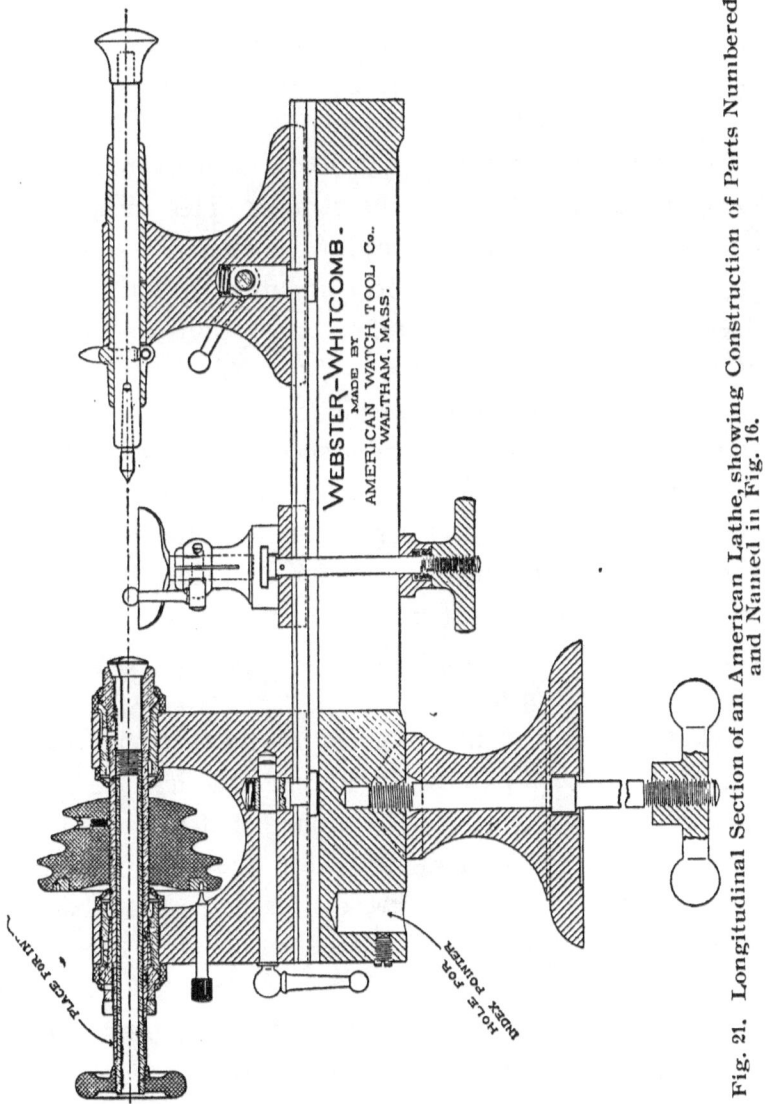

Fig. 21. Longitudinal Section of an American Lathe, showing Construction of Parts Numbered and Named in Fig. 16.

the American; the curved interiors of the lower portions of the head and tail stocks are purposely made so that they will spring to fit the curvature of the bed and the total effect is that we have still the narrow base of the triangle as exhibited in the old mandrel, Fig. 19, and which years ago was discarded as insufficient.

When we consider how much of our work must necessarily be done outside of the straight lines inclosing the triangle of forces, it will readily be seen how immensely superior is the American form of lathe, conforming, as it does, so closely with the mathematical requirements of this class of machinery.

In the Geneva pattern (see Fig. 20 and Fig. 23) the head stock, tail stock and slide rest shoes are bored out to fit the bed, and then faced off to suit the guides and a flat clamp added. In the American pattern the castings are simply clamped bottom up and milled before being bored for the spindles, so that any mechanic can see the greater chance for accuracy of fitting that must be reckoned in 10,000ths of an inch.

These considerations have led to the gradual discarding of the Geneva pattern of lathe in America. In investigating this question, the writer found that only the largest tool and material dealers now keep the Geneva form of lathe; a visit to eight dealers disclosed the fact that only two of them had any Geneva lathes on hand and they were on shelves in the original packages, while a full line of the American patterns, of both American and foreign manufacture, was displayed in the show cases.

Of more importance than either the form of lathe, or the truth of alignment of guides and spindles, is the shape, size and proportions of the head spindle. In fact, the whole truth or falsity of the lathe is there, for nine-tenths of the

THE AMERICAN LATHE. 33

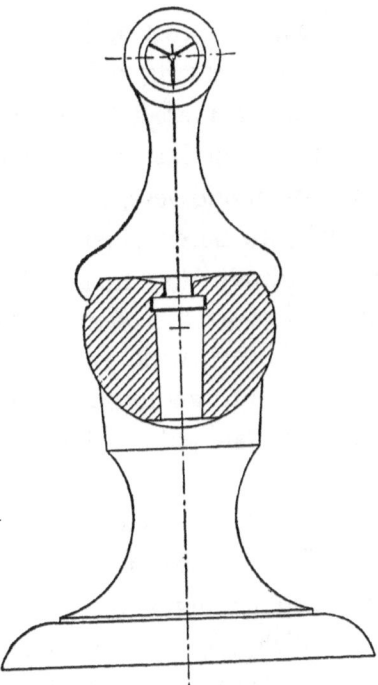

Fig. 22. Section of American Lathe in Front of Headstock. One-Half Size.

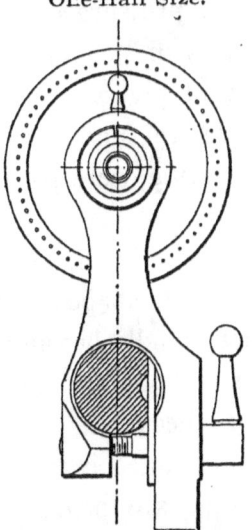

Fig. 23. Section of Geneva Lathe in Front of Headstock. One-Half Size.

watchmaker's work. By far the largest part of his work is done with tail stock, slide rest and all other attachments removed from the lathe, leaving only the hand rest, head stock and chuck to be considered. The hand rest does not move and only requires to be held rigidly where it is placed. The head stock is also motionless, so that only the spindle and chuck have really to be considered.

Fig. 21 shows a longitudinal section of the American lathe and Fig. 24 shows a full-sized section of the head stock, in which we can see the head stock, front and rear bearings, their means of adjustment, method of oiling, dust caps, the head stock spindle, the cone pulley, the draw-in spindle and the chuck.

We will consider first the shape and size of the lathe spindle bearings. The front bearing is a cone, neatly fitted in the head stock and having a three-degree taper on its inner surface, to which the front spindle bearing is also ground. This bearing is tapered forty-five degrees in front to form the thrust shoulder, which receives the end thrust of the spindle whenever pressure is applied on the work in line with the spindle, as in turning a wheel, or the barrel of a watch, shoulders of pivots, etc. Its shape is such as to keep the spindle central under end pressure, which it might not do if the bearing were parallel and the shoulder straight.

The rear bearing is fitted in the head stock in the reverse direction, and has a similar shape; mounted on the rear of the spindle is the rear spindle bearing, shaped like that of the front spindle, but adapted to slide on the spindle and be held in place by a check nut. It will be seen that by having taper bearings mounted in opposite directions means of adjustment for wear are provided, in order that the spindle may be delicately adjusted, so as to be without per-

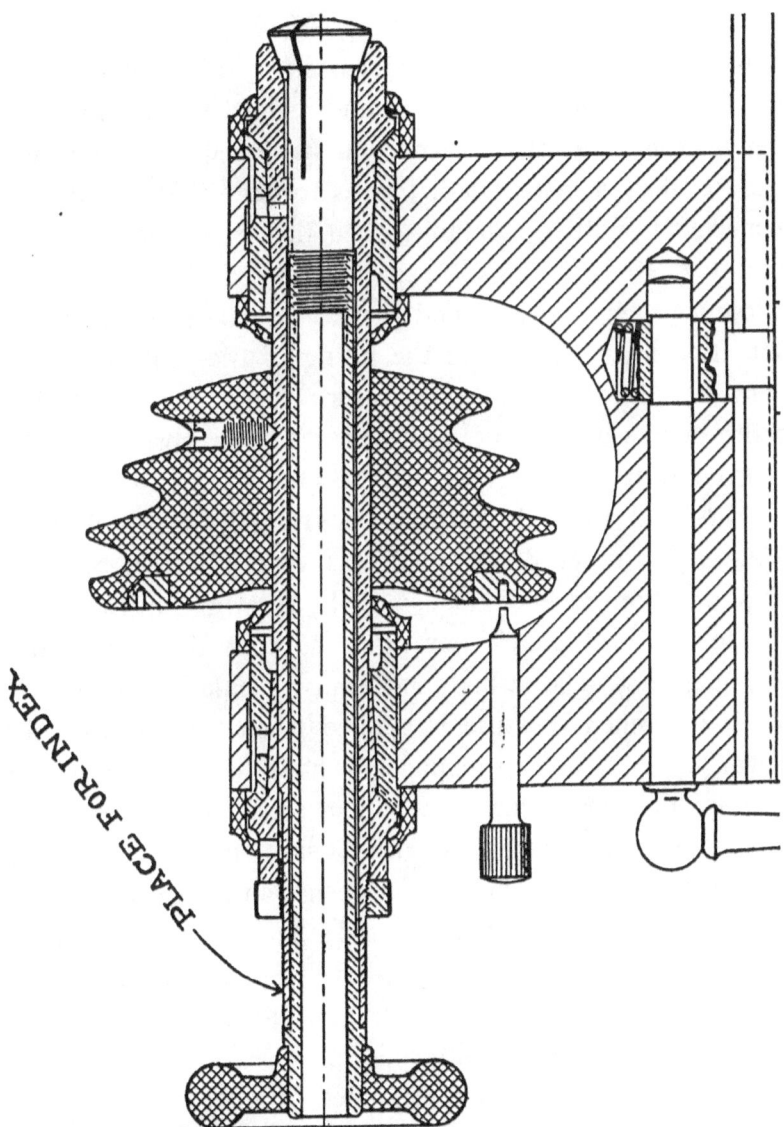

Fig. 24. Longitudinal Section of Head Stock of American Lathe.
Full Size.

ceptible side or end shake and having the least possible friction. These bearings are of gun metal, or of fine grained cast iron, hardened, ground and polished.

Now we come to the spindle itself. This is a piece of the finest tool steel, bored out, and reamed to size, so as to get a true hole; then turned on hardened and polished dead centers in a true lathe, so as to have the central hole concentric with the spindle; then the spindle is hardened and tempered, and finally again mounted on centers and ground to accurate size and shape. In this process special attention must be paid to the fitting of the centers, or the central hole will not be concentric. All spindles spring more or less when hardening and if a badly sprung spindle is ground up true, its walls will be so thin that it will spring in the head stock if the pulley fits loosely, if the draw-in spindle is tightened too much (as very powerful pressure is put on both ends of the spindle by screwing up the draw-in spindle and chuck too tight, so that the head stock spindle, being held at both ends, must buckle in the center), or if too much pressure is applied when turning with the face plate. Many watchmakers have seen lathes where the spindle would run true with a solid chuck, but would not do so with a piece of work in a split chuck; or the work would be true when held in an open split chuck, but would be out when the chuck was closed. Of course they blamed the split chuck, when it might have been the spindle. Both chucks and spindle must be true; an untrue chuck and true spindle or vice versa will not do.

In this connection I am reminded of a controversy which arose between a manufacturer of chucks who claimed absolute truth for his product and a prominent and skilled watchmaker, who had always maintained that perfect accuracy could only be had by cementing. The controversy got into the trade press and was carried on with considerable heat on both sides. Finally the manufacturer agreed to prove his assertions by supplying the watchmaker with a full set of split chucks, to be paid for if true and to be given, if fault could be found with them. The only condition was that the lathe head stock was to be furnished him, so that the chucks might be properly fitted, which was done. It was discovered at the factory that the spindle was too light and would spring; so they made a new spindle with thicker walls, without telling him about it. A week later he paid for the chucks and announced in the papers that ———'s chucks were perfection. He never knew that they had given him a new spindle.

After grinding to truth outside, the best manufacturers fit the spindle carefully in its bearings in the head stock and then grind out the chuck seat with care. This makes a perfect job, as the chuck seat is bound to be central with the spindle bearings, if ground in its own head stock.

In many of the foreign-made lathes of American pattern (which are made to sell at a low price) the greatest economy must necessarily be practiced. They cannot afford to throw away spindles that have sprung in tempering. Only the bearings are ground, leaving the pulley seat untrue. The chuck seat is often not central and the blackened surface shows that it has not been ground out at all. In some cases a chuck will go in too far and in the next lathe not far enough, showing that the seat is either not the proper size or not round. Now these are differences too small for he novice to detect and consequently they pass the buyer, who is looking mostly at the price, and are only found out hen a capable workman commences to find fault with the the, gets out his testing instruments and proceeds to esblish the falsity of either chuck or spindle; he don't know ich.

A nameless "imitation" lathe may or may not have these faults. The trouble is that such a lathe was bought on account of its price, and importer, dealer and manufacturer all have a tacit understanding that it shall be just good enough to pass. This is the reason that the maker does not put his name on it. The nameless lathe is, therefore, when it gets to America, a sort of orphan. No one is responsible for it. Its maker is unknown; very likely it was assembled from a dozen or more makers of parts—a favorite method of manufacture in Europe. In this case, if it were to be returned to its manufacturer, there is still a division of responsibility and uncertainty as to who was at fault. Therefore, when the dealer gets such a lathe returned to him, he either sends it to a manufacturer in this country to be trued up, or he intimates that the watchmaker has sprung it himself, since it has been in his possession, and endeavors to charge him for all or a portion of the expense incurred in making it true.

The American and reputable European manufacturers stamp their names on their products and thereby guarantee their truth. If fault is found, the lathe is returned to the manufacturer to be corrected at his expense, whereas, no one is responsible for the nameless product. Try to get a guarantee from your dealer when buying a nameless lathe and see how quickly he will drop it and try to sell you one that has the maker's name stamped on it.

It is generally stated that an imported lathe will fit the American chucks, but many of them will not do so for the following reasons: The chuck should fit into the head spindle within one thirty-second of an inch of its largest diameter, as shown in Fig. 25, but many of them will not do so. They may even project as far as shown in Fig. 26. In this case the chuck seat is too small and must be ground out, so that the chucks will fit properly into their seat as shown in the previous figure. Sometimes the chucks appear to fit the seat in the spindle properly, but will not enter the thread in the draw-in spindle, or do so with dif-

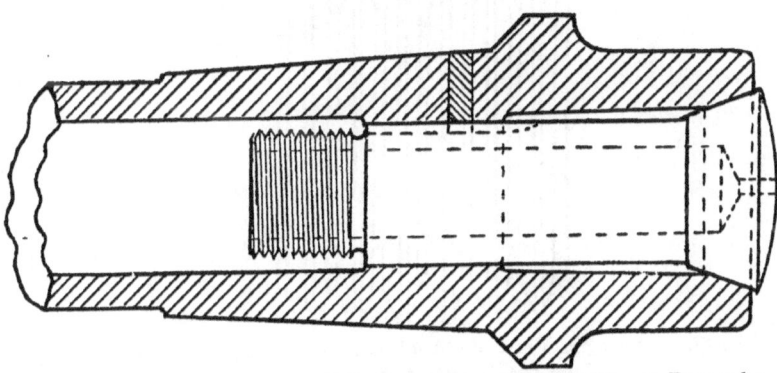

Fig. 25. Enlarged View of Lathe Spindle, showing Chuck Properly Seated. Compare with Fig. 26.

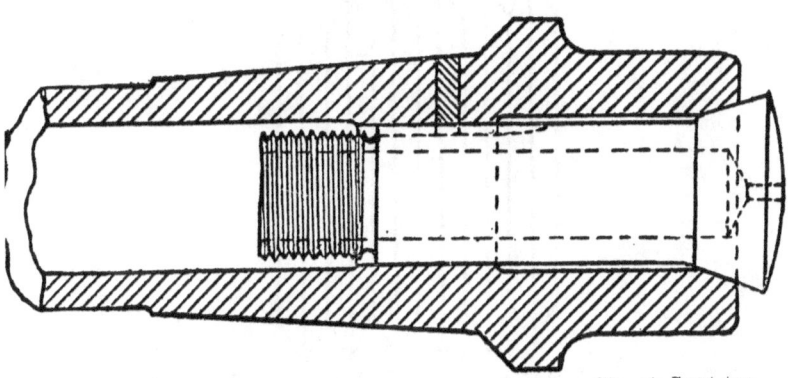

Fig. 26. Enlarged View of Lathe Spindle, showing Chuck Seat too Small. Compare with Fig. 25.

ficulty. The reason is that many of the European makers use a thread that is rounded at the top and bottom as in Fig. 27, while the Americans use a sharp V-thread as shown in Fig. 28. Of course the draw-in spindle must be tapped out, so that room may be provided for the sharp corners of the thread on the American chucks, before they will fit properly. This should always be done, when this defect is found, as it has an important influence on the seating of the chuck in delicate work, or where extreme accuracy is required. If this is not done the threads on all

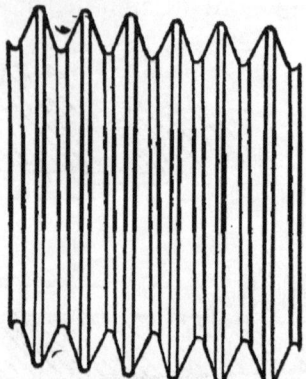

Fig. 27. Enlarged View of Chuck End, showing Round Thread Used by European Manufacturers.

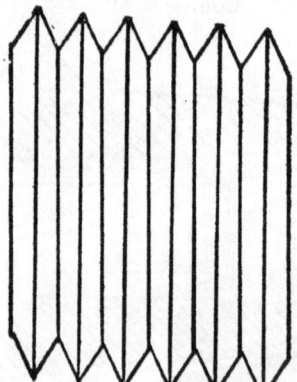

Fig. 28. Enlarged View of Chuck End, showing Sharp V Thread, Used by American Manufacturers.

your American chucks will be bruised, or your draw-in spindle will be stretched, if it is soft enough, and then the European chucks, which came with the lathe, will be loose in the threads and their accuracy will be affected.

If the lathe spindle has not been ground out after hardening, it may have sprung out of round in hardening and have come to you in that condition; then the jaw of the chuck which comes opposite the flattened side of the chuck seat in the spindle will meet the seat sooner than the others when the draw-in spindle is tightened, and will consequently be pushed past the center before it meets the remaining jaws of the chuck. In such a case a true chuck would work exactly central when loosely inserted, but it would throw the work out of center when tightened. In such a case there is always doubt as to whether it is this spindle or the chuck that is at fault, and the blame is generally laid to the chuck, unless it is found to be true in other lathes. The chuck seat of the spindle should be tested for truth in the round, with a testing lever. Even then, if the spindle be too light, it will be true at rest and spring when tightened, as previously described. The spindles and bearings should be ground true. The fact that there are two angles on the cones (generally three degrees and 45 degrees) to be fitted together, requires a nicety of workmanship few watchmakers appreciate; and it has the disadvantage of enabling some manufacturers to palm off on their customers a very inferior article, which, to the unpracticed eye looks all right, but is in reality, far from it. There are thousands of lathes in use that have the spindles bearing entirely on the 45-degree tapers, while the proper bearing is on the three-degree. The only function of the 45-degree angle is to prevent end-thrust on the spindle from binding or sticking the spindle in the three-degree or long bearing. When the spindle bears on the 45-degree angles only it is really running on a pair of very abrupt cones and the lathe will always run hard, sometimes stick, never run true or stay true, and never give satisfaction to its owner. This vital defect is particularly true of the imported, or imitation lathes. Some of our domestic lathes are also faulty in this respect, and when this is true, the best things about the lathe are the nickel and polish. It looks as pretty as any of them.

This fault can be easily discovered, if it exists. Remove the spindle; clean it thoroughly; replace it in the front bearing; remove the rear sleeve and cone bearing; press firmly on the front end of the spindle with the right hand; then take hold of the rear end of the spindle and try to shake it. If it does not feel as solid and firm as when the rear bearing was in place, the spindle was never right and never will be until reground by a competent workman, and the lathe will never give satisfaction to the user until it is reground.

The most valuable appliance a watchmaker can have on his bench is a *good* American lathe. This involves a live spindle hardened on both ends, ground true, inside and out, and properly proportioned to prevent springing, as detailed at length in what has just been said. The rear end of the spindle should be hardened, to prevent the dry draw-in spindle from injury and from scarring the back end of the live spindle, as it often does when they are both soft.

The draw-in spindle should be of soft steel, case hardened at both ends, at the front end to prevent wear of thread, where it engages the thread on the chucks, and at the other to prevent seizing and sticking in the bearing and shoulder of the live spindle.

The spindle should run in hardened steel, or hardened cast iron bearings. The babbitt, brass and gun metal bearings used in the "soft" lathes are a thing of the past and never had anything to recommend them but cheapness. The "soft" lathe had a spindle which was not hardened and ran in brass boxes. The "half hard," used a hardened spindle with soft boxes. Both have been displaced in American practice by the "full hard" lathe—hardened steel spindles, hardened draw-in spindle and hardened bearings. Even these terms are now obsolete in the trade and the "full hard" lathe is always understood when an American lathe is spoken of. Soft lathes are still imported, however, as they are much cheaper to make and the buyer of cheap imported lathes is very apt to get one if he is not on the lookout.

These remarks should be sufficient to show the importance of that hidden piece of machinery, the lathe spindle, and why it is wise to buy only guaranteed lathes, stamped with the name of the maker, as it is a difficult proposition to prove the untruth of a thin spindle and a sprung spindle, or one with improper chuck seat, while easier to detect, always causes an annoying delay, while it is sent to a factory to be corrected.

The sizes of lathes have undergone a gradual evolution. The principal manufacturers originally made three sizes of lathes, the smallest of which had a chuck of .24-in. diameter. The next size was .31-in. diameter. The distance from bed to center of the small size was 1¾ inches, and of the next size 2 inches. Only these two sizes were sold to repairers, the larger sizes being designed for manufacturers and tool makers. The test of long-continued use led to the gradual discarding of the smallest size, principally on account of the weakness and small capacity of the chucks, and this feature will be taken up in full under the subject of chucks. The height of the chuck from the bed and other dimensions of the smallest sized lathe made it a favorite among repairers, however, and this difficulty was met by bringing out, some years later, a lathe retaining the outside dimensions and "swing" of the small lathe, but having a spindle that would take a chuck .31-in. in diameter. Moseley was, we believe, the first to do this and he called the new size 1x2; that is, the No. 2 size chuck and the other dimensions of the No. 1 lathe. The American Watch Tool Co. quickly made similar changes in their Whitcomb lathe and called it Webster-Whitcomb. Others quickly fell into line, and the incident is of importance as showing the dimensions which have stood the test of time. There is now a marked movement towards the No. 2, which has four inches swing, a longer and larger chuck and heavier dimensions throughout. The larger head gives more room to swing large pieces. The chucks have a larger capacity for occasional jobs and many men with large hands have found difficulty in working at the small lathe; hence the growing tendency to larger sizes. American manufacturers generally have discontinued making the lathe taking the small chuck.

Fig. 29 shows the construction of the head stock and spindle of the Rivett lathe. This lathe has the usual front bearing of three and forty-five degrees with a parallel bearing in the rear which is adjusted by a compression sleeve and screw in the tapered rear seat in the head stock and a flat collar between the head stock and pulley which is adjusted by a thread on the spindle and set by a locking screw in the collar. It makes a very good bearing for the purpose for which it is used and the iron sleeve on which the hard rubber pulley is carried extends from the front bearing to the rear adjusting collar and thus tends to re-enforce the spindle and prevent springing in the middle when the draw-in spindle and chuck are strained tighter than they should be.

Fig. 30 illustrates a spindle designed and made by Hardinge Bros., Chicago, and which they consider as nearly perfect. They have had it in use for several years, and have studied it carefully, with a view of discovering any faults which might exist, but still consider it as nearly perfect as it is possible for them to design a spindle.

THE AMERICAN LATHE.   45

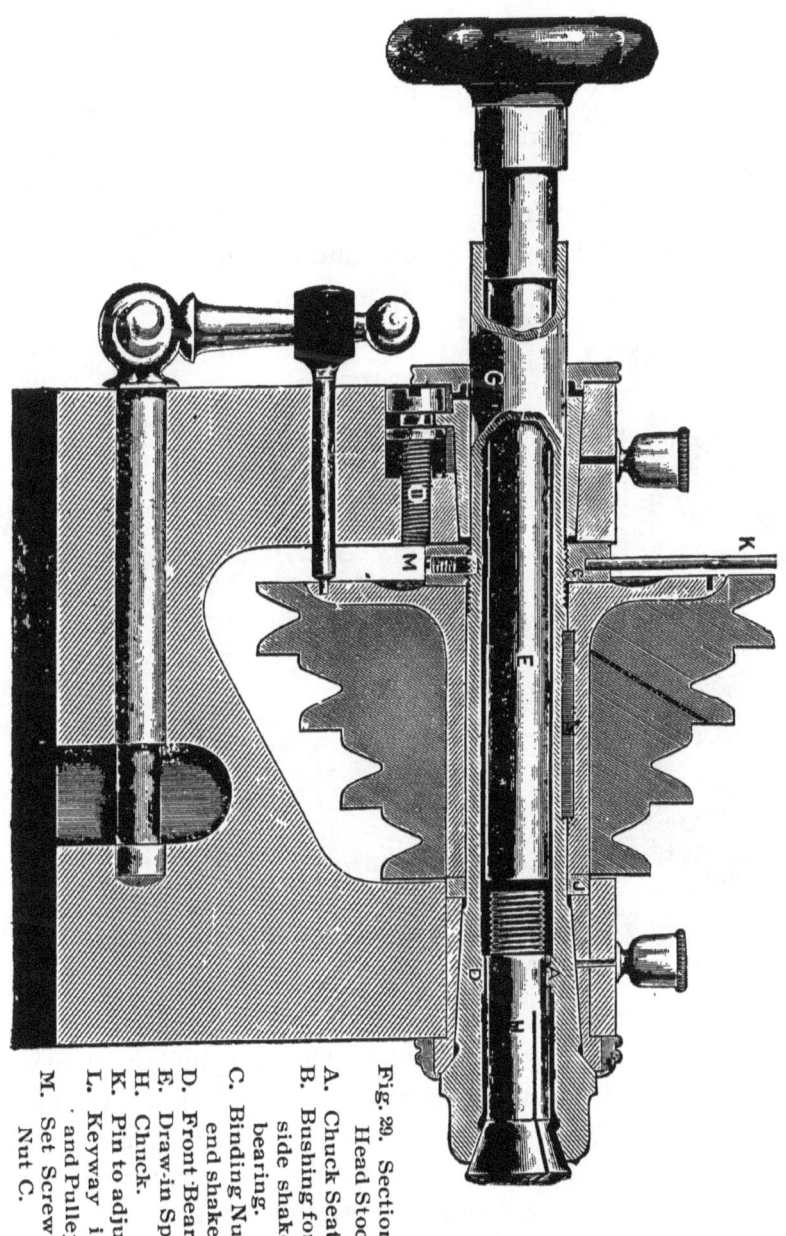

Fig. 29. Section of Rivet Head Stock.
A. Chuck Seat Pin.
B. Bushing for taking up side shake of rear bearing.
C. Binding Nut to take up end shake of spindle.
D. Front Bearing.
E. Draw-in Spindle.
H. Chuck.
K. Pin to adjust Nut C.
L. Keyway in Spindle and Pulley.
M. Set Screw to tighten Nut C.

It has but 3 degrees at front bearing A and E is a hollow space. This space is left to collect all fine material which may work in between the spindle and dust band F and preserve the bearing from being injured by the dirt. G is a space, or ring, turned out in the head, which is a reservoir for oil, and is kept full; if the bearing heats it expands this ring of oil, which naturally runs into the hole on the top of

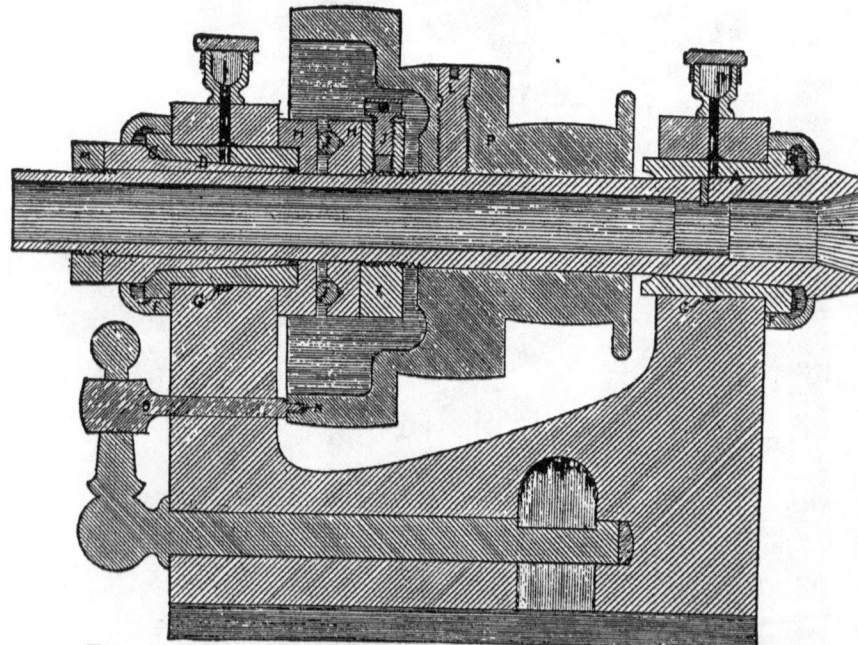

Fig. 30. Section of Hardinge Spindle, with Pulley for Flat Belt, as used by Toolmakers.

the hardened bushing B and lubricates the spindle. H represents the ball-bearing seat, which is hardened and ground perfectly flat and presses over the hardened bushing, seating against the rear head stock-standard. I represents the balls, and H the hardened and ground conical ball race, which, with H, gives us a three-point bearing for the balls I. K represents the take-up nut, and J the binding screw. For the rear bearing 3 and 45 degrees are used at C and D, as the wear is about equal in this bearing and drilling does not have a tendency to bind the spindle. With these bearings so constructed, all possible shake can be taken from the front journal of the lathe and still allow it to revolve freely. The ball bearing and rear bearing are then adjusted to leave no end shake and there will be no binding, and the wear of the spindle is reduced to a minimum. This lathe is known as the "Dale," and is having a considerable sale as a speed lathe for toolmakers, and also with grooved pulley for many watchmakers.

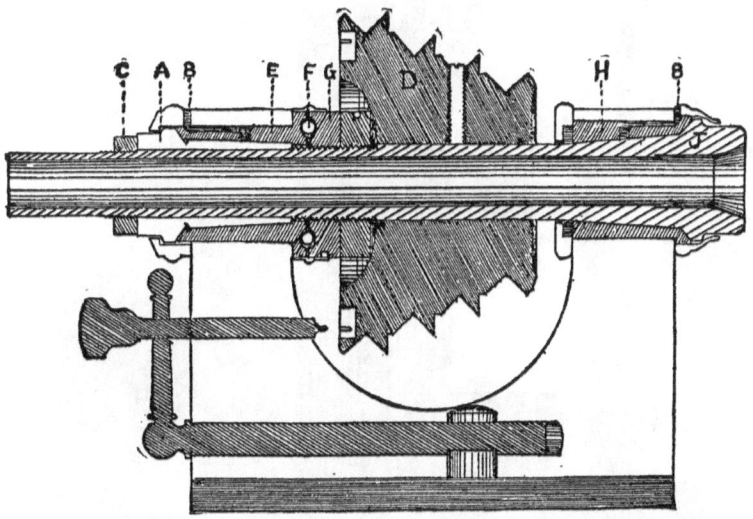

Fig. 31. Section of Headstock of Hammel, Riglander & Co.'s Lathe, showing construction of parts.

Figs. 31 and 32 show a lathe that is having a considerable sale in America, although it is made in Europe. The lathe is of the Moseley pattern (i. e., it has center guides), and the headstock is made one-half inch longer, to give room on the spindle for the ball bearings. H and A are the front and rear bearings; B. B. oil holes; E and G, the two parts of the ball bearing—the seat and race; F the balls. It will be noticed that in this lathe the rear cone

Fig. 32. Hammel, Riglander & Co's. lathe with center guides and ball-bearing spindle.

bearing of the headstock is simply enlarged and grooved at its inner end, to make the ball seat; also that the ball race is screwed on the spindle, instead of sliding upon it, so that it is adjusted by turning the race, whereas in the Dale the race slides on the spindle and is pushed forward by turning the nut K behind it. In Fig. 31 the nut shown on the same thread with G is simply a jamb nut, to hold G in position after it is adjusted. Both G and its jamb nut are worked by a pin wrench. The next point of difference is that this is a two-point bearing, while the Dale is a three-point. If the reader will examine the construction of H, I, H, Fig. 30, and E, F, G, Fig. 31, he will readily see the difference. In Fig. 30 the balls, I, touch on three plane surfaces, while in Fig. 31 the balls F roll in a groove, which is an arc of a circle of larger diameter than the balls. To go into the merits of these different forms of ball-bearing construction would be to quote a controversy that would last as long as the bearing, and would take the reader into plane and spherical trigonometry, calculus and questions of shop practice, only to find out at the end that either form will answer for such light work as is here indicated. The student who desires to inquire further into the subject is referred to the manufacturers, either of whom is competent to give the reasons for adopting the form he has chosen.

The object of introducing ball-bearing thrust collars is to reduce friction from end thrust, and in order to do this the spindle must be adjusted so that all end thrust is taken by the balls while the end shake is taken up by the rear thrust collar, leaving the front spindle bearing running on the three-degree taper only. For this reason the front thrust collar is omitted in the Dale, and it serves no purpose in Fig. 31, while the balls are in use. The only reason we can see for leaving it on is that if for any reason the balls should get lost, or broken, the owner would not be deprived of the use of the lathe until they were replaced.

The lathe is well made, hardened throughout, and can be used with American chucks after taking the precautions noted previously concerning the seating of the chucks and the draw-in spindle.

CHAPTER III.

THE CONSTRUCTION AND USE OF THE SPLIT CHUCK.

Having now a fair understanding of the construction of our lathe bed, headstock and spindles, we will take up the study of the chucks we are to use for holding our work. Incidentally, we shall find that while there are upwards of one hundred variations of this useful article, they may all be classed as of two kinds of bodies, split and solid, the variations being confined chiefly to the formation of that portion which projects from the lathe, while the truth and accuracy of this work-holding device has to do chiefly with that portion of the chuck which lies within the spindle when the chuck is performing its proper office.

Let us first consider it mathematically, just as we did the construction of our lathe, because by so doing we shall see the reasons for many things that will be developed as we get farther along, and many points will be made plain to the novice which he might not so readily grasp if he did not thoroughly understand the theory upon which the chuck is built. The split chuck is a clamp, forced along an inclined plane by means of the screw thread at its inner end. The inclined plane is the conical mouth of the lathe spindle, and in action the chuck is drawn into the cone (and towards the smaller diameter of the cone), thus forcing the several jaws of the chuck to close slightly and exert a clamping action on the piece of work that is being held.

The jaws of the chuck are the base of a triangle, and the apex of the triangle is that point on the outside of the chuck jaw riding on the incline of the lathe spindle. The lines f forces exerted in this clamping action are represented in the partial drawing (Fig. 33) of a lathe spindle, with a chuck in position to act, by the dotted lines as follows: A and B are points at the mouth of the spindle cone at which the apices of the several triangles rest and in action are drawn along c c; the apices of the triangles are the radial lines of force derived from the hand wheel on the back end of the draw-in spindle, at c, and are shown by the dotted lines d d. These lines express the direct line of the prime force, terminating at the apices of the triangles shown at the mouth of the chuck. At this point the prime force is deflected at an angle terminating at the bases of the triangles, which form the clamping surfaces of the several

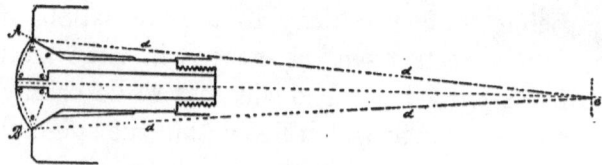

Fig. 33. Showing lines of force in clamping a chuck.

jaws of the chuck. The deflection of the prime force at this point is caused by the opposition to its action of the inclined plane of the spindle, and while the prime force is one of tensile strain, the resultant one is that of compression, resulting in the clamping action at the base of the triangle, and is the force found in the jaws of the chuck.

It will be seen that if the chuck seat is too small the chuck will not have its angles A, c, c, and B, c, c equilateral triangles, and the resultant compression will not pass through the centers of the jaws in the line A, B, but will pass nearer to the inner ends of the jaws, in proportion as the seat is too small; in this case we will have the work held by the inner ends of the jaws only, allowing the outer ends to slip or remain free of the work entirely, when any considerable pressure on the work will allow it to slip out of center. Similarly, if the chuck seat is too large the outer ends will receive the force of compression and the inner ends of the jaws will be without proper bearing on the work, and it will slip as before. If the chuck seat is not round, the jaw which comes opposite the flattened side of the chuck seat will come into action sooner than the others, and tend to push the work out of center.

If we have properly fitting and true chucks we can still affect their truth and accuracy of holding work on just these lines in several ways. If we force too large a piece into the chuck, we shall spring the jaws outwards, and practically enlarge the outer diameter of the chuck so that the seat will no longer fit the chuck, and we have the same results as if the chuck seat were originally made too small. If we use the chuck on too small a piece of work, then the jaws of the chuck will close further than they were intended to do, and the second set of conditions confronts us. Hence we see that in order to obtain the proper direction of the line $A.B$ of the force of compression, which holds the work properly, we must keep our chuck nearly the proper size, so that the line of force may pass midway of the length of the jaws. When this is the case, the bearing is such that all forces are balanced within the triangles $A\ c\ c$ and $B\ c\ c$ of the jaws, and there is no strain on the springs which hold the jaws in position and form part of the body of the chuck.

Further, if the piece of work be much too large, or much too small, the jaws will not be parallel when they are closed upon it, and we then have the work held by one end only of each jaw. This would not be so bad if that jaw were rigid, but it is not; it is held in place by a spring. And we then have a bearing along either of the lines $A\ c$ with the base of the triangle completed by the spring which holds the jaw. Of course, any considerable pressure will then cause wabbling of the work, and this will be greater as the spring is weaker, and less as the spring is more powerful. It was this tendency of the workman to use the chuck to hold improper sizes of work that was primarily responsible for the prevalent notion that good work could not be done with split chucks. It was also responsible largely for the general discarding of the small-bodied chuck, generally known as No. 1, manufacturers having found that this tendency to the abuse of chucks could not be wholly prevented, and that the longer and larger bodies enabled them to get more metal in the springs of their chucks, so that they were stiffer and would stand up better when improperly used, as explained above. The larger hole was, of course, an advantage to the workman, but the real reason for their increase in favor was the increase in the size of the springs holding the jaws. No. 1 chucks are still in use, and are supplied when called for by those who have the No. 1 lathes, but they are not recommended by the manufacturers to the purchasers of new lathes.

This brings up the practical question of how far a chuck will spring and still do reasonably good work. For extremely accurate work, one-fourth of a size should be the limit. Chucks are generally sized with a unit of measurement of one-tenth of a millimeter, or its equivalent in thousandths of an inch. Thus No. 4 chuck means that the jaws are parallel when the hole is .4 mm.; No. 4½ equals .45 mm., etc. A reference to the scale of sizes given by the manufacturers will show half sizes from No. 3 to No. 10; thence forward they increase by tenths of millimeters to No. 70, which is seven millimeters in diameter. Thus if a workman has a piece of work between No. 5 and No. 5½, he will not have to spring his chuck jaws more than one-fourth of a size to fit it. The use of half sizes is strongly recommended for the further reason that many staffs and arbors are made to half sizes, or nearly so, and in such cases the work will be found to fit the chuck perfectly, with, of course, a great gain in the truth and accuracy of the work to be performed upon it. Above No. 10 the amount of work is much less and consequently the need of half sizes is not so great, although they would be an advantage. The workman may (and many do habitually) turn their work to a size that will fit their chucks, or nearly so, and the resulting gain in accuracy is an important one; below No. 10, however, it is best to provide yourself with half sizes of chucks and not attempt to disturb the carefully thought out proportions of a fine watch.

This brings us to the consideration of the bodies of our chucks, and in order to understand it properly we shall have to know something of its history and the successive changes incident to its growth.

In 1857 or 1858 Charles S. Moseley was designing machinery for the Boston Watch Company, Roxbury, Mass., afterwards known as the American Waltham Watch Company; John Stark and Ambrose Webster were also employes of the same company at that time. Mr. Moseley and Mr. Stratton, his associate, were at work upon a device for holding and releasing work in watch factory lathes which should do away with the necessity which then existed of putting lathe dogs on every piece which had to be turned. The original chuck made by Mr. Moseley had four jaws, because they did not have at hand any means of accurately splitting the chuck in three sections. So the first chuck (and only the one chuck) was split by making two cuts clear through it, at right angles to each other, thus producing four jaws. Finding it likely to be a success as a work-holder, they fitted up a slitting machine and thus the first split chuck was born.

It was at first used as a holder for work that was already cut off, and a solid draw-in spindle was used to tighten the jaws of the chuck. Then it was pointed out that by making the draw spindle hollow the stock could be fed through it, and the work cut off after being partially completed.

The device was designed for and first used with the old two-bearing watch factory lathe, but was rejected after some trials, because the chuck would not go back into the same place every time if some pieces were larger than others.

Mr. Moseley then modified his lathe so that the chuck was held in a fixed position and the lathe spindle advanced upon and receded from the jaws of the chuck to open and close it. This device is one of the most important features of all automatic machinery today, and has spread from watch factories into dozens of other metal-working lines, as it is the only known means of practically holding a piece of work true and gripping and releasing it instantly.

John Stark, C. S. Moseley and Ambrose Webster, each utilized their experience in the production of automatic watch-making machinery to design and build watchmakers' lathes, after severing their connection with the Waltham factory. All of them used the split chuck in their new productions, and they made them light and delicate because their watch factory training had been entirely upon the lines of having tools enough to do work well within the capacity of those tools. The watch repairer, however, did not understand the necessity of having so many chucks, and attempted to get along with less, so he sprung his chucks and then condemned the principles upon which they were made. The controversy thus started has continued until the present day, but is steadily growing less as watchmakers are coming to understand the limitations of the device and comprehending that they must work within those limitations or take the consequences.

Fig. 34 is one of the first chucks put on the American market. All these cuts are actual sizes of the chucks they represent. This chuck was generally left soft. I have come across a good many of them; they are generally split to within a very short distance of the rear end, which, together with the small diameter of the body (3-16-inch) allows them to spring all over; in fact, about the only thing a chuck of this design will do successfully is *spring*, and it is this very element of springing which must be eliminated as nearly as possible to get good results with a chuck. If, after the work was in its place and gripped sufficiently tight to hold it, the slots could be eliminated, you would then have a solid holder, the very thing wanted, for solidity is a very important element in close work; but since they cannot be dispensed with on account of the necessity for gripping and releasing the work quickly, the only thing left is for the designer to make them as short as possible,

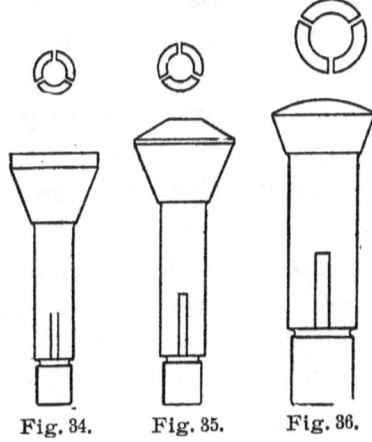

Fig. 34. Fig. 35. Fig. 36.

consistent with the length and general dimensions of the chuck and make the body as large as possible.

Fig. 35 is the second chuck brought out by John Stark, Sr., of Waltham, about 1870. The head of this chuck is about ½-inch diameter, and body 1-32 of an inch larger than his first No. 1. One-half inch diameter has proved to be large enough for the head of any watchmaker's chuck and the body should be smaller than the head by just the amount that is necessary to leave sufficient length of angle on the head, so that it will draw into the spindle firmly, without putting too much strain on the threads of the chuck and draw-in spindle. This angle varies with different makers, but the majority of manufacturers are making watchmakers' chucks with a 20-degree angle of head and the others are gradually coming round to that angle, as it seems satisfactory after years of use.

Fig. 36 shows the popular dimensions of the modern chuck, in which the reader will note the shortening of the angle of the head (20 degrees) and the consequent enlarged body. The heads of Figs. 35 and 36 are the same size; it takes the same amount of stock and labor to make them; yet the difference in strength and durability is immense, as will be seen by a glance at the small cuts, which represent the same chucks with their heads cut off. Either of the previous two will go inside of Fig. 36, and the difference of the amounts of material and consequent strength of the springs is immense. In addition to these structural differences there is a great difference in the size of wire that will go clear through the chuck.

The shape of the face of the chuck has also been the subject of evolution; all chucks were at first made with a flat face; this was found to bring the work too near the spindle, making it difficult to get at; then they were coned, as shown in Fig. 35, and use developed the fact that the further projecton of the jaws of the chuck interfered with its accuracy of holding work. Finally a compromise resulted in grinding the face of the chuck to an arc of a circle, which gave freedom of access while greatly reducing the extension of the jaws beyond the spindle. This was found satisfactory to the majority of the trade, and was universally adopted.

In 1893 Hardinge Bros., of Chicago, produced a flat-faced series of chucks in half sizes that were made with special care, and intended to prove that the use of wax and cement on balance staff work was totally unnecessary. This course was actuated by the following reasoning:

"In the two sectional views here shown, Figs. 37 and 38, the difference between the old style round-faced and new style flat-faced chuck is readily apparent. The lines terminating in the center of inside bearing of chuck which holds the work, show the direction of pressure on both inside and outside of chuck when in use, and its relation to the spindle. The old style is practically a shoulder chuck up to No. 10, as all, or most of the bearing is outside of the spindle, and the truth of the chuck is dependent upon the strength of each section; the weakest of the three will spring most. In most designs and all chucks of small

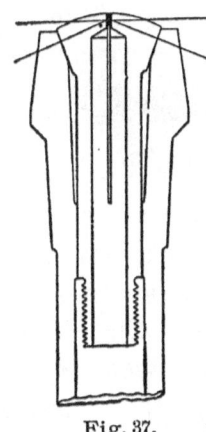
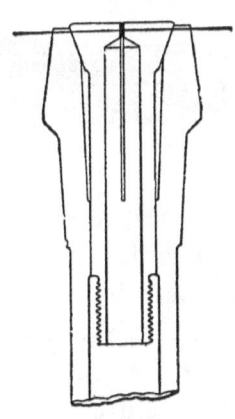

Fig. 37. Fig. 38.

diameters, each section is weak and springs easily. In the flat face the bearing is under the head and the pressure direct as it should be. This is the only correctly designed chuck yet produced. With Dale chucks like this, in full and half sizes, the finest staff and pinion work can be done. We make them for any lathe, from No. 3 to No. 30, and in any size for Moseley No. 2, on account of conoidal design."

The other manufacturers' immediately denied the force of this reasoning, and a controversy ran for some time. Mr. Hardinge claimed the accuracy of his position, and the others claimed its value was largely imaginary and was offset by the inconveniences of having to work closer to the lathe spindle. Neither side ever convinced the other, and we give the controversy, without expressing an opinion of our own, chiefly on account of its historical value, as the date of the reintroduction of the flat-faced chucks. A very large number of these chucks have been sold, and have given satisfaction to their purchasers.

Another special form of chuck is the conoidal, Fig. 39, invented by Mr. C. S. Moseley, for his No. 2 and larger lathes. The reasoning was that such chucks could be manufactured with more uniform accuracy, as the gradual taper from jaw to spring made them less liable to crack in hard-

Fig. 39. The Conoidal Chuck.

ening, and also less liable to wabble when the chuck was used beyond its proper range. It is a very satisfactory chuck as made by the Moseley Lathe Co., but considerable trouble has been found in using imported chucks of this pattern, for the reason that if they are not evenly split and tempered the greater strength of the thicker springs in them will accentuate the difficulties of drawing the several jaws to a true center. Also, if the arc to which the chuck is ground and that of the lathe spindle do not coincide, the greater length of the taper increases the difficulties which would otherwise be encountered.

For these reasons other manufacturers have clung to the conical head, and preferred to use a short head, join it to the body as nicely as possible when grinding, and take chances on having them snap off at the joint when hardening.

Perhaps it may add to the reader's knowledge of the subject if we briefly summarize the process of manufacture of these indispensable articles. There is no secret about the manufacture of a chuck; any one that is near enough to a factory in which they are made may enter and see it done; but unless he possesses the necessary personal skill, he can never make a uniform product. That is the whole secret—skill in working, hardening and tempering steel. Briefly it may be summarized into the knowledge necessary to build automatic machinery that will run with perfect truth, and this carries with it the knowledge necessary to successfully operate such machinery after it is built, for in this case uniformity of production is a necessary concomitant of accuracy and to secure uniformity handwork must be eliminated as far as possible. For this reason all chucks are made upon special tools, built in the factory.

The blank is formed on the end of a bar of the finest tool steel, in a specially constructed turret lathe, which performs eight distinct operations, including the cutting of the thread and the final one of cutting off the blank, a proper margin of stock being left for the subsequent operations. The blanks are then reduced to the proper external dimensions in a grinding machine, which takes very light cuts, and work and wheels revolve in opposite directions at great speed. Everything is measured by micrometers and brought to exact size; great care is used and the work is never hurried. After grinding, the threads are sized by a standard die and the chucks are keyseated by a milling tool carrying a cutter corresponding to the make of lathe for which the chuck is intended. Then the heads are rounded to the precise arc required (which also varies with different chucks), and they are stamped with the name of the manufacturer. The chucks are next "back drilled;" that is, the large holes clear through them are made by placing the blanks in the head spindle and the proper sized drill in the tail spindle of another machine. This hole extends nearly to the face of the chuck, falling short by just the amount necessary to give the proper length of the jaws of the chuck. This length of grip is carefully proportioned to the size of the hole, so as to give the greatest holding power, which is a point in which many chucks are deficient. Too short a jaw reduces the time required in grinding the jaws to truth, and hence reduces the factory cost at the expense of the holding power of the chuck, while too long a jaw adds to the expense of manufacture without adding to the value of the product.

The blanks are then stamped with the number or size of the finished chuck, after which they are "front drilled" on another machine, the drills entering from the front and making the hole which forms the jaws of the chuck, sufficient stock being left for grinding the hole to truth after splitting.

They are then split to a standard depth of spline, carefully proportioned to the size of the particular chuck in hand, and varying with each size. This is an important point in which many makers of chucks have failed, for unless a chuck be properly split it will not hold the work with any degree of accuracy. The splitting is done by means of small steel circular saws, which are proportioned in thickness to the work to be done, and they require another special machine to keep them in order, which is done, like the rest, by grinding.

After splitting, the jaws of the chucks are ground out by means of revolving laps, and either emery, carborundum or corundum and oil, to nearly the desired size, after which they are hardened and tempered. In many factories this completes the job; many Swiss and some American chucks show the blackened surface in the jaws, left there by the hardening process. In the best factories, however, they are again ground and polished inside and out, in order to remove any inequalities caused by hardening and tempering, and are not allowed to leave the factory until they are perfectly true, inside and outside.

Of course, it is only natural that such processes should leave traces of their presence or absence on the work, and any one knowing them can readily judge of the quality of workmanship by inspection of the chuck, if he knows where to look at it.

When split chucks were first made they were sized by Stubbs' wire gauge, as they were intended to use wire, chiefly, and Stubbs' gauge was then in universal use. Ambrose Webster was the first man to make them to millimeter gauge; he reasoned, correctly, that the chucks used by watchmakers were chiefly for repair work, and therefore should be adapted to the measuring instruments in use by watchmakers. These were at that time nearly all imported from Europe, and were consequently on the metric system. Therefore he made his unit of measurement one-tenth of a millimeter, and numbered them so that the number of the chuck should express the number of tenths of a millimeter of the diameter of the hole. By this system the smallest practicable chuck is No. 3, which is three-tenths of a millimeter, and the largest No. 70, which is seven millimeters, the largest practicable size for the No. 2 lathe. The convenience of having chucks to correspond with the gauges in use was immediately recognized and the system was followed by others as the demand for it grew.

Tool makers in America, being accustomed to work by thousandths of an inch, and having their gauges on that system, demanded chucks on the same system, and tool makers' chucks are generally sized in that way.

We, therefore, have three systems of sizes in more or less general use today, as follows: Stubbs' wire gauge, in which the holes get smaller as the numbers increase, and the metric and decimal systems, in which the holes increase with the increase of numbers, indicating their sizes.

The following tables were compiled by Mr. Franklin Hardinge, a manufacturer of chucks; they give the dimensions of all chucks in common use among watchmakers, and a close study of the tables in connection with what has been said concerning the design and manufacture of these useful articles should prove very interesting:

TABLE GIVING DIFFERENT SYSTEMS OF MEASURING CHUCKS AND THEIR EQUIVALENTS.

Stubs.	Metric.	Decimals of Inch.	Stubs.	Metric.	Decimals of Inch.	Stubs.	Metric.	Decimals of Inch.	Stubs.	Metric.	Decimals of Inch.
80	3	.0118	----	11½	.0452	35	----	.108	16	----	.175
----	----	.013	----	12	.047	----	----	.1.9	----	45	.177
79	3½	.0137	----	----	.049	34	28	.110	15	----	.178
78	----	.014	----	12½	.0492	33	----	.112	14	----	.180
----	----	.015	55	----	.050	----	29	.114	----	----	.1811
77	4	.0157	----	13	.0511	32	----	.115	----	46	.181
----	----	.016	----	----	.052	----	30	.118	13	----	.182
----	----	.017	----	13½	.0531	31	----	.120	----	----	.184
76	4½	.0177	54	----	.055	----	----	.121	12	47	.185
----	----	.018	----	14	.0551	----	31	.122	----	----	.188
----	----	.019	----	14½	.057	----	----	.124	11	48	.189
75	5	.0196	53	----	.058	----	32	.126	----	----	.191
----	----	.040	----	15	.059	30	----	.127	10	----	.1929
----	----	.021	----	----	.061	----	33	.1299	----	49	.192
74	5½	.0216	52	16	.063	----	----	.130	----	----	.194
73	----	.022	----	----	.064	----	----	.133	9	----	.1969
----	----	.023	51	----	.066	----	34	.1339	----	50	.196
72	6	.0236	----	17	.067	29	----	.134	----	----	.197
----	----	.024	50	----	.069	----	----	.136	8	----	.199
----	----	.025	----	----	.070	----	35	.1378	7	----	.200
71	6½	.0255	----	18	.0709	28	----	.139	----	51	.201
----	----	.026	49	----	.072	----	36	.1417	6	----	.2047
70	----	.027	----	----	.073	----	----	.142	5	52	.204
----	7	.0275	----	19	.0748	27	----	.143	----	----	.207
69	----	.029	48	----	.075	----	37	.145	4	----	.208
----	7½	.0295	----	----	.076	26	----	.146	----	53	.209
68	----	.030	47	----	.077	25	----	.148	----	----	.2126
67	----	.031	----	20	.0787	----	38	.1496	----	54	.2125
----	8	.0315	46	----	.079	24	----	.151	----	55	.216
66	----	.032	45	----	.081	23	----	.153	2	----	.2195
65	----	.033	----	----	.082	----	39	.1535	----	56	.2204
----	8½	.0334	44	1	.085	----	----	.154	----	57	.224
64	----	.035	----	22	.086	22	----	.155	1	----	.227
----	9	.0354	43	----	.088	21	----	.157	----	58	.228
63	----	.036	----	23	.0906	----	40	.1575	----	59	.2322
62	----	.037	----	----	.091	----	----	.160	----	60	.2362
----	9½	.0374	42	----	.092	20	----	.161	----	61	.240
61	----	.038	----	24	.094	----	41	.1614	----	62	.244
60	----	.039	41	----	.095	----	----	.163	----	63	.248
----	10	.0393	40	----	.097	19	----	.164	----	64	.2519
59	----	.040	----	25	.098	----	42	.1654	----	65	.2559
58	----	.041	39	----	.099	----	----	.166	----	66	.2598
----	10½	.0413	----	----	.100	18	----	.168	----	67	.2677
57	----	.042	38	----	.101	----	----	.169	----	68	.2637
----	----	.043	----	26	.1024	----	43	.1693	----	69	.2716
----	11	.0433	37	----	.103	17	----	.172	----	70	.2755
56	----	.45	36	27	.106	----	44	.173			

THE AMERICAN LATHE

TABLE SHOWING DIMENSIONS OF CHUCKS OF VARIOUS MANUFACTURES.

NAME OF CHUCK	Dia. of Head	Dia. of Body	Dia. of Thread	Pitch of Thread	Angle of Head	Total Length less curve	Largest Hole clear Through	Largest Hole in Front
Dale No. 1	.500	.335	.295	40 Eng.	15°	1.437	m.m. 5.8	m.m. 6.5
Dale A	.500	.335	.325	40 "	15°	1.437	" 6.5	" 6.5
Dale No. 2	.625	.450	.395	30 "	15°	1.812	" 8.	" 10.
Dale B	.625	.450	.435	30 "	15°	1.812	" 10.	" 10.
Dale No. 3	.890	.650	.560	24 "	15°	2.250	" 10.	" 14.
Dale C	.890	.650	.635	24 "	15°	2.250	" 14.	" 14.
Dale No. 4	1.125	.825	.700	20 "	15°	3.125	" 14.	" 18.
Dale D	1.125	.825	.810	20 "	15°	3.125	" 18.	" 18.
Hopkins No. 1	.435	.2285	.187	48 "	25°	1.031	" 2.8	" 4.2
Hopkins No. 2	.530	.325	.250	36 "	25°	1.187	" 4.4	" 6.5
Hopkins No. 3	.460	.260	.220	40 "	25°	1.—	" 3.8	" 5.
Hopkins No. 3 & 4	.530	.3255	.285	40 "	25°	1.360	" 5.2	" 6.5
Hopkins No. 4	.850	.605	.545	24 "	20°	2.437	" 10.	" 13.
Rivett No. 1	.500	.300	.265	40 "	20°	1.250	" 4.8	" 6.
Rivett No. 3	.825	.590	.525	26 Eng.	20°	2.125	m.m. 10.	m.m. 13.
Rivett No. 4	1.025	.750	.665	20 Eng.	20°	2.750	" 13.	" 17.
Stehmens J. & S. No. 1.	.650	.370	.320	34 "	20°	1.812	" 6.5	" 7.
Stehmens J. & S. No. 2.	.650	.380	.325	32 "	20°	1.812	" 6.5	" 7.
Moseley No. 1	.430	.240	.208	48 "	25°	1.250	" 3.8	" 4.7
Moseley No. 1 x 2	.500	.3135	.270	40 "	20°	1.250	" 5.	" 6.5
Moseley No. 2	.500	.314	.270	40 "	Condl	1.562	" 5.	" 6.5
Moseley No. 3 Conoidal.	.600	.400	.350	36 "	Condl	1.750	" 6.5	" 7.
Moseley No. 3, 15 degree	.625	.400	.350	36 "	15°	1.844	" 6.5	" 7.
Moseley " 4, Bench Lathe	.875	.590	.490	25 "	20°	2.312	" 9.5	" 13.
Whitcomb No. 1	.375	.1965	.168	55 Met.	20°	.936	" 2.5	" 3.6
Whitcomb No. 1, Watch Factory	.435	.236	.182	63 "	20°	1.093	" 3.3	" 4.4
Whitcomb No. 1¼	.435	.255	.220	63 "	20°	1.140	" 3.8	" 5.
Webster Whitcomb	.500	.3147	.270	63 "	20°	1.312	" 5.	" 6.5
Whitcomb No. 2 Watch Factory	.560	.355	.278	.71 Met.	20°	1.500	m.m. 5.5	m.m. 7.
Whitcomb No. 2¼ "	.750	.4725	.370	.85 "	20°	1.531	" 7.	" 9.
Whitcomb No. 3	.865	.590	.508	1. "	20°	2.125	" 10.	" 13.
Whitcomb No. 3 Large Thread	.865	.590	.587	1.25 "	15°	2.187	" 13.	" 13.
Whitcomb No. 4	1.080	.747	.665	1.25 "	15°	2.875	" 13.	" 17.
Whitcomb No. 4 Large Thread	1.080	.747	.745	1.63 "	15°	2.875	" 17.	" 17.
Triumph or Elgin	.500	.275	.250	48 Eng	25°	1.218	" 4.4	" 5.
Mansfield	.500	.300	.270	40 "	20°	1.250	" 4.8	" 6.
Hinkley	.475	.280	.250	40 "	20°	1.312	" 4.2	" 5.5
Stark No. 1	.435	.1875	.165	48 "	22½°	1.108	" 2.3	" 3.5
Stark No. 2	.500	.2205	.185	48 "	22½°	1.250	" 2.8	" 4.2
Stark No. 3 Watchmaker.	.500	.245	.185	48 "	20°	1.218	" 2.8	" 4.5
Stark E	.500	.300	.270	40 "	20°	1.250	" 4.8	" 6.
Stark N	.625	.355	.305	40 "	20°	1.750	" 6.5	" 7.
Stark No. 3 Bench Lathe	.875	.590	.508	26 Eng.	20°	2.125	m.m. 10.	m.m. 13.
Stark No. 4 " "	1.430	.998	.990	20 "	15°	2.312	" 25.	" 25.
Geneva	.425	.235	.200	71 Met.	20°	1.156	" 3.5	" 4.7
Kearney	.500	.300	.265	44 Eng.	25°	1.531	" 4.8	" 6.
Tarrant Bench Lathe	.800	.550	.475	32 "	25°	2.500	" 9.	" 12.
Springfield No. 4	.800	.500	.425	32 "	25°	1.875	" 8.	" 11.
Olin Watchmakers	.500	.311	.270	40 "	20°	1.250	" 5.	" 6.
Pratt & Whitney	.850	.600	.500	24 "	20°	2.063	" 10.	" 13.
Automatic Special	.475	.281	.248	32 "	20°	1.500	" 4.	" 5.5
Ballou & Whitcomb	.475	.3147	.270	63 Met.	15°	1.937	" 5.	" 6.5
Lapper Special	.760	.495	.430	40 Eng.	20°	2.125	" 8.	" 11.
Star Special	.600	.320	.260	40 "	25°	1.563	" 4.8	" 6.5
Ide Bench Lathe	.800	.500	.425	32 "	20°	2.	" 8.	" 11.
Special Tool makers	1.650	1.125	1.125	18 "	12°	7.	" 22.22	" 25.4

TABLE OF DECIMAL EQUIVALENTS OF MILLIMETERS AND INCHES FOR TRANSLATING EITHER.

MM. Inches.	MM. Inches.	MM. Inches.	MM. Inches.	MM. Inches
1-100 = .00039	21-100 = .00826	41-100 = .01614	61-100 = .02401	81-100 = .03189
2-100 = .00079	22-100 = .00866	42-100 = .01654	62-100 = .02441	82-100 = .03228
3-100 = .00118	23-100 = .00905	43-100 = .01693	63-100 = .02480	83-100 = .03267
4-100 = .00157	24-100 = .00945	44-100 = .01732	64-100 = .02520	84-100 = .03307
5-100 = .00196	25-100 = .00984	45-100 = .01771	65-100 = .02559	85-100 = .03346
6-100 = .00236	26-100 = .01024	46-100 = .01811	66-100 = .02598	86-100 = .03386
7-100 = .00275	27-100 = .01063	47-100 = .01850	67-100 = .02637	87-100 = .03425
8-100 = .00315	28-100 = .01102	48-100 = .01890	68-100 = .02677	88-100 = .03465
9-100 = .00354	29-100 = .01141	49-100 = .01929	69-100 = .02716	89-100 = .03504
10-100 = .00394	30-100 = .01181	50-100 = .01969	70-100 = .02756	90-100 = .03543
11-100 = .00433	31-100 = .01220	51-100 = .02008	71-100 = .02795	91-100 = .03582
12-100 = .00472	32-100 = .01260	52-100 = .02047	72-100 = .02835	92-100 = .03622
13-100 = .00511	33-100 = .01299	53-100 = .02086	73-100 = .02874	93-100 = .03661
14-100 = .00551	34-100 = .01339	54-100 = .02126	74-100 = .02913	94-100 = .03701
15-100 = .00590	35-100 = .01378	55-100 = .02165	75-100 = .02952	95-100 = .03740
16-100 = .00630	36-100 = .01417	56-100 = .02205	76-100 = .02992	96-100 = .03780
17-100 = .00669	37-100 = .01456	57-100 = .02244	77-100 = .03031	97-100 = .03819
18-100 = .00709	38-100 = .01496	58-100 = .02283	78-100 = .03071	98-100 = .03858
19-100 = .00748	39-100 = .01535	59-100 = .02322	79-100 = .03110	99-100 = .03897
20-100 = .00787	40-100 = .01575	60-100 = .02362	80-100 = .03150	1 mm. = .03937

10 mm. = 1 Centimeter = 0.3937 inches.   10 dm. = 1 Meter = 39.37 inches
10 cm. = 1 Decimeter = 3.937   "   25.4 mm. = 1 English inch.

CHUCK GAUGE SHOWING ACTUAL SIZES OF CHUCKS ACCORDING TO THEIR NUMBERS ON THE METRIC SYSTEM.

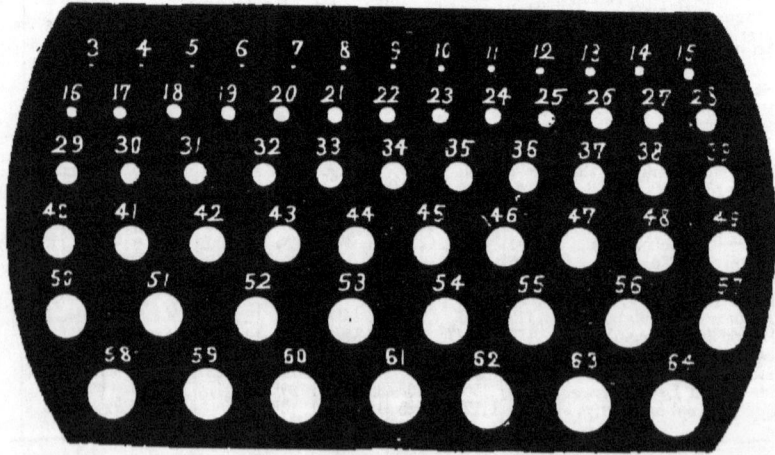

In view of the detailed reasons which we were careful to set forth at length when considering the construction of split chucks, a comparison of the early and present forms of chucks is given in Figs. 40 and 41. Placed in this way the reader will at once see the immense superiority in strength, durability and capacity of the modern chuck. Probably more of the Moseley 1x2 and Webster-Whitcomb chucks are now in use than of all others put together, but

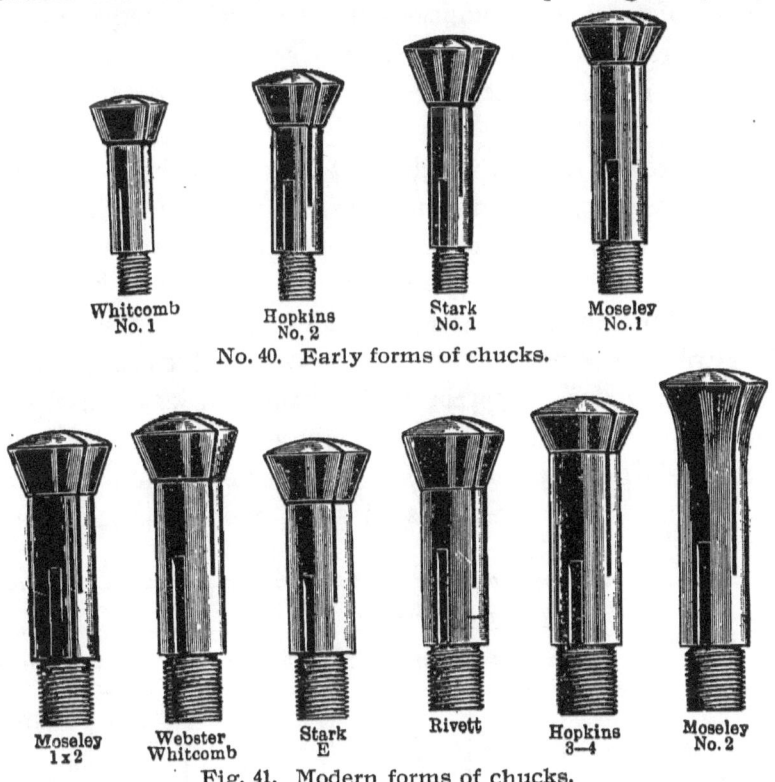

No. 40. Early forms of chucks.

Fig. 41. Modern forms of chucks.

this may, perhaps, be attributed to the superior enterprise of those manufacturers in pushing their product, rather than to any inherent excellence of workmanship or design, as close study will reveal that there is little substantial difference between the modern chucks, while there were marked differences in proportions and design of the earlier forms. The workmanship on the earlier forms was uniformly excellent, but the proportions were found, in use, to be not of the best, and hence they were discarded in favor of others which were found to have greater capacity and more durability under strain.

The final point to be considered in the split chuck is its accuracy and durability in the hands of a competent workman. In this connection we cannot refrain from giving the results of some tests published in the *American Jeweler* several years ago by Mr. A. S. Henry, together with a description of the process of testing them, as described by him:

"The set of chucks which were tested had been in daily use for seven years and much of the work in which they were used was heavier than the ordinary work of the watchmaker. Under these circumstances it is but fair to the maker to say that we consider that the error shown is attributable more to the heavy work which they have done than to any inherent fault of the chucks themselves, and while some of the errors, may, at a glance, seem extremely large, yet they are in reality very small, and in many instances the error is so small as to approach perfection very closely.

CHUCK No.	OPEN			CLOSED		
	Spline 1	Spline 2	Spline 3	Spline 1	Spline 2	Spline 3
11	0	5	10	0	−15	−10
12	0	2	15	0	− 5	5
13	0	4	6	0	4	0
14	0	3	5	0	− 7	−10
15	0	24	15	0	6	4
16	0	− 9	− 8	0	− 6	− 7
17	0	−10	15	0	0	− 3
18	0	− 1	1	0	− 1	1
19	0	0	− 1	0	− 3	−10
20	0	1	0	0	− 8	− 5
21	0	6	10	0	− 9	− 9
22	0	− 3	− 3	0	− 2	− 2
23	0	2	11	0	− 9	3
24	0	1	6	0	1	2
25	0	− 3	− 5	0	− 2	− 4
26	0	− 5	2	0	−10	− 5

"In the above table one division on the scale represents one twenty-thousandth of an inch, so that the chucks were practically perfect after seven years of steady usage.

"The length of lever used was ten inches from the arbor to the outer end, and from arbor to the end resting in the chuck was one-eighth of an inch, thus increasing the error 80 times at the outer end. An accurately made scale, graduated to one two-hundred and fiftieth of an inch, was set at the outer end of the lever, from which the extent of the motion could be read by means of a double eyeglass. The mouth of the lathe spindle was thoroughly cleansed with gasoline and wiped with tissue paper, and the air ball was used to remove the last traces of fibre or dust. The chucks were treated in a similar manner, and carefully inserted and drawn into the spindle until they revolved the spindle, which was set so as to be perfectly free. This was done in order that the chuck would be drawn into place, yet was left in the normal state. In this way each chuck could be tested under the same conditions as nearly as possible. The spline bearing the chuck number was selected as No. 1, and the holes in the index were selected which would bring the center of the splines at the top. Extreme care was exercised that the draw-in spindle was not touched so as to change its position, and the index pin, as well, was inserted only sufficiently to hold the index in position while the measurement was being made. The lathe spindle was tightened so that it was barely free, and on trial it was found that the same readings could be made repeatedly.

"At spline 1 the index was adjusted to stand at zero, and this formed the base of measurement with which the other splines could be compared. In the table the absence of sign indicates that the lever went below zero, or the radius was greater than spline 1, while the — sign indicates the lever went above normal. One division on the scale showed the one-twenty thousandth of an inch variation in the chuck. The splines were first tested open, and then at spline 1 the chuck was drawn in until the lever indicated that it had been contracted one-four hundredth of an inch. The index finger was again set at zero and the readings proceeded with as before mentioned.

This testing may be done in various ways, but the easiest and simplest way is to take a piece of pegwood and setting the T rest so it is about one-eighth of an inch from the work, lay the piece of pegwood upon it, when the eccentricity of our work may be judged by revolving the lathe spindle and noticing the outer end of the pegwood stick, which will stand still if the work be true. By using a full length stick, and setting the T rest, as above, we will multiply the error in the work about fifty times. For those who want something more accurate and mechanical looking to test with, a long and light lever may be made of aluminum, which may be made of considerable length, from ten to fifteen inches long. Having the lever made, drill a hole near the larger end, into which is fitted a carefully made, pointed, steel arbor. By making the hole for the arbor one-tenth of an inch from the point where the end rests against the work, and the lever ten inches long beyond the arbor, we can magnify the error in our work one hundred times. To find how many times such a tool would increase the error, divide the length of the lever beyond the arbor by the distance between the center of the arbor and the point where it rests against the work. While a single long lever is, perhaps, not so compact as a system of compound levers, it is more accurate and easier made and less chance for error.

This lever is now mounted between hollow centers, as shown in Fig. 42, which is made to fit the shoe of the T rest. If we constructed the supports of the knife edge form, we would, theoretically, have a bearing with no error, but practically the pointed arbor, if carefully made, will be all that is needed. When using the tool, to know what is the amount of error, it will be necessary to have a finely divided scale at the outer end from which we can read the extent of motion. Supposing that our lever is so constructed as to increase the error one hundred fold, and the end of the lever moves one-fiftieth of an inch, by dividing one-fiftieth of an inch by one hundred we have the one five-thousandths of an inch that our work is out of true at the point supporting the end of the lever. This tool also may be used to measure the error in a balance staff, by putting the tool between one pair of centers while the staff is supported in the other pair of an ordinary depthing

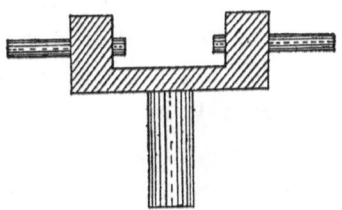

Fig. 42. Yoke for Testing Lever.

tool, and by means of a gauge set the jaws so they are just one-tenth of an inch, or whatever proportion the lever is made for, apart; then by revolving the work the error may be read off from the scale.

The chucks which we have been considering have all had the grip for the work smaller, or no larger, than the hole through the chuck, and were designed primarily for feeding the stock through the chuck when performing work upon it. There are several other kinds, however, that are equally important, those with solid bodies and those with steps or shoulders larger than the hole through them, but which still belong to the first class, in that they are split like them and grip or hold the work in the same manner.

Fig. 43 shows the original form of step chucks. This chuck originated in the days of the old No. 1 lathe, when it was frequently necessary to use a device that would hold work which was larger than the hole through the chuck. It was at one time used for jewel settings, pinions that needed work done on the pivots of their staffs, the crowns of pendants, etc. It is a difficult chuck to make on account of the trouble experienced in getting the end

Fig. 43.

wall of the step true in the flat and joining it with the sidewall in such a way as to keep the corners sharp. In addition the step hole is frequently not concentric with the chuck unless very carefully ground, and the hole is either' too deep or too shallow for most of the work on which it is used, so that a rod must be inserted from the rear through the draw-in spindle and the shallow work pushed out to its proper place after inserting it in the chuck. As used in the watch factory, it gave complete satisfaction, because the step was made to exactly fit the piece it was designed to hold, and it was used for that work and no other, but it was not designed to be a universal appliance, and those who tried to use it as such soon found themselves in difficulty; in addition to its lack of range it was difficult

Fig. 44. Stepping Device. *a*—rests in chuck and should be slightly less than diameter of work. *b*—tightens in rear of draw-in spindle. *c*—turning this regulates depth of step.

to clean; dirt would gather in the corners of the step and affect its truth.

For these reasons the introduction of the larger chucks was soon followed by the stepping device, Fig 44. This consists of a rod having a screw thread at its front end, on which may be placed cylinders of any desired diameter, which should be a little smaller than the hole of the chuck in which it is being used. By having a sufficient number of these removable cylinders any wire chuck may be converted into a step chuck and the objections as to range of work and difficulty of cleaning noted in regard to the solid step do not apply. Jewel settings and other thin, flat pieces which are liable to turn askew in chucking, may be perfectly handled in this way. The step is also useful in chucking short pieces, in order to bring them to uniform lengths after cutting off, and in many other ways. The collar shown midway on the rod should be an easy fit in the draw-in spindle. Its object is to keep the step central, so that the end will enter the chuck jaws easily. In use, the tapered seat *b* is pressed friction tight in the draw-in spindle and the thread used to regulate the depth of step desired, or it may also be used to push out very thin work, if there is

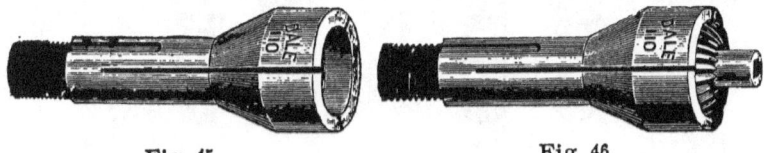

Fig. 45. Fig. 46.

difficulty in withdrawing it from the front. Care should be taken not to do this, however, if working on a number of pieces which should be of the same dimensions, as constantly changing the rod would make it impossible to get the same depth of step for all, as the adjusting thread is coarse, and the rod could not be returned to its exact position every time.

Among the class of shoulder split chucks, Figs. 45 and 46, are the Hardinge Crown chucks. As they are made in properly ranged sizes the objections to the solid shoulder chuck do not apply to these chucks. They are made of fine bar steel, in thirteen sizes, and numbered as follows: 60, 65, 70, 75, 80, 85, 90, 95, 100, 105, 110, 115, 120, 125; 60 being the smallest and 125 the largest. With a full set you can hold all sizes of crowns, from the smallest Swiss to the largest American. They will be found a great convenience in fitting crowns, as they hold them so as to enable the workman to operate on every part without trouble to himself or injury to the crown. Do not expect to hold all sizes of crowns with two or three sizes of chucks.

Another form of shoulder chuck is the auxiliary split chuck for jeweling, Fig. 47; while unnecessary for any one having a full set of chucks and a stepping device, they are frequently useful to those who are not so well provided, and they are cheap. They are made of brass and are stepped for jewels having range from No. 15 to No. 33 in odd numbers, also even numbers if desired. They are to be used in a wire chuck, being made in two sizes of body, viz., No. 38 and No. 50. The steps are five sizes larger than the holes, so that jewels can be reversed in the steps; they are

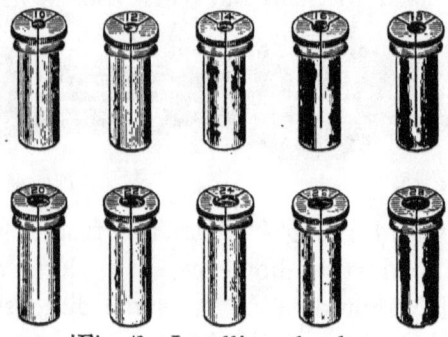

[Fig. 47. Jewelling chucks.

in sets of ten, as above. They are made also without steps, for screws, if desired. A small auxiliary brass chuck, to fit No. 38 wire chuck, is frequently used to hold screws and not injure the threads.

Other chucks for holding crowns and other special devices will be considered when we reach the consideration of that class of chucks having a solid body and holding the work outside of the spindle.

The next variety of step or shoulder chuck is the wheel chuck; these differ from those previously described in having more than one step on the same chuck, Fig. 48.

In the beginning they were made with four-tenths of a millimeter between steps; this did very well while there were few sizes of wheels which the watchmaker had to handle; and five chucks were considered a full set. The addition of sizes of watches, however, made new sizes of wheel chucks necessary, and a full set now consists of ten chucks having steps ranging two-tenths of a millimeter apart from 50 to 228. In order to get sufficient bearing on the back of each step to properly chuck the wheel, the steps on each chuck are ten sizes apart. Thus the first step on chuck No. 1 is 50; the second is 70, the third 90, etc. If we study the table of wheel-chuck sizes, Fig. 49, we shall find the first step, No. 50, on chuck No. 1; No. 52 is the first on chuck No. 2; 54 is first on No. 3, 56 on No. 4, and so on

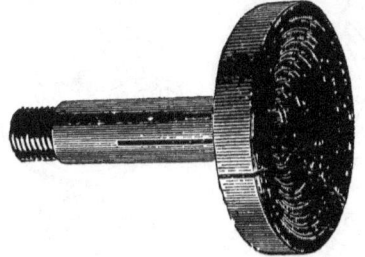

Fig. 48.

until we reach 68, on No. 10. Returning, we repeat the steps on the next round, and so on until we reach 228 on the last step of the last chuck. In this way we secure 90 steps on ten chucks, while giving a proper bearing to each.

In step chucks the important points are that the steps shall be round, concentric and that the side walls of each step shall be straight and square with the bottom, so that they shall grip the wheel properly. Brass wheels, crossed out in the middle and with the rims still further weakened by the teeth cut into them, are very much weaker than a solid disc would be, and therefore they are easily sprung out of round. When this happens, there is trouble with the depthings, unless the rounding-up tool is used, so that it is better to avoid it by seeing that the chucks fit your wheel in such a manner that they will hold it securely without using pressure enough to throw it out of round. There-

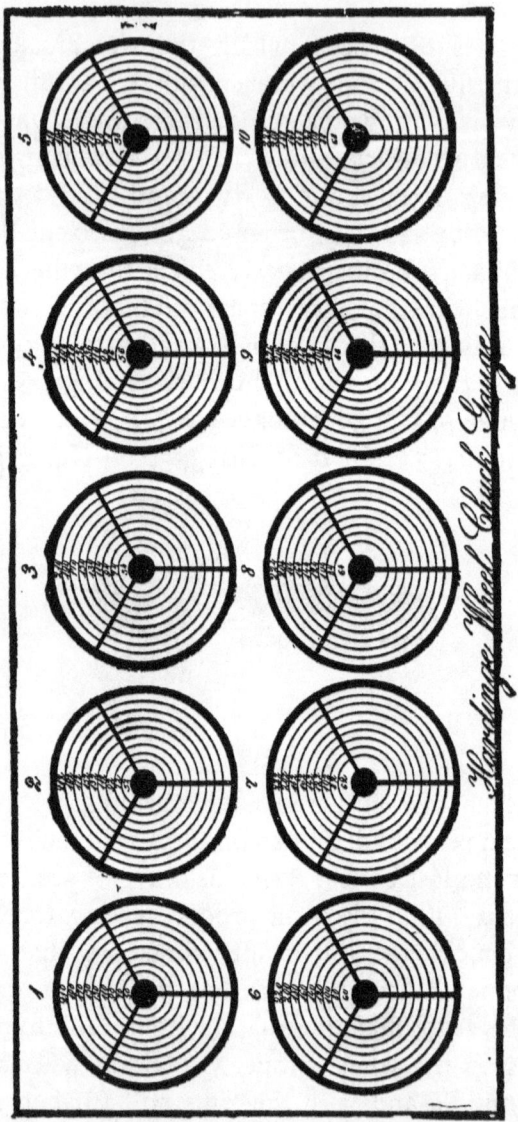

Fig. 49.

fore have plenty of wheel chucks and get a close fit, so that the wheel will be gripped by practically a complete circle instead of by three points only; otherwise you are certain to make trouble for yourself. If you cannot get a fit with the wheel chuck do not use it, but cement the wheel on a cement chuck, or use the face plate, Fig. 50, if the wheel is large enough so that the plate will take it.

CHAPTER IV.

FACE PLATES AND LARGE CHUCKS.

Work that is larger than the spindle must necessarily be held outside of it, and for large work that is capable of being held by it, there is no better device than the universal face plate of the machine shop, which is shown in two of

Fig. 50. Universal Head.

its adaptations for watchmakers, in Fig. 50, the universal head, and Fig. 51, the universal face plate. The universal head, Fig. 50, is the truest, most durable and most expensive of these devices. It consists of a complete, independent headstock for the lathe, having the front end of its spindle extended far enough to receive a hardened steel plate, which is shrunk or soldered on to the spindle, so as to be permanently fastened to it. The spindle is hollow, and is pierced at the front end by a pump center, having a male center that is operated by a rod extending through the spindle. Tapering peep holes in the plate are provided so that the workman may see the point of his center when placing the work before fastening it on the face plate. This is shown more clearly in the rear view of the universal face plate, Fig. 51, in which the point of the center may be clearly seen through the hole. Three jaws to hold the work

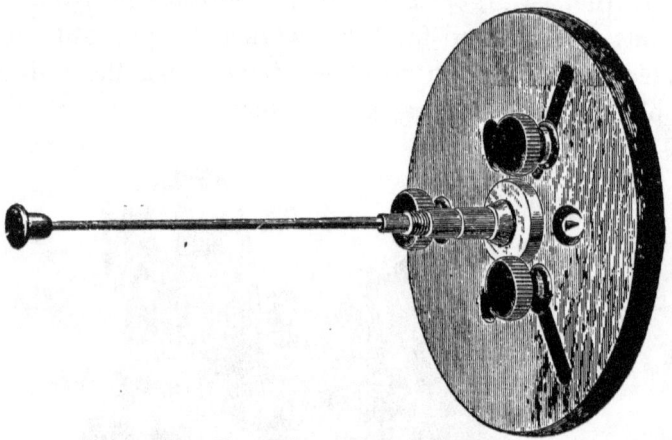

Fig. 51. Universal Face Plate.

are arranged to slide back and forth in radial slots in the face plate, to provide adjustment for varying sizes of work. They are fastened by thumbscrews at the back, and carry

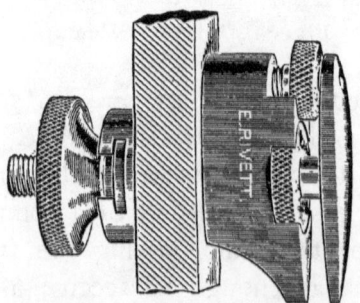

Fig. 52. Enlarged View of Jaw.

clamps upon their faces, which are operated by two screws. The screw in the middle of the jaw regulates the width of opening, while that at the outer end presses up on the end of the jaw and thus exerts a downward or clamping force upon the work. Fig. 52 shows an enlarged view of the jaw in which the action is clearly shown.

Everything about the appliance is made and fitted with the utmost care and the plate is ground off after it is mounted on the spindle in its own headstock. The only objection to the universal head is its cost and this, amounting, as it does, to a sum equal to the cost of the lathe, is practically prohibitory, so that very few of them are used.

The universal face plate, Fig. 51, is the same appliance, mounted on a chuck, so that it can be put in the headstock and held in place by the draw-in spindle. The pump center rod is screwed into the pump center, and is unscrewed be-

Face Plate, showing Circular Slots.

fore inserting the chuck in place. It is then passed into the draw-in spindle from the rear, and screwed into the pump center again, when the face plate has been fixed in its position, after which it is operated as described for the universal head. Nearly all workmen buy this plate instead of the universal head, as its cost is low, and while not as strong as the head, it has been found sufficient for the class of work it is called upon to perform. It should be handled and used with care, however, as, if sprung, all work done upon it would be thicker on one side until it was sent to a factory to be corrected. All parts of it are hardened, and the watchmaker would only make matters worse if he attempted to repair the damage himself. With proper usage and care it will stay true as long as the lathe, and every owner of a lathe should have a face plate, if he has not a universal head.

We have always recommended the universal head as the most durable and accurate device, and where economy is not absolutely necessary we should advise its use rather than the universal plate. The universal plate is subject to the errors which creep in from worn throats of lathe spindles, and also the wear and tear of the stem of the chuck on which it is fitted, and the risks of getting dirt in between the mouth of the spindle and the chuck. When all these points are properly watched and guarded against, accidentally bringing the hand rest against the jaws when revolving would be sure to break the chuck pin of the lathe, or injure the jaws, and might spoil the universal plate.

The centering from the back is provided for the reason that it is truer and more convenient than to center with a male center in the tail stock, as is done by the machinist, or with a peg wood or graver point from the T-rest. If the slide rest is on, the tail stock cannot be brought close enough to use in this way, and if it could be so used the taper in the tail stock might not be exactly centered, so the independent center has been provided. Ambrose Webster is said to have first made the taper peep holes in the plate, and C. S. Moseley was first to curve the radial slots, so that the jaws should be brought nearer to the center.

Rivett makes his plates of solid nickel.

A question often asked is: Why is the face plate not made to screw on, as it is on the machinist's lathe, so that any chuck could be used with it? This is not done for mechanical reasons in the manufacture. The spindle could be extended and a screw nose put on it, to take the face plate, as is done in engine lathes, were it not for the fact that the spindle is hardened and the threads could not be trued up after hardening. The face plate is also hardened, and if they were put together in this way each face plate would have to be put on the spindle it was intended for, and ground up true on its own spindle. This would prevent making face plates and keeping them in stock, and if the plates should get mixed in shipping a consignment of lathes from the factory, there would be further trouble. The present arrangement answers all purposes, and is decidedly the best that has yet been evolved. In inserting the work the jaws should be moved towards the outside enough to allow the work to pass between them. The clamps on the jaws are now opened by loosening the knurled nuts at the back. Withdraw the pump center so that the work will not strike it, and insert the work. One jaw should now be lightly clamped so as to hold the work while adjusting the small stop nuts, which will be seen in Fig. 52, between the base and the top of the jaws, which should be so adjusted that when the jaw is clamped it will come down squarely on the work.

While looking through one of the peep holes from the rear, press forward the pump center until it meets the hole or centering point of the work, and look through each of the three peep holes of the plate, to make sure the pump center is where it appears to be on the work, as it is easy to be deceived on this point, owing to the way you are looking at it. When you have centered the work, hold it lightly in position by means of the knurled nuts at the back. Now bring forward the pump center firmly and bind the knurled nuts down securely in position. By proceeding in this way you get the work centered absolutely, which could not be done otherwise if one jaw was open more than the others, which would allow the work to tilt, thus throwing the center of the work, when clamped to one side of the lathe center. In using the face plate to upright, fasten the two pieces together and mount the work as above, using the pointed center in the tailstock for locating the required point in the work.

Fig. 53 illustrates a live center with dog face plate. This attachment is intended for turning work between centers by means of a dog. The work is first centered and then center drilled to a 60-degree angle, the same as the center. Centers should always be ground to a known angle, generally 60 degrees, so that in drilling for centers, you can drill to the same angle, and thus have your work fit the cone instead of bearing on the point only. The work is

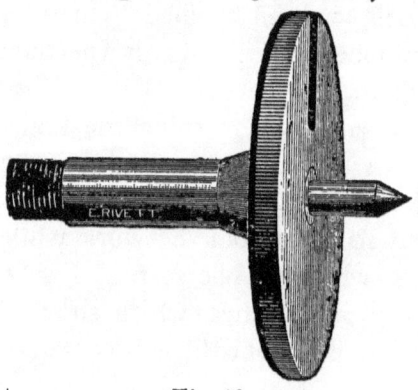

Fig. 53.

rotated by a dog clamped on the work, or by a stud bolted in the slot of the face plate.

By substituting a female for the male center, Fig. 54, this attachment will be found useful in clock, music box and the heavier work having pivots, with which it is desirable to have the other portions concentric. Female centers should

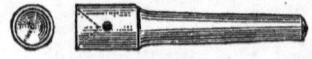

Fig. 54.

be cross-drilled, as shown in Fig. 54, so that they may be readily cleaned out, as dirt is liable to clog the point of the cone and interfere with the accuracy of the work if this point is not attended to.

Where a workman is provided with a full set of accurate split chucks the dog face plate is of little real use, as the chuck will receive and drive any work that is small enough to go into the dog, while the other end is carried on the tail stock center, as it would be with the dog face plate in use. This face plate is really a survival of the machine-shop practice, in which the American watchmaker's lathe had its origin. There the work is entirely on rough castings, as a rule, and the workman centers and dogs his work and then turns up his journal bearing at the tail stock center, turns the work in the lathe, puts the dog on the turned portion, and then proceeds with the work. The same method should be followed in using the dog face plate on the watchmaker's lathe, if the work is new, as it is the only practicable method of getting the centers accurately in line. Special attention should be paid to getting the tail stock center fitted snugly in the tail stock spindle; there should be no play in the tail stock spindle, or between the work and the center, as any looseness here would make a side

Fig. 55.   Fig. 56.

shake while turning, so that the work would not be round when finished. For the same reason, the taper of the tail stock center and of the hole in the work should be the same, so that they will fit accurately as mentioned above. For repair work, however, it is generally sufficient to chuck the work in a split chuck, support the other end in the male or female center in the tail stock, and proceed as usual. If the work demands great accuracy, and the workman doubts his chucks, or if he has no chuck that will fit, the dog face plate is a necessary appliance. It requires great care, however, in the fitting of centers, if accuracy is to be maintained.

There is one point on centers which it may be well to elaborate here. A center, Figs. 55 and 56, is not parallel anywhere on its surface. It is tapered in the shank, as well as on its working surface. This is done so that it shall fit snugly, for its entire length in the chuck or tail stock spindle. If the taper hole is not drilled at the same angle as that of the taper, it will not fit as intended. If the taper of the center is too great, the center will bear only at the mouth of the hole, and the back end being free, it will wabble when the tool exerts side pressure on the work. If the taper of the center be too small, the back end only will bear, and the taper will be free to wabble at the throat of the chuck or spindle in which it is used. Truth is impossible in either case, so the reader will see the importance of hav-

Fig. 57.

ing his tapers fit for the entire length, not only in the shank, but also in the work.

Fig. 57 shows a four-jaw chuck mounted on a solid chuck and adapted to be used as a face plate, or machinist's chuck. It has jaws which are adjustable independently, so that work may be held out of center if desired. In such a case, the point to be centered is tested with a center in the tail stock, or by means of a pegwood on the T-rest, or the point of a slide-rest tool, if the slide rest is on. It is useful for the heavier kinds of work which are too thick to be held in the jaws of the face plate, such as a heavy piece of brass for making a barrel, or other work of that nature.

Fig. 58 shows a Snyder bezel chuck, which differs from

the others in that it is intended for a special class of work, as its name indicates. It will hold bezels, caps, etc., by either the inner or outer edge, and is extremely serviceable when working upon cases, removing solder or changing the groove in thin bezels, etc. The six jaws are operated simultaneously by rotating the milled ring which is seen at the back. There are several forms of this chuck, and they

Fig. 58.

are mounted on a solid chuck, as shown, and also upon a stem, to be held in the largest size of split chuck. The latter is done to effect a small saving in price, but the mounting is so much weaker that it is generally better to pay a dollar or two more and get the stronger form of mounting, as shown. This also holds true in regard to crown chucks.

Figs. 59 and 60 illustrate the Gem pivoting chuck which is intended to do away with any necessity for wax by carrying auxiliary chucks for holding the work, as shown, spinning the work to center and then clamping the holder firmly in position. Its construction will be readily understood by a study of the illustrations. N shows a wheel in position for work on its pivot; G shows a staff chuck, M is the clamping ring of the holder, which is tightened after spinning the work to center; pressure on the ball is obtained by rotating K, Fig. 60, which tightens the clamps C on the ball B, and holds the chuck, G, when it has been centered.

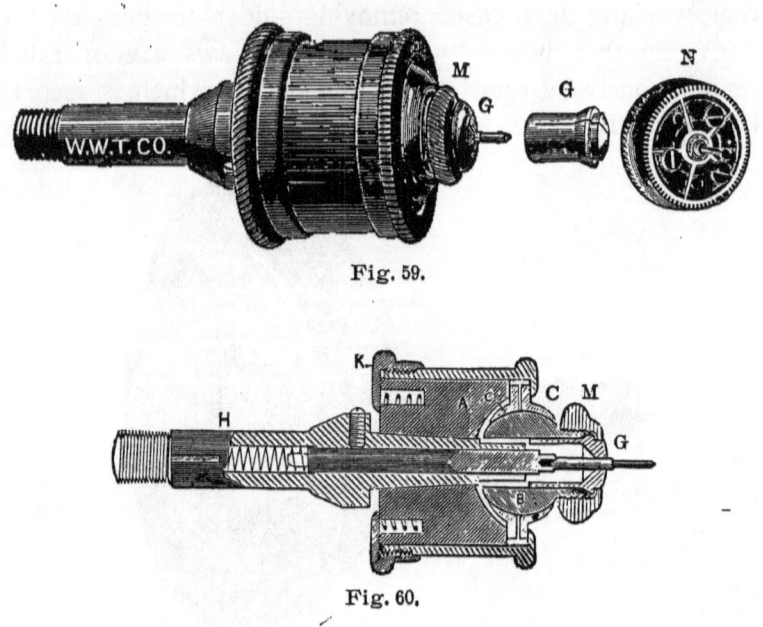

Fig. 59.

Fig. 60.

Fig. 61 shows the Johanson Crown chuck. It consists of an adjustable center, C, with left-handed thread, a number of caps, A, with varying sizes of holes, to fit the various sizes of crowns, and the body, B, with right-hand thread for the caps, so that the center will not run down when the caps are screwed down to hold the crowns in place. This is a favorite form of crown chuck, if we may judge by the number sold; it is mounted on a solid chuck, and also on the stem, as shown.

We also show the Scholer Crown chuck, which is very similar to the other in principle. The crown is held in position by a small brass ring, as shown in the illustration, and it can be made to fit any size crown by using a few rings with different sized holes. A set of four rings accompanies each chuck, and one can easily make more if necessary. It holds

THE AMERICAN LATHE.

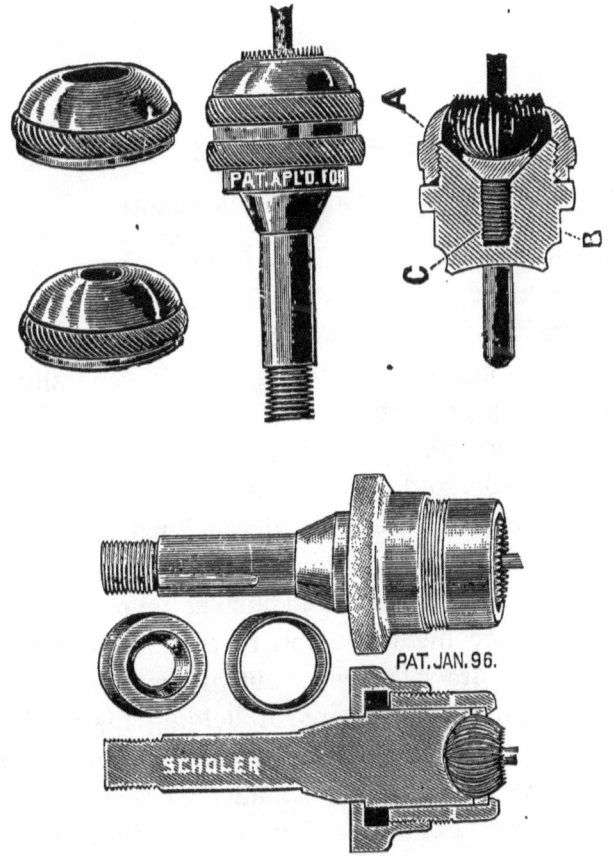

Fig. 61. The Johanson and Scholer Crown Chucks.

the crown by the screw cap shown, which draws the brass ring against the crown, and thus retains it very firmly. This is also a popular form of crown chuck.

CHAPTER V.

CEMENT CHUCKS AND CEMENTING WORK IN POSITION.

The cement chuck is the oldest form of chuck that is used in watchmaking. Previous to the invention of the split chuck it was the only known means of holding work that could not be hung between centers. It is generally utilized today by European watchmakers and while requiring considerable skill on the part of the workman before he can use it accurately and quickly, it will probably never be entirely displaced from the list of watchmaker's attachments on account of certain peculiar advantages inherent to its nature. For instance, the watchmaker who has learned to accurately center his work and to so manipulate his wax that it will not draw the work out of center while cooling, has at his command a means of holding his work which, although slow and troublesome, enables him to successfully handle, on an untrue lathe spindle, work demanding the finest accuracy. For work that is too thin to be successfully held in a split chuck, cementing frequently offers the only practicable means. This is often the case with a very thin jewel setting; also when it is desired to lighten a 'scape wheel by turning or grinding it thinner. In such a case the arms, teeth and rim are all held rigidly by the cement and there is much less danger of bending or stretching any part of the wheel than if it were held in a split chuck. Of course, if the steps are properly turned out, a 'scape wheel may be firmly held in a split chuck and we know that it is done every day; but, for all that, the student should become conversant with cementing his work in its various forms, as it may happen any time that he will get a piece of work which his chucks will not fit, particularly if he has just bought a lathe and only a few chucks; or if he has lost, broken or sprung the only chuck that will hold that particular piece of work, he will have to cement it, or wait till he can send and buy a chuck to replace the one that was lost or damaged.

Cementing requires practice, on several accounts. First is skill in centering the work; it is not so easy as it looks when it is done by an old hand at the business. There is a knack in feeling when one end of a revolving staff is standing still, or moving very slightly about the center; in one case the work is truly centered and in the other it is not and we believe that fully as much work is improperly centered in wax as there is in split chucks and always has been, notwithstanding the showers of abuse that have been hurled at the split chuck for years.

The next point is the manipulation of the wax and this will vary according to the wax you are using. Probably half the trade use gum shellac. It is thin, easily applied on a large flat cement brass, or softened over a lamp and rolled into about the right size lump for a staff. It cools quickly and draws a good deal when cooling. It is the strongest cement and is easily and quickly dissolved when the finished work is boiled in alcohol. Pure sealing wax is also used; this does not have such a tendency to draw out of shape when cooling, as the coloring matter in it prevents it from shrinking so much. On the other hand, it is decidedly brittle and cannot be used over again for nearly as long a time and a chance blow or too great pressure of the graver will be liable to loosen it and let the work fall off the chuck. Many watchmakers use a mixture of half shellac and half sealing wax, melted together in a gentle heat, well stirred and run into sticks to cool. Many of the kinds of lathe wax sold by material dealers are mixtures of shellac and pitch with coloring matter added. The pitch, if in the right proportion, adds elasticity to the wax, so that it holds on under undue pressure and it can be used again repeatedly. Too much pitch makes the wax too soft and the work takes too long in cooling, as it hardens slowly when melted, while sealing wax hardens very quickly and is brittle when cold. From the above it will readily be seen that the workman must get used to his wax, before he knows how hot to make it when chucking and how long to hold on when centering.

Fig. 62 shows the screw chuck, which is generally part of the outfit which comes with the lathe at the time it is

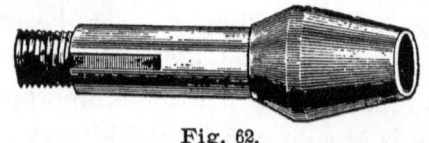

Fig. 62.

purchased. With this screw chuck are sent a number of cement brasses having a thread cut on them to fit the thread in the screw chuck and these brasses are so cheap that they may be purchased by the dozen or singly in varying sizes from ¼-inch up to 2½ inches, which is large enough to hold a watch plate and allow any part of it to be centered.

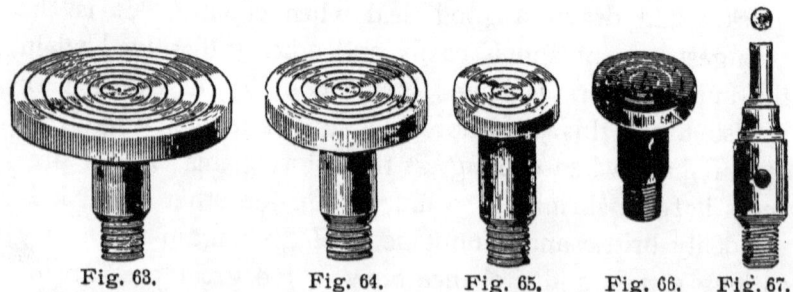

Fig. 63.   Fig. 64.   Fig. 65.   Fig. 66.   Fig. 67.

Figs. 63, 64, 65, 66, and 67 show various sizes of these brasses after they have been put in the chuck and turned up true on the lathe by the watchmaker. The rings on the faces of the brasses are added as a guide in placing the wheel before spinning it to center. Fig. 67 shows a ¼-inch cement brass turned down for small work and a hole drilled in the shank to insert a pin for use as a wrench when screwing or unscrewing the brass from the chuck. This is often done in small brasses, while the larger ones offer sufficient hold for the hand so that a pin wrench is unnecessary.

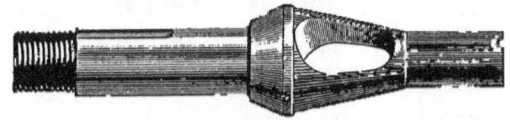

Fig. 68.

. Fig. 68 shows a solid steel chuck which is of the form generally used in watch factories. It is ground true all over and the airhole is put in for two reasons; it enables the wax to cool quickly, thus saving time, and it prevents the heat from reaching the spindle of the lathe, which it would do if the chuck were constantly heated and cooled throughout a full day's work. This chuck has a general sale among watchmakers who believe in cement work and do much of it.

Fig. 69. Wax or Cement Chuck, with Sliding Sleeve

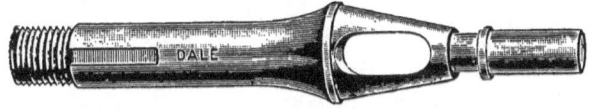

Fig. 70. Wax or Cement Chuck with Sliding Sleeve and Air Hole.

Figs. 69 and 70 show steel wax or cement chucks with a sliding sleeve. This is a device which is much admired by some and considered unnecessary by others. The wax will not harden as quickly within the sleeve and it is more apt to draw the work out of center when cooling, unless care is taken to see that the wax is evenly distributed all round the interior of the tube and that no air-bubbles get in. On the other hand, it is a decided protection to the work and is of assistance when using old wax that has become too brittle through repeated heating and cooling.

Fig. 71 shows a steel taper chuck, with various forms of tapers. The taper blanks may be purchased, either hard or soft, at a low price, just as cement brasses are. Many watchmakers therefore use the tapers and taper chuck for cement work instead of the forms shown in Figs. 68, 69 and 70. In fact, the latter are comparatively recent among repairers and we give the older method, although the special chucks have rendered it unnecessary.

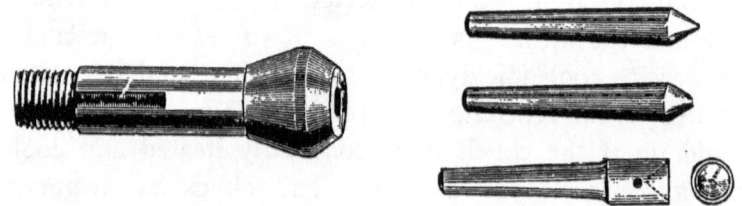

Fig. 71. Taper Chuck with various forms of tapers.

The first requisite is a true taper chuck; and it is well to purchase an extra one to be used solely for this purpose, so that you will be prepared at all times for staff work. Select a good steel taper, and having placed your chuck in the lathe, see if your taper fits well by inserting it in the chuck while running slowly. If it fits well, it will be marked almost throughout its length. Insert again in the chuck, and with a few light taps of the hammer set it firmly in place, so that you know that there is no danger of its working loose. The taper will then project about three-quarters of an inch from the face of the chuck. By means of a sharp graver, make the projecting surface of the taper smooth and straight, and cut off the taper end. Now with a long-pointed sharp graver proceed to cut a nice V-shaped center with an angle of about 60°. The all-important point in the use of wax chucks is to get a perfect center. If you are not careful you are liable to leave a small projection in the center as shown at Fig. 72. Care must be taken that the center is quite true, and that no projection is left like that illustrated in Fig. 72, no matter how minute it may be.

After you have carefully centered your wax chuck and made sure there is no oil or grease on it to prevent the wax from adhering, place a small alcohol lamp under the chuck, add a sufficient amount of wax to imbed the work so that

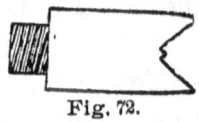
Fig. 72.

it will be well covered, and heat it until the wax will just become fluid and yet not be hot enough to burn the wax. Revolve the lathe slowly and insert the staff so that the pivot rests squarely and firmly in the center. Now re-heat the chuck carefully in order that the wax may adhere firmly to the staff, keeping the lathe revolving meanwhile, but not so fast that the wax will be drawn from the center, and at the same time apply the forefinger to the end of the staff, as shown in Fig. 73, and gently press it squarely into place in the wax chuck.

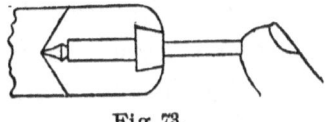
Fig. 73.

The lines in Fig. 73 designate about the right amount of wax after the work is ready, but it is well to add a little more than is shown and you should be careful to keep the wax of equal bulk all around, or when it cools it will have a tendency to draw the staff to one side. Now remove the lamp and keep the lathe revolving until the wax is quite cool, when it should be removed, by means of a graver, down to the dimensions designated. When this is accomplished re-heat a little, but only enough to make it soft, but not liquid, and placing a sharpened peg-wood on the tool rest proceed to the final truing up, by resting the pointed end against the hub, and rapidly or slowly revolving the lathe as the case may require.

If it is desired to use the sleeve the procedure is as follows: Mark a point on the taper about one-fourth of an inch from the end and proceed to turn down the diameter from this point to the end, leaving that portion of the taper about two-thirds of its original diameter, and finish with a nice square shoulder. Now with a long-pointed sharp graver proceed to cut a nice V-shaped center with an angle of about 60°. When you have proceeded thus far you will find that you have an implement resembling that shown in Fig. 74.

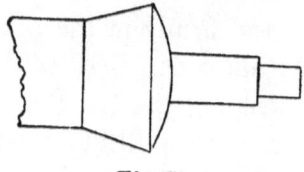

Fig. 74.

Care must be taken that the center is quite true, and that no projection is left like that illustrated in Fig. 72, no matter how minute it may be. Now examine the center by the aid of a strong glass, and after you are satisfied with its appearance proceed to test it. Take a large sized pin with a good point, and placing the point in the center, maintain it in position by pressing upon the head, and while revolving the lathe slowly proceed to examine by means of your glass. If the center is a good one there will be no perceptible vibration of the pin.

Now procure a piece of small brass tubing with an internal diameter a little less than that of the turned down portion of your taper. If the brass tubing cannot be procured readily, you can substitute a piece of brass wire a little larger than the taper, and by means of a drill a little smaller in diameter than the turned down portion you can readily make a small tube about one-half inch long. Now by means of a broach proceed to open the tube to a point one quarter inch from one end, and carefully fit it on the turned down portion of your taper. After fitting tightly to the shoulder of the taper, proceed to turn out the other end until it will take in the hub of your staff easily and leave a little room to spare. Now turn your tube down in length until a little of the hub is exposed either way you put the staff in. Turn the outside of the tube smooth and to correspond with the outline of the taper, so you will have a nice looking job when completed. Just below where the hub will come drill a small hole in the tube and remove all burr, both inside and out, that may have been made in drilling, so that the shellac or wax will not adhere to it. This little hole acts as an outlet for the air in the tube; and as the hot shellac enters at the end of the tube the air is expelled through this vent. It also helps to hold the cement firmly in place. Now try your staff in the tube again, and be sure that it is quite free, and that you will be able to work on the portions of it above and below the hub, according as one end or the other is inserted.

You are now ready to insert your staff and proceed with your work. Hold your shellac in the flame of your lamp a moment until it is quite liquid, and then smear both the inside and outside of the tube with it. Heat the shell or tube gently by means of the lamp, keeping the lathe revolving slowly all the while, and taking the staff in your tweezers proceed to insert it carefully into the tube. Press firmly back, making sure that it has reached the bottom of the V-shaped center. Pack the cement well in around the staff, and while centering remove the lamp and allow the wax to cool, keeping the lathe revolving until quite cool. Now remove the superfluous cement by means of the graver, and heating the tube again slightly, proceed to center the staff exactly by means of a pointed pegwood, resting on your T-rest to steady it. Turn slowly in the lathe and examine with a glass to see that it is quite true. Your completed instrument will resemble Fig. 75. It is well to employ a taper chuck exclusively for this work, and not attempt to use it for any other, for if you try to remove your taper and replace it again, you will surely find that your work is out of center, and you will be compelled to remove the brass shell and find a new center each time you use it. You can avoid all this trouble, however, by purchasing an extra chuck and devoting it exclusively to wax work. Of course, the brass shell can be removed and placed in position again without in any way affecting the truth of the center, and any number, shape and size of shells can be made to fit the one taper, and these shells will be found very useful for holding a variety of work, aside from balance staffs.

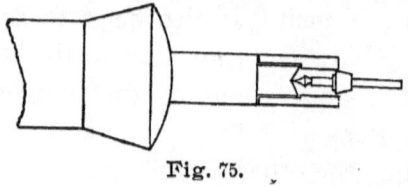

Fig. 75.

Flat pieces, such as wheels, are cemented by first heating the cement brass, while revolving slowly, applying cement, and when it is sufficiently melted to spread evenly over the surface, owing to the centrifugal motion, apply the wheel or jewel setting, as the case may be, and spin to center with a peg wood in the hub of the wheel or either the outer rim or hole of the jewel as desired. If the outer rim and hole are concentric, either may be used; if not the hole should be selected unless you are chucking the setting to take out a poor jewel, then of course the rim should be used.

After finishing the work, it is taken off by again holding the flame of the lamp under the chuck and revolving it until the wax becomes fluid enough so that the work may be removed without bending it; it is then placed in alcohol in a small metal pan, called a boiling-out pan, and held over the flame of the lamp until the wax has all been dissolved off the work. It is then taken out, clean and bright and dried either in an old cloth or in boxwood sawdust, or by

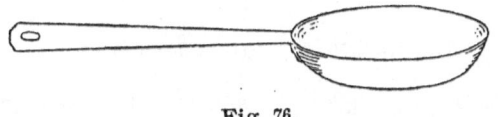

Fig. 76.

being held over the lamp until it is perfectly dry. In the boiling out care must be taken not to draw the temper or discolor the work from the heat, by proceeding too rapidly, as if the alcohol is allowed to boil there is danger of its boiling dry and leaving the work exposed before the workman is aware of it and a hard staff will then be softened and discolored, so that it must be repolished.

CHAPTER VI.

CHUCKS FOR SPECIAL PURPOSES.

There are many chucks for special purposes and whether they should be purchased or not depends largely upon the value of his time to the workman and this, of course, is decided by the amount of work he has to do and also how much work he has of the kind for which that particular chuck is intended. Where several workmen are employed in a shop and a number of them have similar lathes, then a number of these special tools, if purchased, may be used in common. In such cases, the shop may own the tools, and where this is done the lathes should always be identical, so that the purchase of a full set of tools and accessories for each lathe may be avoided. Of course, those chucks most in use should be provided for each lathe and where the workman owns his tools he should endeavor to keep on buying until he has a full and complete outfit that will enable him to do quickly and properly everything he may be called upon to perform. The chief and almost the sole advantage of the American watchmaker over his European competitor lies in the speed with which his tools enable him to do his work. This is what governs the earning power of the man at the bench, and it furnishes the only reason for the fact that the European watchmaker is working for from one-third to one-half of the amount generally earned by an American of no greater or even less skill. European watchmakers are constantly coming to nearly every large city in the United States. They secure positions in the larger repair shops, employing from ten to thirty workmen. They bring their tools with them and do work as they have been accustomed to do it in Europe. This is not tolerated long; the foreman notifies the newcomer that he is too slow and he finds that in order to accomplish what is considered a full day's work in that shop he must buy American tools and use American methods. He is allowed to retain his position because, as a rule, he knows more of the theory of watchmaking than the Americans employed in that shop; he is equally as rapid in fitting and adjusting and he has greater skill in shaping and finishing. So he is retained at wages corresponding to his output, as compared with that of the others in the shop, until he has learned to work with equal rapidity by acquiring a full set of American tools and becoming familiar with American methods. From this time on he is the equal and frequently the superior of his American fellow employes, and his earning power is equal to and often greater than that of those around him.

This is being demonstrated every day in every large city in the United States and it furnishes the strongest possible argument for the superiority of the American tools and appliances, as time savers.

It is solely in this respect, we think, that the purchase of the numerous forms of special chucks should be considered; if their use will occasionally increase the output of work to an amount equal to or beyond that of their cost, they should be considered a good investment and purchased accordingly, as time is the most expensive thing an employer of labor has to buy, and the vast trade in ready-made material from the factories has been built up solely on the ground that a busy man finds it cheaper to buy a staff or pinion from the factory or material dealer, than to pay a watchmaker for making it. It does not alter the value of this argument, either, to say that a proprietor of a store does his own work. In that case he is merely hiring himself to do work and he frequently does this when good business policy would suggest that he hire a cheaper man to do his watch repairing and use his own time in a way that would be more productive.

Among the special chucks above referred to are a number that are especially contrived to hold the balance staff for pivoting without taking off the balance and roller table.

Fig. 77 illustrates such a device; it is called the Jumbo

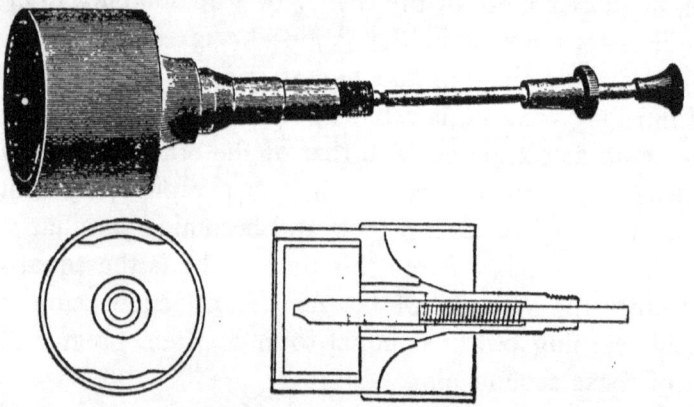

Fig. 77. Jumbo Chuck.

Chuck, and consists of a chamber having a central hole in front and a pump center at the back for the centering of the staff. The sides of the chamber are cut away to allow of the insertion of the balance and, when it is in position, with

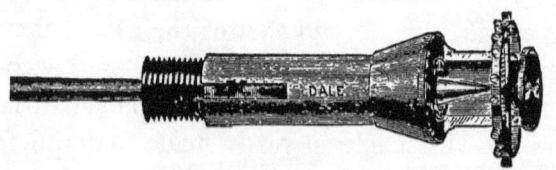

Fig. 78. Balance Chuck.

one end projecting through the central hole and the other held by the pump center, a sliding cover is pushed forward so that the balance is completely inclosed and protected from accidental injury. Its construction will be readily understood from the drawings.

Fig. 78 is similar in principle, but the chamber is smaller, and cut away from one side far enough not to interfere with the balance arms, while the balance is not enclosed.

Figs. 79 and 80 show two forms of cylinder chucks for turning the lower pivots on cylinders without wax. They are very convenient, and turn the pivot true with the cylinder. Nos. 8, 9, 10, 11 and 12 take all sizes, and the same chucks can also be used for staff work. These chucks are split and the work is placed in position by a rod inserted through the draw-in spindle as indicated in the Fig. 79 or from the recess shown in Fig. 80. The work is held in posi-

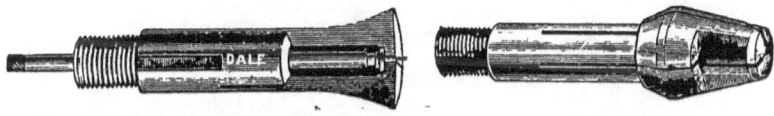

Fig. 79. Cylinder Wire Chucks.   Fig. 80.

tion by the jaws of the split chuck when the draw-in spindle is tightened as in an ordinary wire chuck.

Fig. 81 is a split chuck designed to hold a balance staff with roller table on, the roller pin going into the hole shown at one side of the center. Fig. 82 is an enlarged front view which shows the construction more clearly. Nos. 5, 5½, 6, 6½, 7, 7½ constitute a set and will take all sizes of staffs. Fig. 83 is also designed for the same work, the hole being

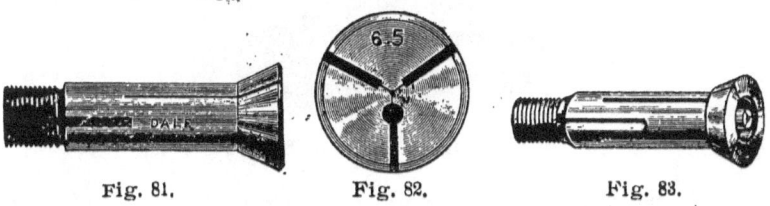

Fig. 81.   Fig. 82.   Fig. 83.

replaced by a circular groove for the reception of the roller pins.

Fig. 84 shows a chuck for finishing the ends of screws. It consists of a steel chuck with a threaded plug, on which are screwed recessed caps which, when screwed up tight, hold the screw by its head firmly against the end of the steel plug, as will be readily understood by a study of the illustration. Extra caps of brass or steel are supplied as desired.

The soft-jeweling chuck, Fig. 85, is the same as is used for jeweling in all watch factories. This chuck is one of the most useful in the watchmakers' outfit, as when the step wears out, or gets out of true, he can turn it down and true it up again himself, as the chuck is soft.

This chuck is furnished with the step cut all ready for jeweling, or in the blank, ready for steps to be cut by the workman. Those who use this form of jeweling chucks generally prefer to cut the steps themselves.

Fig. 84. Screw Finishing Chuck.

Fig. 86 shows a true taper chuck for holding laps, etc., for truing up when they get out of round in use or need the shape changed for special purposes. The taper on the plug is made to coincide with that of the spindle of the pivot polisher, so that the laps may be firmly mounted and held and they are then trued up, either by turning in the lathe or grinding with another lap on the pivot polisher, or both. It is also useful for holding large laps for grinding and finish-

Fig, 85. Jeweling Chuck of Soft Steel.

ing flat steel work which is very hard and from which, for various reasons, it is not desirable to draw the temper. Much work can be done in this way, with the proper sizes and shapes of laps, at a considerable saving of time over the usual methods of flattening, graining and polishing steel by hand. This is especially true of repeating mechanism, with polished edges of the steel parts, etc. Diamantine can be safely used on the lathe in this way, provided that it is wet with oil, so that it will not fly about and care is taken to keep it where it should be and wash up cleanly with oil after finishing the operation in which it is used. It is also a good plan to lay a cloth over the lathe bed and remove the hand rest, tail stock, etc., when using the lathe for grinding and finishing with large laps in this way. Those who become proficient in lapping their work with a proper assortment of varying thicknesses and shapes of laps will be surprised at the gain in time and the ease with which intricate curves and corners may be finished, at the same time keeping the edges and corners sharp.

As to the laps they may be of soft iron, block tin, copper, brass, fine grained wood, ivory, or anything else that is softer than the work to be done, so that the pressure of the hard material to be worked will force the powder into the

Fig. 86. True Taper Chuck.

softer lap, instead of allowing it to crumble and fly off; once forced or rolled into the lap, the material of which it is composed should be strong enough to retain its shape and the powder or other abrasive material imbedded in its surface, under light and steady pressure of the material to be ground. Copper answers these purposes admirably. This is the reason it is used for the very thin saws used in splitting the hard iridium points of gold pens, as it has been found that a very thin copper disc, well charged with diamond powder will retain the powder and hence do effective work longer than any other material. On the other hand, copper is too soft to keep its shape under the greater pressure used in diamond cutting and polishing, so that iron gives better service under the greater pressure. Tool makers working very hard steel use laps made of lead, rolled up with emery; where large surfaces are to be worked this makes a cheap and fast cutting lap, but it takes some skill to keep it in shape, as the material is so soft. We think the above is sufficient to convey the idea to the reader; he must obtain the rest by practice, taking care never to use the different kinds and sizes of powder on the one lap, but to have a different lap for each powder and also for each size of that powder, otherwise he will find that the coarser particles sticking in the lap will make scratches when he tries to polish his work. As the laps in question are of such cheap material, and the watchmaker can make them himself, he can easily comply with the conditions set forth by making separate laps as indicated for each grade of the powder he wishes to use. They should then be plainly marked and kept separated from each other when not in use.

Fig. 87 shows a chuck with a wood screw and plate on which to chuck a piece of wood which it is desired to turn.

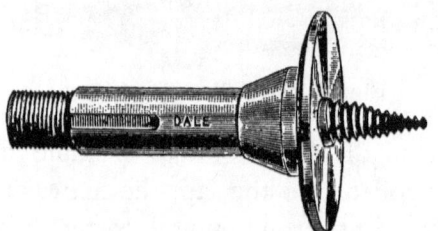

Fig. 87. Wood Chuck.

This is often convenient for many purposes in the jeweler's repair work and it is a very useful chuck.

Fig. 88 is made with a tapered screw of coarse pitch on which to mount buffs for finishing watch cases, finger rings, etc. Where the watchmaker can afford it he should have a foot power polishing lathe on which his buffing should be done, as the flying powder gets all over the bench and into everything. Still in a pinch he may do buffing on his lathe by using the above chuck, but the practice is not recommended for the reasons given.

Fig. 89 shows a chuck for holding stone settings. The body of the chuck is tapped to receive a screw which is passed through the setting and holds it in the chuck with its claws supported by the walls of the recess in the chuck. This enables the work to have the same depth and angle on each claw, so that the seat for the stone will be perfectly formed and the mounting is stronger than it would otherwise be. The groove may be cut in the claws with a graver or with a burr mounted on the pivot polisher, the latter method being preferable as it is quicker and more exact.

We now come to the arbor chuck; this is in many respects one of the most important forms of the chucks having solid

Fig. 88. Buff Chuck.

bodies; its use has been gradually extending as the various attachments have been added to the lathe, until it is at present used for quite a variety of purposes. Fig. 90 shows the arbor chuck with screw of the arbor adapted for a pin wrench; Fig. 91 shows the same chuck opened that its action may be understood. This chuck is also made with a thumb screw if desired. Fig. 92 shows the arbor chuck with an elongated arbor. This arbor chuck has two collars for filling up the space, while using different widths of emery

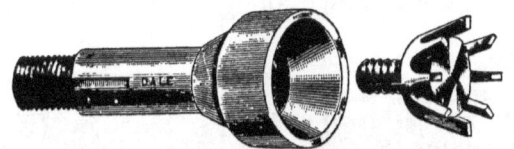

Fig. 89. Stone Setting Chuck.

or oil stone wheels or saws. The collars at A, B are removable leaving a space of ½ inch if desired.

Fig. 93 shows it as used to carry rounding-up cutters in conjunction with a wheel cutter, thus making it unnecessary to purchase a rounding-up tool, if one has the wheel-cutting attachment for his lathe. It is also used to carry fine steel circular saws, which will be found a great saving of time in cutting out from the sheet the flat steel work used in watches and bringing the pieces nearly to shape before filing or grinding to exact size, slitting screw heads, or sawing out the spaces between the teeth of steel pinions before beginning on them with the forming cutters. It is used to carry the cutters in wheel-cutting. It has lately had extended use with the smaller sizes of carborundum wheels used by dentists, these wheels taking the place of hand-filing in

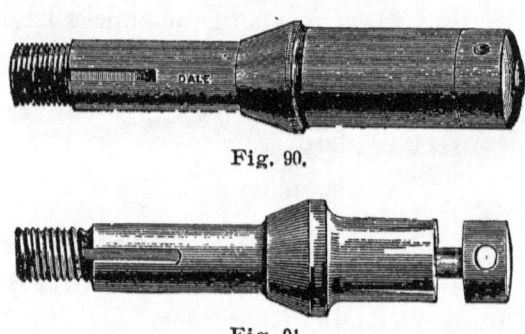

Fig. 90.

Fig. 91.

finishing the steel work referred to above. Fig. 94 shows a special form of arbor chuck on which the wheel is carried on a loose pulley mounted on the arbor. In this method the lathe spindle stands still and the wheel is driven by a belt from the speed wheel on the countershaft running over the small-grooved pulley shown alongside the wheel in Fig. 94.

Fig. 92.

The increase in speed and consequent gain of time by this method is very considerable and it has the further advantage of giving sufficient peripheral speed to the wheel, so that it will not fill up with metal and refuse to cut.

There is a proper speed for each grade or kind of manufactured wheel; above this speed the heat is such that the bond will be softened and then the wheel will either crumble or be burst by the centrifugal force. With large wheels bursting is always attended with considerable danger from the flying fragments, loss of life not being uncommon in such cases. Below the proper speed, or with too much pressure, the wheel will glaze over; that is, its surface will be-

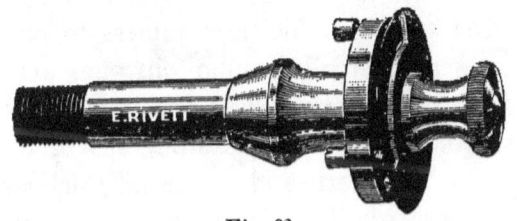

Fig. 93.

come filled with fine particles of metal and cutting is delayed or stopped until this is removed by turning down with a diamond, wasting the wheel and delaying the work. With large wheels it is easy to get a very high speed at the

Fig. 94.

circumference, and users have to be cautioned not to exceed the safe speed of the wheel. With small wheels, on the contrary, the difficulty is generally found in getting a sufficient speed to prevent glazing, especially if used in the watchmakers' lathe spindle. In using such wheels the pressure should be light and intermittent—never put your work against the wheel and hold it there steadily, but take it away frequently and grind a little here and a little there until it is brought down to size. In this way you do not heat your work enough to discolor it, and you do not glaze your wheel.

Emery, carborundum, and oil-stone wheels may be purchased of various shapes and sizes in grades sufficiently fine to do the work satisfactorily. We would recommend buying the first two in sufficient numbers to have a satisfactory assortment. Small circular oilstones are, however, almost prohibitory in price, while the large sizes intended for hand use are quite cheap. A stone 2½ or three inches wide by 8 or 10 in length and the usual thickness may be purchased, cut into squares with a copper lap charged with diamond powder, chucked in the face plate and drilled to fit the arbor with a diamond turning tool, or with the end of a copper pipe charged with diamond powder. It is then mounted on the arbor, or the arbor-bushing as desired, turned into the desired shape and size with the diamond and we have a number of good and cheap oil stones of various grades, shapes and sizes. All the waste should be powdered, graded and bottled for use as oil-stone powder on laps, etc. It is desirable in doing this to buy as wide stones as possible, as the difference in using a stone of large diameter as compared to that of a smaller one is surprising when we multiply the diameter by 3.14156, and that by the number of revolutions per minute, to get the peripheral speed. Stop a moment and figure it out to make the point clear to yourself. Assume a given number of revolutions which shall be the same with each size of stone and take two diameters of wheels well within the capacity of your lathe.

These stones will also be found very useful in sharpening gravers and slide-rest tools, especially if the finishing cut is made with the stone moving parallel to the edge of the graver instead of at right angles with it. The difference will be very apparent in turning steel with gravers sharpened in each way, one leaving the work dull, the other bright, almost polished.

CHAPTER VII.

HAND RESTS AND SLIDE RESTS.

The hand-rest, or T-rest, is that part of the lathe and its support upon which the graver is held when turning by hand. It consists of a slotted cylindrical post, mounted upon a base, bored to receive the stem of the rest and provided with a screw to compress the sleeve at its upper end and thus hold the rest firmly in position. The base has a T-slot by which it is held in position by a T-bolt passing through the shoe and clamped by a nut under the lathe bed. Nos. 8, 9, 10, Fig. 16, show the T-rest standard, 11 the T-rest and 20 and 21 the clamping nut and washer. The T-rest is bent forward so that when turned sidewise it may be brought sufficiently close to the work without the standard catching in the work if it is large, such as a clock wheel, or the jaws of the face plate. T-rests are usually left soft, so that the graver will not slip, as it would do if the edge were hardened and polished. An old rest frequently has its upper edge badly nicked by constant pressure of the angle of the graver bearing upon it. Some workmen who are on watchwork constantly, and are addicted to using gravers long after they should be sharpened, will file notches in the edge of the T-rest so that their dull tools will not slip, but it should not be done, as it seriously interferes with straight turning on longer work, such as clock arbors, barrels, winding wheels, etc. A T-rest which has its upper edge filed level is plenty rough enough to hold a sharp graver and will allow of its being moved evenly and smoothly along when turning straight arbors or flat work, while the nicked surface of the T-rest will show on the work if such practices are permitted.

For special work, such as making jewel settings, or other work requiring the rest to be very close, with frequent measurements or changes of work, a special form of rest, called the "Tip-over T-rest," is in extensive use. Figs. 95 and 96 show this device closed in position for work and swung outward and downward for measurement or removal of the work. It is in universal use in watch factory jeweling departments, and is also on the lathes of many retailers. It is supplied with all Hopkins lathes and on demand for the Moseley, Webster-Whitcomb and Rivett. Those who have tried it long enough to get used to it on any special work

Fig. 95. Closed. Fig. 96. Open.

endorse it heartily as a time saver, as it permits the rest to go back to the same distance from the work every time and thus does not change the leverage on the graver, so that the same pressure of the hand will produce the same results on the work. A rapid workman is guided very largely by his sense of touch and the "feel" of the graver is kept exactly the same if the rest is maintained at a constant distance from the work.

Some of the higher-priced Boley lathes have the standard for the T-rest formed of a split steel tube which is closely fitted on the outside by a loose clamping sleeve, so that it may be turned around at the will of the workman and thus placed so that the lever of the clamping screw will not interfere with any desired position of the T-rest. The split clamping collar conforms to the usual shape of the T-rest standard, so that no difference is noticeable unless the pieces are taken apart. This makes a very nice arrangement, but it is one which is seldom seen in this country, on account of the cost of making it.

The lever of the clamping screw should be below the screw when the T-rest is clamped, as shown in Fig. 95, and they are so when new, but the screws stretch and wear with use until the lever comes up so as to interfere with the T-rest in some positions. When this is the case a steel washer should be placed between the collar and the head of the screw, having its thickness sufficient to bring the lever in the desired position when the sleeve is clamped. This stretching never occurs with some workmen, while with others it is perceptible in a week after the purchase of the lathe. The reason is that the latter class use force enough to stretch the screw every time they adjust the T-rest. This is an abuse, of course, but it is a very common one. The stem of the T-rest should fit the standard so closely that a very slight pressure will hold it firmly; if it is too small to do this throw it away and make another that will fit properly.

The shoe should accurately fit the ways, or guides, of the bed, as the slide rest is fitted to the upper surface of the shoe and if the under surfaces do not hold the shoe at right angles to the line of centers of the lathe, the workman can never be sure of what he is doing. This holds true also of all that class of attachments which are carried on the slide rest or in place of it, on the shoe, so that the width and fitting of this simple piece of the lathe are important. Those workmen who desire to use attachments made by one manufacturer upon a lathe made by another can do so by having a shoe made to fit the appliance which it is desired to add and in this way they may obtain an amount of freedom in the choice of attachments that is very pleasing in some instances; for example, where a bargain is offered in the way of attachments which the workman feels that he ought to have but cannot purchase of the manufacturer who made his lathe on account of the expense of new attachments. This change of shoe is usually made in its thickness, but may also be made in the width and sometimes in the length also. The top should be flat and the sides should fit the guides of slide rest, pivot polisher, etc., smoothly and without play. If the top is not flat the attachments placed upon it will rock when taking heavy cuts, thus causing a chattering of the tool which is attributed to lost motion, loose fitting, or springing of the slides of the slide rest, attachments, etc., when the real trouble lies in the imperfect support offered by an improperly fitting shoe. If the shoe is too narrow the slide rest may be put on square and shifted while working without the knowledge of the operator and thus turn taper when he wants the part straight and vice versa. It should be of equal thickness, as if one end is thicker than the other tools will rise above the center at one end of the slide rest and sink below it at the other. The sides should be square with the line of centers, as if they are not so, flat turning will be difficult when making wheels, plates, etc.

In putting on the various tools, care should be taken to see that the ways of the bed, the top of the shoe and the T-bolt are all clean and free from dirt, filings or chips of metal, as a little dirt under the shoe, or between it and the slide rest will cause chattering as above alluded to. In wheel cutting or other work in which the attachments are built up quite high above the bed of the lathe, or at some distance from the line of centers, a very little imperfection in fastening to the ways of the bed will be multiplied into a serious error at the cutting edge of the tool. The readiest means of cleaning the lathe of chips, etc., is with a clean, dry bristle brush, which should be combed out whenever it becomes filled with turnings and dirt, and washed with soapsuds occasionally to free it from oil and keep it clean and soft.

Although the work for which the lathe was designed is so short and small as to make its use as a speed lathe compulsory and to compel the majority of the work to be done with hand tools, still there is a large part of it for which the slide rest is demanded as a means of obtaining the necessary accuracy of direction in working at a commercial speed. In order to accomplish many of the functions of a machinists' engine lathe the slide rest is made so large as to be utterly out of proportion to those used with any other lathe. The lower slide is long enough so that when desired it may carry the edge of the tool away even further than the center distance of spindle to lathe bed. The middle slide is even longer, and its screw is designed to take the place of the lead screw which feeds the tool against the work in the engine lathe. In addition it has one, and sometimes two, swivels between the slides, which allow of turning tapers to predetermined angles, which are indicated by graduated circles which have the swivels as their centers. In the machinists' lathes tapers are turned by setting the tailstock center away from the line of centers of the lathe; but as the watchmaker's lathe makes comparatively little use of the tailstock on account of a majority of its work being so short, the taper turning is accomplished by swinging the slide rest.

An inspection of the sectional drawings will show that the slides have their bearing surfaces between the various parts fully as wide and generally wider than the ways of the bed that supports the headstock. This is because the slide rest is designed to carry all sorts of attachments, such as wheel cutters, pivot polishers, rounding up tools, traverse spindle grinders and various other devices having working spindles placed as high as the line of centers and sometimes two and a half to three inches to one side of it. Under these circumstances we have five bearing surfaces resting upon each other between the tool and the lathe bed, and at least three of these surfaces must be sufficiently loose to allow of their being moved evenly and smoothly by the feed screws as the necessities of the work demand. It will be seen, therefore, that these surfaces must be broad and closely fitted, or the tool will spring and chatter to such an extent as to make good work impossible. If the fitting of the slides is badly done, so that they are loose at some portions of their travel and tight in others, then in addition to the springing we have the liability of the slide allowing the tool to dig into the work if the tool happens to have too much top rake, or of allowing it to be pushed away if it be dull or the metal being turned is rather hard. In either case the work done will not be of the proper diameter, and it must be gone over again, losing time and perhaps spoiling the work. Many young workmen who have good slide rests think that they will save themselves labor and not wear the slides so much if they loosen the screws which hold the splines against the beveled surfaces of the slides. So they loosen up to where chattering is bound to occur, and then commence to find fault with their cutting tools, wonder why they won't keep an edge, change the angles of the cutting surfaces, try all sorts of patent hardening solutions and look everywhere else for their troubles, which will not disappear until they take the lost motion out of their slide rests. Slide rests will spring when they are closely and properly fitted, and this fact is well known to all machinists and also to many watchmakers.

One day, in talking with a tool maker, he said that when he wanted to take a light cut he did it by springing the tool holder. If tools as heavily proportioned as those used by tool makers and others in the heavier classes of work can be sprung by a simple pressure of the hand, what are we to expect of the watchmaker's lathe, where the pressure, due to the handling, is much greater in proportion to the work done than it is in the large lathes? Any one who is at all skeptical in regard to this matter may easily try it for himself by putting a piece in the chuck and with a keen cutting tool in the slide rest turn it down true and smooth, then, with the hand, press lightly on the side of the headstock so as to press the piece toward the tool; also try it by pressing the tool to the work, and I dare say it will be a surprise to those who have never tried this to know what a small pressure it will take to make a cut of sensible amount. This may also be tried in other ways which will suggest themselves to the workman, a good one being with the pivot polisher and the parallel grinder.

Many of the slide rests are made with the graduated circle for cutting angles so small that it is impossible to cut any given angle with certainty and still more difficult to cut a taper, and then reset the slide rest again after it has been once changed, so as to conform to the first angle. Of course, the size to which this circle may be increased is necessarily limited, but the design in those not so constructed should be changed so as to make this adjustment as accurate as possible.

Another source of trouble lies in the fitting of the feed screws and their nuts. Some of the cheaper slide rests have the feed screws held in place only by a collar at the head of the screw. Where this is the case care should be taken to see that the collar fits the screw closely. They are sometimes left loose by the manufacturer, so that if the nut in which the screw works is not in perfect alignment with the screw the screw may tilt as the nut approaches the inner end of the screw and thus prevent binding at that end. Then the play necessary in the collar will be enough to give sometimes a quarter-turn of lost motion when the nut is between the center and outer end of the screw. This is a great nuisance to a workman who understands the capabilities of the slide rest.

Such a man will have collars on the ends of his feed screws, graduated with reference to the thread of the screw, so that the slide may be advanced a definite amount by reading the collar as it is being turned. For instance, if it be twenty-five threads to the inch, then one turn of the screw will advance the slide one-twenty-fifth of an inch. If we divide our collar into forty parts, then one part equals one-fortieth of one-twenty-fifth, or one-thousandth of an inch. Metric threads will give metric divisions. Having got his work nearly to size, he callipers it closely, finds how much more is needed and then advances his slide one-half the distance, which brings the work to the proper diameter at the next cut.

Now lost motion in the collar of the feed screw or between the nut and screw will render it difficult to tell just when the slide starts moving and so make the depth of cut a matter of uncertainty in fine work, such as taking off two thousandths of an inch. If his slides and nut are loose the difficulty is not as great, but if they are closely fitted, as they should be in such work, he will sometimes be unable to tell just when the slide starts moving toward the work.

Sometimes the screws which hold the nut to the slide are too small for the holes in the wing of the nut and allow it to move about. This is likely to happen when the workman has taken his slide rest apart for cleaning and put it together carelessly. Lost motion will result in such a case, and if the nut be narrow tilting and consequent uneven wear of the nut will result.

Loose handles on the feed screws are another nuisance, for which the workman is generally to blame, as they are caused by carelessness in allowing the screws to work loose, jamming against the bench or drawer, getting tangled up with other tools, etc.

Fig. 97 shows the Moseley slide rest, which has two swivels, one of which is below both slides, and allows the first or long slide, when swung crosswise, to lie flat and firm upon the base, making it very solid, with no tendency to vibrate or chatter when cutting. The other swivel is between the two slides, which allows a hole to be turned taper and the face to be squared flat, or vice versa—the face squared at an angle and the hole turned straight. They use in the long slides an improved detached nut, and the tool or cutter will not show ridges or grooves in the work at each revolution of the screw. The compound tool post is so arranged that an ordinary square tool can be used, or by applying the eccentric quill and clasp it will allow the use of tools made from round steel rod, which many workmen will eagerly adopt when familiar with its advantages. The feed

Fig. 97. Moseley slide rest with two slides. 1. Base. 2, Lower Slide. 3, 4, Center Swivel. 5, Upper Slide. 6, Tool Post Collar. 7, Tool Post. 8, Binding Screw. 9, Gib. 10, Quill with Eccentric Hole. 11, Tool. 15, Lower Swivel Binding Screw.

screws have graduated collars on the end of lead and cross screws, just inside of the handle, to read to thousandths of an inch. Half and quarter thousandths are easily obtained by dividing the spaces by the eye. This enables any one using gauges reading thousandths to readily adjust their tool to avoid mistakes in getting proper sizes, and is a great convenience and saving of time for any one using the rest.

Fig. 98 shows a longitudinal section of the Webster-Whitcomb slide rest with three slides. This is also shown in elevation at Fig. 99. This has proven a very popular form of slide rest and has been imitated by a number of European tool makers. This is the form which is generally meant when an "imitation slide rest" is spoken of. It has one swivel between the lower and middle slides, which is clamped

218 THE AMERICAN LATHE.

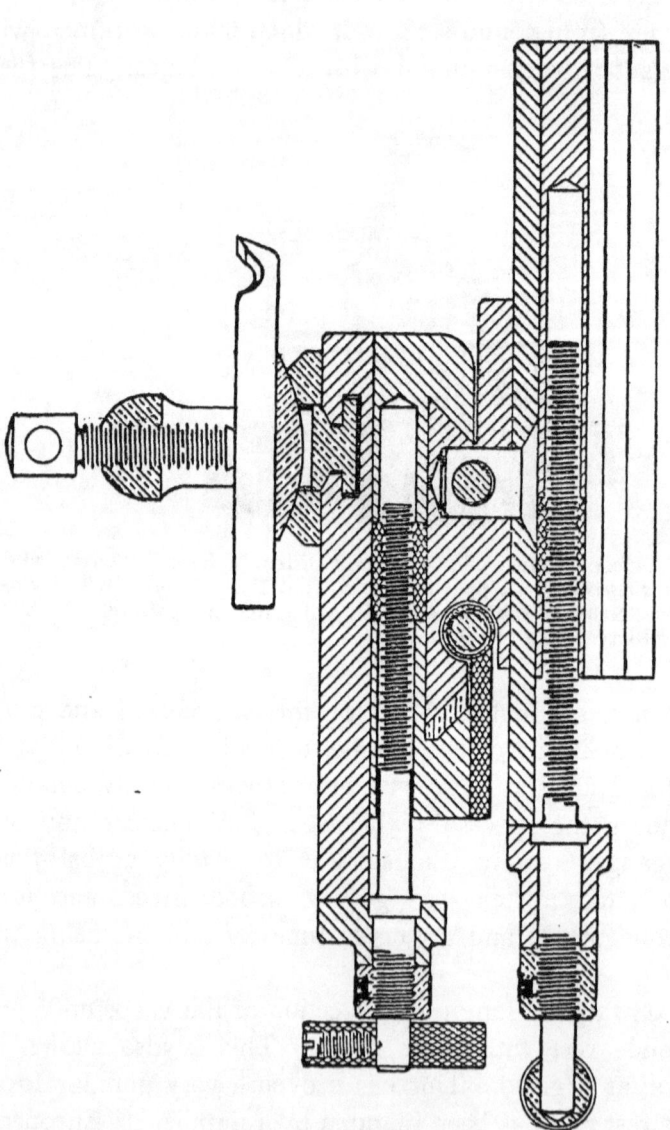

Fig. 98. Webster-Whitcomb Three-slide Rest, Longitudinal Section, showing construction.

by a T bolt and eccentric in the same manner as the head or tail stock of a lathe is fastened. The slot for the tool post is placed parallel to and very close to the end of the upper slide, with the result that a very short tool may be used and still have the slide clear of the work. The slotted tool post is surrounded by a collar which is chamfered out to the arc of a circle, and the tool is carried upon a steel support, which forms a segment of the same circle. This allows the tool to be tilted at pleasure, while still being firmly held by

Fig. 99. Webster-Whitcomb Slide Rest.

the screw of the tool post. This arrangement is common to the majority of machine shops on account of the great latitude of adjustment with simple means. In the better class of slides the nut, which is threaded on the front ends of the lead screws, is divided in millimeters or thousandths of an inch, as previously referred to. Two handles are provided for the lower screws and milled head for the upper screw.

In place of the rocking segment for adjusting the height of tool many workmen use two collars, one of which screws into the other, as shown in the sectional drawing of the Hopkins slide rest, Fig. 100. The advantage of this is that the tool may be elevated or depressed horizontally, so that

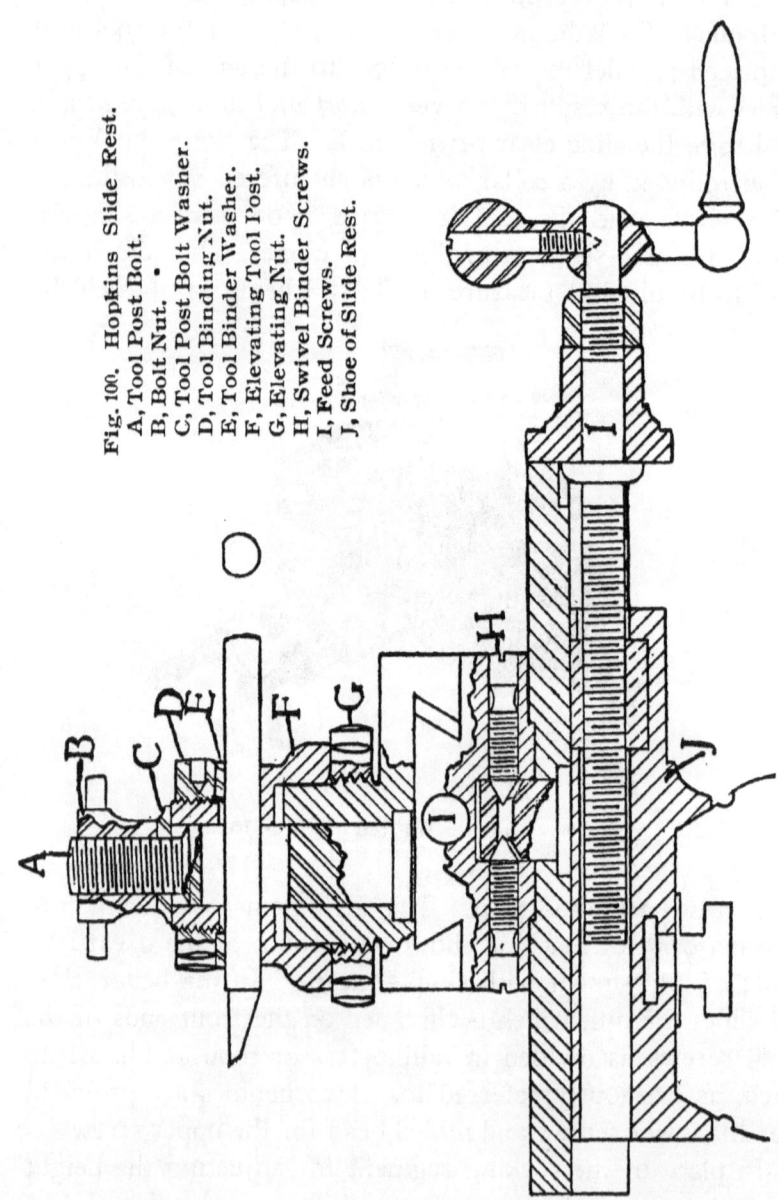

Fig. 100. Hopkins Slide Rest.
A, Tool Post Bolt.
B, Bolt Nut.
C, Tool Post Bolt Washer.
D, Tool Binding Nut.
E, Tool Binder Washer.
F, Elevating Tool Post.
G, Elevating Nut.
H, Swivel Binder Screws.
I, Feed Screws.
J, Shoe of Slide Rest.

the angles of the cutting edges of the tool are not changed at the point where they enter the work. Such a tool as is shown in Fig. 98 will alter its action materially under such conditions, and if it is sharpened on top the cutting edge will be lowered, making elevation necessary to reach the line of centers. The man with few tools prefers to alter the angle at the working point by tilting his tool to accommodate it to the varying qualities of metal, rather than make another tool with different cutting angles, while the man with plenty of tools contends that it is better to have an assortment of tools shaped properly for cutting the various hard and soft

Fig. 101. Hopkins Slide Rest.

metals and to present those tools to the work at known angles by properly forming the cutting edge and keeping the shank of the tools always horizontal. Every experienced lathe hand will admit the justice of the latter proposition and then resort to tilting the tool when he finds himself short of tools of the required shape. So, after all, it is a matter of personal liking or adjustment to circumstances.

Fig. 100 shows a longitudinal section of the Hopkins slide rest, which is shown in elevation at Fig. 101. This is a two-slide rest, with swivel, H, between the slides. Unlike the other rests, this has its shoe formed on the base of the slide instead of fitting the shoe of the lathe. The tool post will hold either square or round tools, and the tool is elevated horizontally by rotating G after loosening B. The wide bearing of the round tool post gives a very firm fastening for the tool, and this is also an advantage in making a rigid

122   THE AMERICAN LATHE.

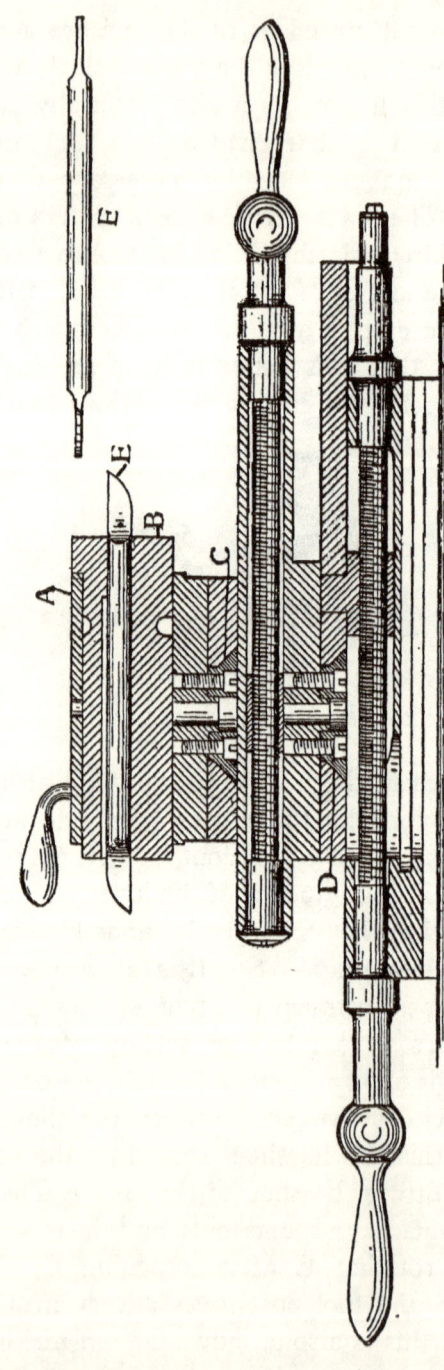

Fig. 102. Longitudinal Section of Rivett Slide Rest and Tool Post. A, Tool Post. B, Elevating Quill. C, Swivel of Tool Post. D, Swivel between Slides.

fastening for the various attachments, which will be discussed later. The tool may be taken out, sharpened and replaced without changing the angle or height.

Figs. 102, 103 and 104 are longitudinal and cross sections and elevation of the Rivett slide rest. As will be seen from Fig. 102, the feed screws are journaled at both ends in this slide rest, the rear sleeves being adjustable to take up any

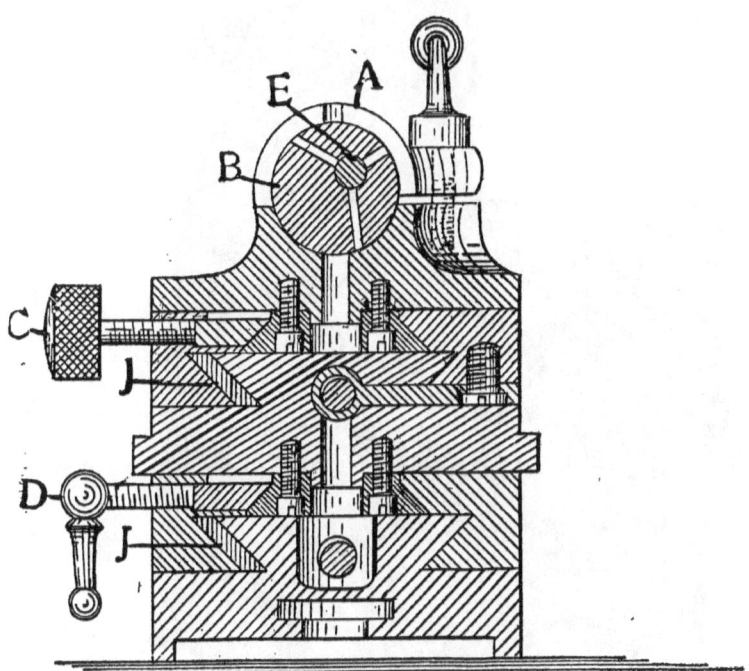

Fig. 103. Cross Section of Rivett Slide Rest. A, Tool Post. B, Elevating Quill. C, Binding Screw of Tool Post Swivel. D, Binding Screw of Swivel between Slides, J, J, Splines, E, Tool.

lost motion; the swivels are conical and screwed into position; the tool post covers the top of the upper slide and is swiveled in the center of the slide. The first feature which strikes us is the great care in fitting and the unusual strength of the slide rest. The bearing for the tool post is extremely wide; the reason for such construction is made plain when we come to consider that all the attachments are held in the

124   THE AMERICAN LATHE.

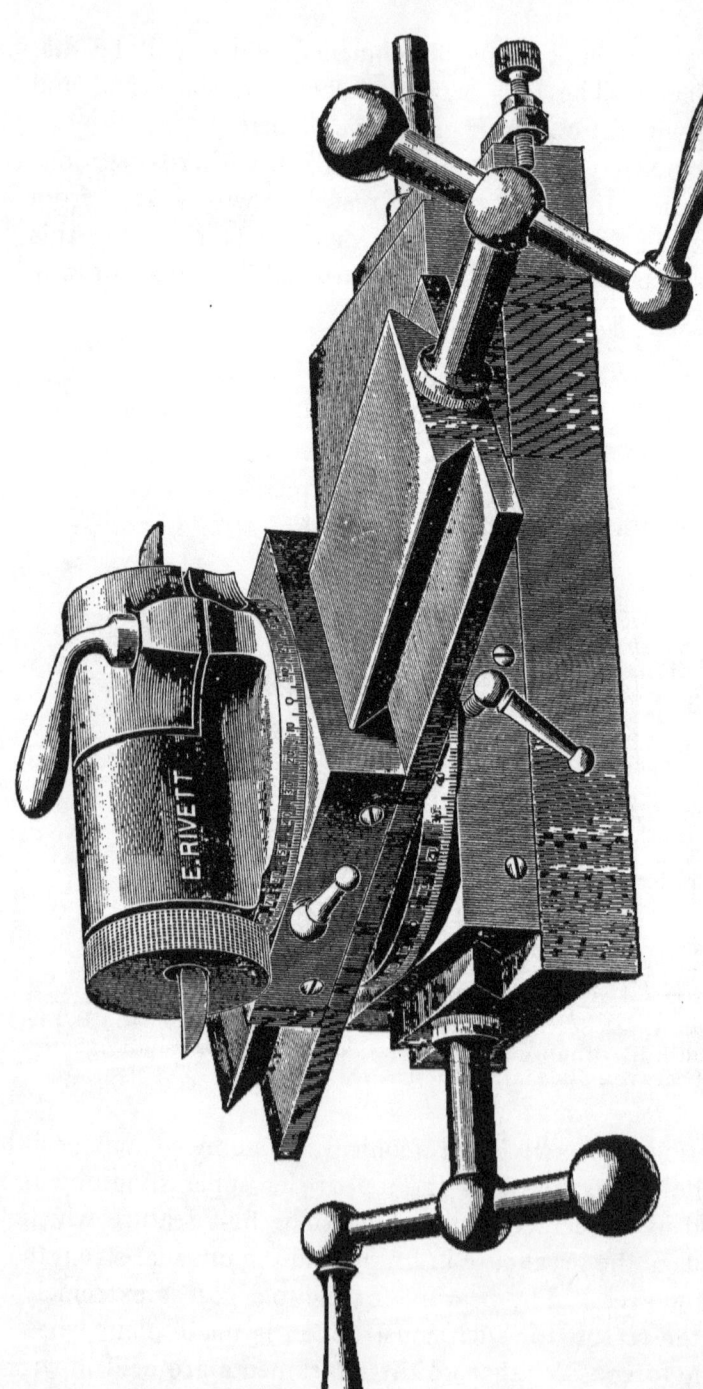

Fig. 101. Rivett Patent Slide Rest. Elevation.

slide rest and that the rest itself is used in a vertical instead of a horizontal position in many operations, under the Rivett system—in wheel cutting, for example. The large graduated circle about the base of the tool holder, although unimportant in ordinary watch repair work and plain turning, becomes extremely so when the tool holder is replaced by the pivot polisher, or the quill for traverse spindle grinder or the chuck for holding the work in wheel cutting.

The quill for holding the tool is another device which has come to us from the watch factory. This is shown at B in Figs. 102 and 103; it consists of a steel cylinder, bored longitudinally to one side of the center and split so that compression will allow it to grip the tool, which is of round wire. Rotating the cylinder will raise or lower the height of the tool and as the tool is round, turning it will restore the cutting edge to its position after the height has been changed. Of course, the tool may be withdrawn and inserted any number of times without changing its application to the work. In manufacturing this item is an important saving of time, particularly where the tools are cutting ten hours per day. In such cases the ability to cut off a piece of steel rod, grind the end to shape, harden and use it as a cutter effects an important saving as compared to the blacksmith's work on tools of the ordinary shape. Of course, its importance diminishes as the volume of work decreases, but its convenience in the preparation of tools in a country jewelry store, for instance, where machine shops are scarce and dealers in machine steels are conspicuous by their absence, is such that it is rapidly winning friends in the watchmaking trade, as round steel may be ordered from the material dealer and kept in stock. Then the making of cutters take only a few moments' time.

CHAPTER VIII.

VARIOUS FORMS OF TAILSTOCKS AND THEIR USES.

The tailstock is a part of the watchmaker's lathe whose capabilities are but little understood by the average repairer of watches. Here and there we find one with factory experience who has become an adept in their use, but the average watchmaker of ten or fifteen years' experience is apt to show you a lathe with the nickel all worn off the bed, the edges of the slide rest rounded from wear and the tailstock as bright as if he had used it for six months. He will tell you that he does his drilling with a pin vise and that he only uses the tailstock occasionally to drill a long hole or on the rare occasions on which he has to swing work on centers. He only has the push-spindle tailstock and he doesn't see much use in it. On the other hand, if we go into a factory we shall find the tailstock in use more often than the slide rest, and the number of operations performed with it is surprising to the class of man referred to above, as is also the amount of work which is turned out. He will find the tailstock in so many forms, varying from the simple push spindle up to and including the automatic turret carrying a dozen tools, that he may well ask himself whether he cannot adopt some of these devices with the result of greater accuracy and speed. For the American is prone to run to extremes, and having discarded turning between centers —and accustomed himself to sneer at European methods as old-fashioned and slow, he wants to discard the tailstock altogether, and many do so to the detriment of their work and peace of mind. To the European watchmaker, with his greater knowledge of the business, brought about by a long and arduous apprenticeship, it is more important to get a hole straight and of proper size than to get one quickly, and the tailstock is never absent from his bench. He generally has two and frequently three of these useful appliances, and his tailstock spindles are fitted with all the appliances which have been presented for his consideration by the manufacturers and which on trial he has found useful.

There are some advantages in having to learn your trade twice. The European watchmaker, on his native heath, has as large a percentage of botches as the American, probably, for human nature does not differ greatly between nations when considered in mass. But the man who has learned European methods, where the work is chiefly done looking to the right, and then come over here and learned to work with different tools and looking to the left, has had his wits exercised rather more than the man who has been content with one method—either one.

The tailstock, while it was primarily devised to hold one end of the work in position, and while it is still used for that purpose chiefly in the engine lathe, has been developed into a tool-carrying device of great utility for work which can be held by one end. The majority of the watchmaker's work is of that description, and therefore the chief utility of his tailstock is as a tool carrier. We will therefore consider the various tailstocks in that connection.

The tail stock usually found in the repairer's outfit is the push-spindle; it is shown in elevation in Fig. 16, and in longitudinal section in Fig. 21. As will be readily seen from Fig. 21, it consists of a casting shaped to fit the ways of the bed, provided with a T-bolt and eccentric for clamping and bored to receive a tube which should be accurately fitted to the spindle within it, and exactly in line with the center of the lathe spindle. Great pains is taken to preserve the truth of this alignment in the manufacture, as it is vital. In one of the factories this point is tested by locking four of these tail stocks, end to end, on a lathe bed and pushing a tail stock spindle clear through the four; alternate tail stocks are then turned end for end and the test repeated. This is done before nickel plating; after nickeling it cannot be done with the first four tail stocks that may be picked up, although it may be done with two and sometimes with three, if they are selected. Only a skilled mechanic will understand the severity of the test with four tail stocks and an accurately fitted spindle. Turning alternate tail stocks end-for-end doubles any error there may be in the alignment of the bore.

The fitting of the spindle should also be carefully looked after, and this is done in the best makes. Cheaper lathes frequently have the bore of the tail stock smaller in the middle than at the ends. Then, if the spindle is clamped at the front end, the spindle is thrown out of line by clamping. It will also be put out if the spindle fits too freely. Sometimes we find a case in which the center is larger than the ends of the bore, and if such a lathe is put in the hands of a careless man, he will often clamp the spindle tightly enough to spring the spindle. The spindle should occupy practically the same position when loose or clamped and with either end of the tail stock next to the lathe head, as tested by putting a needle-pointed center in the tail stock and another in the arbor chuck in the lathe spindle, bringing the two together and revolving them slowly, under a strong glass, first in the same and then in opposite directions. Of course care must be taken to center both needle points accurately before commencing. You may be sure of the practical efficiency of a tail stock which will stand this test.

The spindle should fit closely enough so that it will not be thrown out of line by clamping, and if the workman can have several spindles for the same tail stock he will frequently find that it will save him a great deal of time, as they can be fitted with the tools he uses most frequently and the constant centering of such tools be thus avoided. If the tool mounted on any spindle be too large to pass through the tail stock, he may remove the rubber push button and insert the spindle from the forward end.

The holes in the ends of all spindles should be of exactly the same size and taper and they should be cross-drilled at the extreme ends of the hole. All tapers should be of the same size and long enough to reach the cross-drilled hole. Then inserting a taper plug in the cross-drilled hole and tapping it slightly will at once start the tool out of its seat in the spindle, with no injury to the tool. This point should be insisted upon, as it is not only a saving of time and temper, but it prevents injury to delicate and expensive tools. The workman caught hammering a taper to loosen it in a machine shop would be discharged if the superintendent had any pride in the condition of his tools, and if heavy engine lathes and radial drills suffer from such practices, how much more is the injury to watch tools, a drill chuck, for instance?

One of the prominent lathe manufacturers sends out the following: "If the chuck comes to us true it will run true after mounting. Our liability ceases after it leaves the factory. We guarantee nothing but the mounting." This was made necessary by the tendency of workmen to clamp the spindle and twist a closely fitted taper out of the spindle with the fingers, or to place a screwdriver or file against the back of the chuck and drive it out with a hammer. There is no quicker way to impair the efficiency of such tools.

If the workman is buying his centers he should try all of them for fit as soon as they are received, rejecting all which are long enough to close the hole, and also those which are not long enough to reach it. The former should then be turned off and the ends rounded so as to half close the cross-drilled hole when inserted in the spindle. The short ones must either be ground down to a proper fit, or returned to the dealer. In this connection it would be well to refer to our remarks on centers and their proper fitting in Chapter V. If the watchmaker prefers to make his own tapers, this is easily done by setting the slide-rest at a proper angle, putting a rod of steel in the chuck, and turning down the taper so that it will fit the conditions shown above. In doing this it will be best to round the ends and cut off the taper of the desired length with a hand graver, without disturbing the slide rest, as after once getting the slide rest set to the exact taper required for a perfect fit, it is not easily changed and reset again for every piece; for the same reason it is better to make up a number of them at once, as the time taken in getting the taper right is then done but once for a number of tapers. In thus making them for stock it is better to employ as large a rod as your largest chuck will take and to leave the unfinished ends long enough so that they may be formed into cutting tools, stems for mounting, or be drilled and taper ground to receive the ends of broaches,

Fig. 105. Drill Socket.

drills, reamers, etc., as shown in Fig. 105, thus making what the machinist calls a socket. In this case the taper holes should also be cross drilled as described at length for the spindles. By mounting a number of his tools in sockets, in this way a watchmaker may rapidly insert one tool after another in his tail stock spindle while swinging his work in the face plate or chuck, and the rapidity with which he can center, drill, broach and countersink when uprighting a pair of plates, for instance, is only limited by the number of tools which he has already mounted in sockets of uniform size, all ready to be put in or taken out of the push spindle of the tail stock as desired. Drilling with the push spindle keeps the hole straight and round and preserves the edges of the drill, as the pressure is only in the direction of the work to be done, while if the drill is held in the pin vise there is always more or less side pressure on the drill. Many watchmakers hold that in enlarging a cannon pinion, for instance, the drill is not so likely to be broken if held in the hand. Perhaps this is true, if the drill is not right, but not otherwise; and many a pivot drill has been broken and its maker condemned when the real trouble was that it was broken by side pressure, caused by improper methods of holding.

One of the most useful adjuncts to the push spindle tail stock is a series of drilling rests, Fig. 106, made of brass, of various sizes, and mounted on tapers as described above.

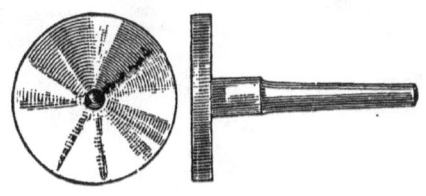

Fig. 106. Drilling Rest.

The advantage of using large stock for tapers will be seen here, as it permits a substantial shoulder to support the plate. In making them, mount heavy sheet brass in the face plate, face off, drill and cut out of the desired diameter, of course making the central hole small enough so that you can make a shoulder on your taper. Turn the shoulder straight and have the hole in the brass a little larger outside, so that the

Fig. 107. Square Back Center.

brass may be held by upsetting the end of the taper slightly. Face off and round the edges of the plate and it is done. They should vary in size from a quarter of an inch to two inches and will be found extremely convenient in holding work at right angles to a drill or other tool held in a chuck in the lathe spindle.

Another extremely handy appliance is the square back center shown in Fig. 107, and the workman should have several of them for use in drilling round objects. Both these and the drill rests may be purchased or made, as desired.

Figs. 108, 109 and 110 show various forms of pivot drill chucks, on tapers to be used in the push spindle. They consist of a small split chuck with three jaws covered by a

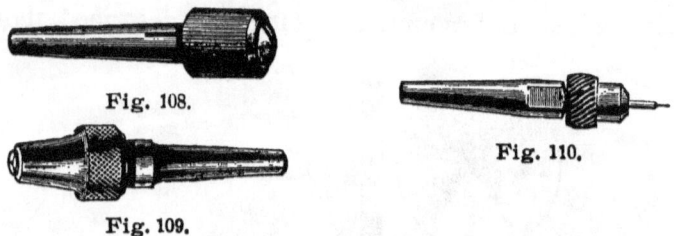

Fig. 108.

Fig. 110.

Fig. 109.

compression sleeve, as shown on a larger scale in Fig. 111, in section, with the sleeve removed. Although very small, they are quite true if not abused, and if the watchmaker will make his drills on the lathe and sharpen them with the pivot polisher (as will be described later in the chapter on drills and drilling) so that the point of the drill is exactly

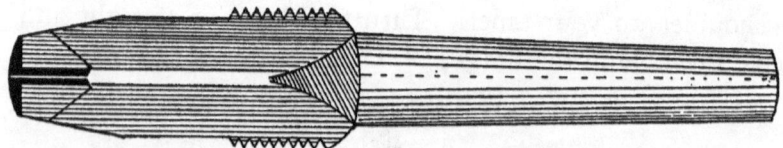

Fig. 111. Enlarged Section of Pivot Drill Chuck.

central with the shank, very excellent results will be obtained with drills held in this chuck in the push spindle. It is only of late years that machinists have concluded that they have not the skill to keep their drills accurately centered when sharpening by hand, and they have introduced drill grinders for that purpose, as they have found that a few thousandths out of center seriously impairs the efficiency of the drill. How much more necessary, then, is truth where the entire diameter of the drill is only a few thousandths of an inch and it is to drill hard steel altogether. Pivot drills should always be put in a chuck and sharpened with the pivot polisher, so as to keep the point central.

Sometimes a watchmaker decides to use two or three of these drill chucks, in which case he orders the holes of different sizes and sends a taper which exactly fits his push spindle, so that the chucks come to him true and accurately fitted. He then has a very convenient set of chucks for drilling, and if he will put all his drills in a split chuck and grind down the shanks to fit one or the other size of his drill chucks, he is doubly fitted. When the work is in the split chuck of the lathe, he can drill with the drill chuck in the push spindle of the tail stock; when the work is out of the lathe he can still fit his drills in the split chuck and rest his work against the drilling plate in the tail stock spindle; and in either case he is sure of a hole that is round and at right angles to the face of the work.

Besides its use in centering and drilling, the tail stock is regularly used as a stop, or gauge, in cutting off pieces which are desired to be of the same length. In this case the slide rest is set so as to carry a parting tool close to the chuck in the lathe spindle, care being taken to set it as nearly on the line of centers as can be, so as to leave as small a tit as possible when the piece which is being cut off falls from the bar. Measurement is taken by running the cutting edge of the tool up to the line of centers and bringing the tailstock spindle with a center or drill rest into position, so that the desired length may be measured between the back edge of the tool and the rest which is to serve as a stop. This is readily and quickly done by inserting a piece of the proper length between the back edge of the tool and the rest. The tailstock and spindle are then clamped in position and a rod of the material to be cut inserted in the chuck through the draw-in spindle, the end of the rod faced off, the tit removed with a file, graver or oil stone; the rod is then pushed forward till it strikes the stop and the chuck clamped on it, when it may be cut off and the operation repeated as often as desired. In doing this, many use as a stop a hollow or female center, a little smaller in diameter than the rod to be cut, but large enough so that if the end is not flat the tit will strike the hole in the center and not alter the length of the rod by preventing it being brought squarely to the stop. By paying attention to these points stock may be rapidly cut with practically no variation in length. By taking care to get a flat end every time before cutting off, the workman is sure of his lengths and the tit left on the other end is removed after the desired quantity of stock has been cut by putting the stepping device, Fig. 44, in the draw-in spindle, putting the lengths of wire in the

Fig. 112. Screw Tailstock.

chuck, one at a time, and finishing the other ends. In doing this, it should be born in mind to place the stepping device so that enough of the piece may project from the chuck to allow it to be inserted and withdrawn easily from the front of the chuck, so that the step need not be moved after being placed in position.

Fig. 112 shows the screw tailstock. This differs from the push spindle in having a hollow spindle with a nut at its rear end and a spline or slot to keep it from revolving in the tailstock. The nut engages a screw, which is journaled at the rear end of the tailstock and enters the tube of the spindle. Turning the hand wheel on the rear end of the screw revolves the screw in the nut of the tailstock spindle and thus advances or retracts the spindle with a power proportioned to the pitch of the screw and the size of the hand wheel. The thumb screw shown in the center is used to clamp the spindle in position. The tailstock screw should be long enough to push the tool out of the spindle when it is drawn clear back, in which case a cross drilled hole in the spindle to remove the tool will be unnecessary. The taper hole for the reception of tools in the front end of the screw tailstock spindle should be of the same size and taper as that in the push spindle, so that the tools will fit either and thus

Fig. 113. Half-Open Tailstock.

avoid the duplication of tools, sockets, tapers, rests, etc. For large and heavy work, the screw tailstock is almost a necessity, as it allows very powerful pressure to be put on the work and avoids chattering, breaking of drills and glazing over in the bottom of the hole when drilling hard steel, and secures round, straight holes in thick brass clock frames, music box work, model making and the numerous other jobs, aside from watch work, which a watchmaker is often called upon to do.

Fig. 113 is called a half-open tailstock. It is chiefly used in manufacturing, where the amount of work done is considerable, but not enough to make the purchase of a turret or automatic machine advisable. It is fitted with any number of spindles, each carrying a tool and having a clamp with a set screw clamped on it. This clamp is split at its lower end to engage a guide or steady pin inserted in the rear end of the tailstock. In practice these spindles are laid in a rack at the rear of the tailstock and are rapidly picked up, laid in the forks of the tailstock and run forward until the screw stop strikes the tailstock, when they are removed and the next in order substituted until the piece is completed. Drilling, boring, reaming, counterboring, chamfering, etc., are rapidly done with accuracy in this manner, and where the volume of work is considerable they will pay a profit on their cost. They are not a repairer's tool, however, be-

Fig. 114. Traverse Spindle Tailstock.

ing designed as a substitute for a turret, with the advantage that any number of tools may be used without the loss of time that would be incurred in using a large turret with only a few tools in it.

Fig. 114 is a traverse spindle tailstock, so called because the spindle, slides or traverses longitudinally while revolving. It is about the finest drilling fixture made, consisting of a true spindle running in hardened steel bearings, inserted in the tailstock and fitting so closely that while they work freely there is no play when the spindle is oiled. Like the preceding, it is a factory device. It was designed for drilling round straight holes; the work revolving one way and the drill the other. Later it was found useful in piercing or opening and polishing the holes of jewels, as with jewel and drill or lap, both revolving at high speeds, much time was saved. It was frequently purchased by watchmakers who had to make a jewel occasionally and who also found it useful for drilling, but with the introduction of the pivot polisher and the quick facilities for ordering material by mail, its use has gradually fallen off. The pivot polisher offers a traverse spindle which may be moved about and used at various angles, and while it is not as strong as the tailstock, it can be used oftener.

We now come to the jeweling caliper, or swing tailstock. This most useful tool should be in the hands of every jeweler, as by its use much time is saved and a perfect fit is assured. It is scarcely necessary to point out that the uprighting of the staff and consequently the depthing of wheels and pinions, depends to a very large extent upon perfectly centered hole jewels and perfectly fitting jewel settings, so that any lack of accuracy here will have a direct effect upon the performance of the watch.

There is some doubt as to who invented this jeweling appliance, although all agree that it was done about 1860. It has been attributed to two men, N. B. Sherwood and E. Howard. Ambrose Webster credits it to E. Howard, of Dennison Howard & Davis, the proprietors of the first watch factory in America, afterward known as the Boston Watch Co., and now the American Waltham Watch Company. This story has been widely copied, but we have never seen anything more than the assertion and both Mr. Howard and Mr. Webster are dead. Mr. E. A. Marsh, general superintendent of the company at present, says: "It has been understood in this factory for many years that it was invented or adapted by N. B. Sherwood. We feel that as originally made it was not designed for the setting of jewels, but for the opening of holes in the barrel, to fit the barrel arbor. It has been a matter of great regret with the writer that, contrary to his special orders, the original machine of this kind was destroyed; it was intended to have it kept as a curiosity. This machine had an upright spindle, with an arm which swung out horizontally, the extremity of which calipered the barrel arbor while the tool, midway of the length of the arm, was adapted to bore the hole in the barrel." Mr. H. E. Duncan, at our request, undertook to reconcile these two stories, and after questioning all the old employes at Waltham, says: "But one man comes out strong on the question, P. McNamee, a jeweler. He states that the principle of the swing caliper was known and that the first one for jeweling was made about 1860, in the machine shop of the company, by Deacon Farmer (he was a regular tool maker), and when done was put in his (McNamee's) hands and proved a big success. He also states that the end shaking tool was designed by Sherwood and the first one made under his supervision, and when done, came to McNamee to use and that was a success." This leaves the matter in doubt as to whether Howard invented the caliper for a different purpose, Sherwood adapted it and Farmer made it, or whether the credit of the initiative as regards its present use in jeweling should be given to Farmer. Sherwood is credited with its application in jeweling in the "American Horological Journal," in 1872, while he himself, in "Watch and Chronometer Jeweling," which was written by Sherwood and first published in that paper, in serial form, in 1872, credits the invention of the swing rest to Mr. Howard and states that it can be applied in many ways.

Its application depends upon the fact that angular measurement, considered with reference to linear measure, is a variable quantity, and thus the actual size in inches or meters of a given angle depends upon how far from the center that distance is taken. This will be made clear if we will place a watch dial over the center of, say, a ten-inch clock dial, so that all figures will be in line with each other and the center when a rule or straight edge is laid over them. The minute in each instance equals 360 degrees divided by 60 or six degrees, while the hours equal 360 degrees, divided by 12, or 30 degrees; yet the sizes of the minutes and hours on the clock dial are many times those of the watch, if we measure them with a rule. The student should try experiments enough to get this idea of the variation in actual size of a given angle thoroughly into his comprehension, as it will aid him greatly in studying wheel cutting, escapements and all other constantly recurring divisions of circular or angular measure. The next thing to bear in mind is that a tool in the lathe will cut a circle of twice its distance from the center; thus a tool half an inch from the center will cut a circle one inch in diameter, etc. Now if we place our tool with its cutting edge at the center of the lathe and extend the arm which carries the tool far enough above the tool, then we can find a place on that arm sufficiently far from the center so that the actual size of the angle will measure twice the distance we moved the tool, just as we can make a clock dial with minutes twice the size of those on a watch. Having found this distance from the center and placed a stop there to measure against, then any objects placed between the stop and the arm carrying the tool will move the tool one-half the distance from the line of centers and consequently cut a circle of the size of the object held between the arm and the stop.

This will be more plainly understood by reference to Fig. 115, where AB is the line of centers and AG the center of the swinging arm; C the lathe center; D the tool, carried on the arm AG; F the jewel, whose seat is to be cut in the setting. It will be seen that by moving the stop E up or down on the arm which carries it (not shown here), we can adjust the size of the angle to keep the cutting edge of the tool where it should be, although it wears away as we sharpen it. We can also advance or retract the stop E with reference to the line of centers, AB, by screws at the back of E. If we provide a number of these stops, side by side, we can have one to cut the opening through the setting, one for the counter sink to hold the jewel and form its seat, and one for the outside diameter of the jewel setting. Then if we have cutting edges on the end and both sides of our tool, we can pierce our hole, cut the jewel seat, burnish it in and cut the outside of the proper diameter at one operation with one tool. This is not often done, however, as it is better practice to use separate cutters, each mounted in separate push spindles, as a tool with three cutting edges must be sharpened on top and soon wears too small to be of service, so that separate cutters for the different opera-

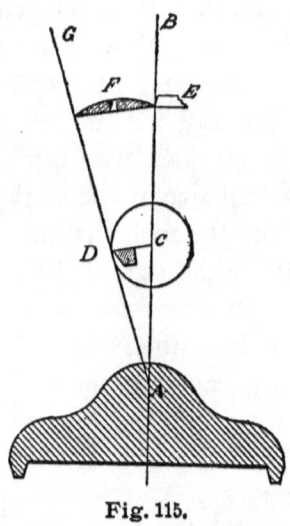

Fig. 115.

tions are better. For this reason, several of the manufacturers provide but two of the stops E on their swing tailstocks, although others make three, as stated above.

The tools are best made from round steel, with shank ground to fit the hole in the push spindle, cut off, chucked and filed down to center with the filing rest set level, and with the index pin at zero in the lathe head, then turned over a stated number of degrees, say to the eighteenth hole, and sufficient clearance given on the cutting edge to just clear the smallest circle it is intended to cut; file the front edge straight and give clearance to the other, so it will enter the hole; harden and then smooth the edges with a fine oil stone or with a lap on the pivot polisher. The tools should be as hard as possible without being brittle, as they will hold the cutting edge longer and thus make frequent adjustments unnecessary. The smoother you make your cutting edges the brighter your work will be, and the longer your tools will last if they are of the proper temper. This can be easily done by lapping and polishing with the lap set

Fig. 116. Moseley Swing Tailstock. 1, Base; 2, Standard Carrying Stops; 4, Swinging Arm Carrying Spindle; 7, 8, Clamp and Set Screw for depth of cut: 9, Spindle; 10, Steady Pin; 13, 14, Nut and Clamp for Feed Screw; removing 14 allows arm to drop forward; 17, 18, Stops or Gauges between which jewel or setting is placed; 18 may be adjusted by rear screws 19; 20, Pivot on which arm swings.

so that its motion is parallel to the cutting edges of the tools. If the polishing is finished with Vienna lime and oil under a strong glass, so as to get a finely polished and very sharp edge, the work done by the tool will surprise you with its beauty. After making, the tool is sharpened on the end only, as all the cutting is done on the end, the tool being always held at right angles to the work by the spindle.

The use of the pivot polisher with its various laps, in tool making, is little understood and deserves more attention by watchmakers generally. By using round steel and setting the index pin at zero, you can file your top flat, with the filing fixture set level; then you can turn your lathe spindle and pin it again at a stated number of holes in the lathe head, and you can thus give a known angle of clearance to the cutting edge of the tool. After hardening you can insert the tool in the chuck again and grind to exactly the same angle any number of times by using the same holes in the index head and the same angle on the pivot polisher every time. In this way you always know what you are doing and your tool will always cut the same way. Few watchmakers use their tools hard enough for the best work, and

Fig. 117. Hopkins Swing Tailstock.

they do not polish their cutting edges because it is too much trouble with a hard tool. A touch or two with a good lap will do the business in a moment, and by working to known angles of cutting edges and clearance it is no trouble to set the lathe head and pivot polisher to do the business perfectly and quickly. The laps will wear so long that their cost need not be taken into consideration, as you can make them yourself. This applies to tools used in the slide rest as well as to those for the tailstock.

Fig. 116 shows the Moseley swing tailstock, while Fig. 117 shows the Hopkins, the latter having a straight arm to carry the stops, while that of the Moseley is curved.

This tailstock is made by all manufacturers of lathes, there being minor differences in each make, but all work on the same principles, as already explained at length. The watchmaker should buy the one which fits his lathe, as then his tapers and push spindles will be all alike, or should be, and he thus saves the duplication of tools. Do not buy an imitation tailstock unless you have an imitation lathe, for the reasons just given. Two spindles should be ordered, so that one may be kept ready for jeweling and the other for general work, and it should be insisted upon that the spindles be interchangeable with those of the ordinary tailstock for your lathe.

Fig. 118. The Clement Swing Tailstock.

Fig. 118 shows the Clement swing tailstock, which is the latest development of the tailstock, as a tool carrier for watchmakers. It is made to fit any make of lathe and consists of a base pivoted on a shoe, which fits the lathe bed. The rear end of the base is graduated so that it may be set to known angles and returned to line by inserting a taper pin at the rear. The spindle is pushed or may be fed by a screw and both screw and steady pins are graduated so that exact depthings may be obtained. There is but one spindle and it is adapted to carry any number of tools, such as filing fixtures, pivot polisher, cutters, etc. The figure shows outside and inside cutters, 7 and 8, in the spindle, 7 being brought into line by the adjusting screw 4. The pivot polisher is shown below, detached. A socket is furnished to fit the tools of the ordinary tailstock. The attachment for turret tools is very ingenious and simple, and is capable of further development along the same lines, so as to replace many of the other fixtures which now come with this attachment. We have no doubt that this will be done. The tailstock has three stops instead of two, and a right and left thread on the swing feed screw, thus giving a rapid swing which may be further increased by disconnecting the feed and swinging by hand. The clamp and right and left screw for the spindle feed is graduated to thousandths of an inch and allows it to be used as a push or screw tailstock in place of the regular tailstocks for the lathe, as well as giving it a rapid feed for cutting tools. The fixtures are so many that they cannot be illustrated here for want of space, besides which the tool is so new that they are constantly being changed and added to. The workmanship is first-class upon all of these tools which we have seen and the new attachment is being purchased very largely by those in the trade who are not already provided with the separate tools for which this attachment is designed as a substitute.

The swing tailstock is used principally for boring, opening barrels to fit arbors, opening wheels to fit pinions, opening plates to fit jewel settings and opening settings to fit jewels when mounting them. It is simple and efficient in its action and when properly set will measure correctly any object that is placed between the stops, and cut a sink of the same diameter. There are several points that should be observed in its use. First, the cutters that go in the spindle should be cut exactly in half; that is, they should be filed exactly to the center. To find the exact center, turn the steel to a point; file it flat until the point is reached, taking care not to go any further, by using your filing fixture set level and at the proper height. Then turn your piece in the chuck one-quarter round and three spaces by, for clearance. If you started with the index pin at zero, this will bring you to the eighteenth hole. File the front edge straight and reduce it in size as much as is necessary for the size of hole it is intended to cut. Then shape it; the shape is just the same as if it was intended to go in a slide rest for the same purpose, perfectly straight on its front side and end, the other side of a size and shape to go into the sink it is intended to cut. Temper and polish as previously described. The object in filing the cutting tool perfectly straight on its front side is so as not to change the cutting angles, as the cutter is sharpened square with the side and only on its end, never on the side, after it is first done. To adjust the cutter, put on the universal head or face plate; put the cutter in the push spindle and the spindle in the swing tailstock; put the latter on the lathe close to the face plate; then adjust one stop or finger so that when the arm is brought against it the front edge of the cutter will be exactly in line with the point of the pump center in the face plate or universal head; turn the lathe slowly, to see if your face plate is on true; if so the point of the pump center will not change its position. To prove that the cutter is in the correct position, put a piece of brass wire in your chuck and drill a hole in it; then take a jewel, place it against the stop which you have adjusted and press the swinging arm back against it; push the spindle forward and cut your sink. If the sink is too large for the jewel the swing stands too far forward and the stop, or finger, must be turned back a trifle; if the sink is too small, the stop is too far back and should be set forward; when the exact size is reached, fasten the stop in position by the screw. This ensures exactness in future operations without resetting every time it is used. The hole under the stop is used for many purposes. If we are opening a wheel, we place the pinion in the hole, bring up the arm, push forward the spindle, and the hole in the wheel is the exact size to be staked on the pinion; so also with the barrel arbor or any other object, such as the screw head.

The swing tailstock is often used in the place of the slide rest, in facing off, turning barrels, etc., but unless you have the Clement, which is designed expressly for that purpose, it should not be done, as a rule. When taking a light cut, the cutter can be swung around quickly, but there is always danger of the cutter catching or breaking unless care is used. If you have no slide rest, you can use the swing with a heavier cutter in the spindle than you can use for jeweling, but it is well to make haste slowly until you are used to handling the tool in this manner. The Clement is stronger, has a longer support for the spindle, and the spindle is heavier, so that the tool is more firmly held. It has been tried and found very satisfactory to those who have no slide rest.

CHAPTER IX.

CUTTERS, DRILLS, AND HOW TO MAKE THEM.

How to make proper tools and keep them in order is one of the most important questions which occur to the every-day mechanic. Having good tools alone is not sufficient for a thorough mechanic; he should possess a thorough knowledge of the principles upon which they are formed; then he can keep them in order, and, should occasion demand it, he can make his own tools or a tool for a special job, so as to get the best results.

In addition to a knowledge of the underlying principles may be included that of setting the tool in position and guiding it to get the best results. The requisite skill necessary to sharpen and set a tool correctly is only acquired by long experience, and this knowledge, when acquired, is highly valued. A poorly ground tool may be used by a skillful man, because his experience has taught him how to place it so as to make it cut; that is, how to present the cutting edge to the work in such a way that it will form the proper angle with the work. While the setting of the tool may, in many cases, be slightly modified to compensate for an improperly formed cutting edge, it should be the aim of the workman to always form his tools with correct angles.

Of all the operations requiring the use of cutting tools, there is none which is accomplished with the same accuracy and rapidity as that of turning, the tool being held by the hand or in a fixture made for that purpose and presented to the work while it is revolving in the lathe, so that the cutting is continuous.

However, all that can be expected from even the finest lathe is that it will revolve the work with the least amount of variation possible while the tool is traversing the work. No machine, however costly or elaborate, can produce fine or accurate work if the cutting tools are poorly made or improperly applied, and it is for this reason that the watchmaker should give that care to both the quality and form of the tool which its importance demands. When any man has thoroughly mastered the principles underlying the formation and use of lathe tools, he will have no difficulty in making any special tool that may be required, for these principles will apply equally well to any other metal cutting tool.

Lathe tools are divided into two principal classes, viz.: hand tools and slide rest tools, both classes being made of a special grade of steel known as tool steel.

To the watchmaker hand tools are known as gravers. When using a graver it is not so important that an exact angle should be obtained when sharpening it as in a slide rest tool, for, in the former, the hand is at once able to detect if the graver is not properly cutting and with the range of adjustment possible the operator can at once place the cutting edge in such a position that it will cut smoothly, while in the slide rest tool the same extent of adjustment is not possible, and we have not the delicacy of touch to guide us, so that the condition the surface of the work is left in and the appearance of the shaving of metal as it comes from the tool will form our best guide from which to judge if the tool is cutting properly. The tool should leave the surface so smooth as to almost have the appearance of having been polished, but, of course, much will depend upon the coarseness or fineness of the feed and the form of the tool as well. The cutting should come away from the tool in the form of a spiral with a clean cut, lively appearance, the length of the spiral being more or less long according to the condition of the metal being operated upon castings giving shorter and more broken shavings than rolled or drawn metal. Should the tool be dull or not of the correct form, the work will be left rough and the cutting will not be in a spiral, but will be in numberless short pieces, will have a sort of dragging, dead appearance, and will come away with a harsh grating sound.

The old adage that "a workman is known by his chips," was never more true than when applied to the cutting of metals. The edge of a tool can affect the surface upon which it acts in two different ways, depending entirely upon the angles of the tool relative to the surface of the work. These are cutting and scraping. The angle of the edge of a tool must be more or less acute to form a cutting tool; that is, so that the edge of the tool will penetrate below the surface and remove a quantity of the metal. In other words, the cutting tool is a wedge which is used to separate a portion of the metal, by pressing the point or edge of the wedge into it. In scraping, the tool is presented in such a way that it cannot penetrate, thus removing but a small amount of metal at a time. In order to make them cut, all tools must have what is known as clearance, or sometimes, as the angle of relief. This is necessary that the portion of the tool back of the cutting edge will not drag or rub on the work, which would prevent the cutting edge from entering the metal. The amount of clearance should always be the smallest amount possible to give a free cutting tool, as by so doing we leave the metal of the tool just back of the cutting edge, where it is in the best possible position to support and strengthen the edge, which is doing the work. To make a tool cut, it is given an incline on its face which is known as rake, and a tool is made more or less keen by giving it more or less rake; in other words, by making the cutting angle of our wedge more or less acute. There are two kinds of rake, viz: positive and negative rake, but since the positive rake is more often used it is spoken of merely as rake, and if negative rake is meant it is spoken of as such.

Fig. 119 represents a tool which is properly formed and presented to the work where A is the tool and B the work, while C shows the shaving or chip. It will be noticed that the chip comes away in the form of a long spiral, which is a good guide by which to judge the cutting qualities of the tool. The rake of the tool shown in Fig. 119 is positive, the angle of the cutting edge being acute, while that of the tool in Fig. 121 is negative, this angle being obtuse. A tool in which the top face is straight, that is, level with the center of the lathe, is spoken of as having no rake. In turning brass a tool is used which has either no rake or negative rake, as from the nature of this metal a keen cutting tool is very liable to gouge or dig into the work. The strain upon

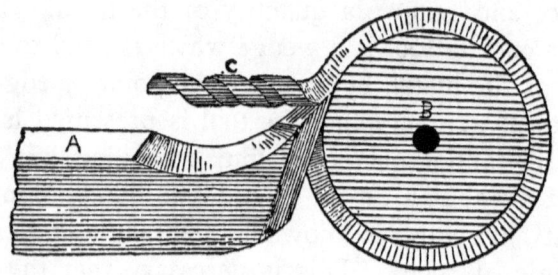

Fig. 119.

the top face of the tool is not that alone due to the actual severing of the metal, but also that of bending the metal after it has been severed. This strain, of course, varies with the depth of cut and the amount of rake given to the tool. The greater the rake the less this strain is. The bending of the severed metal produces a strain in such a direction as would cause it to spring into the work, and so take a heavier cut than intended, unless the tool is made strong enough to resist this strain and prevent springing. A tool which is to be used to take a light cut may be made with very acute angles at the cutting edge, but one which is to be used on heavy work must be made less acute on account of its being too weak, if too acute, so that it will spring and gouge into the work.

The form of a cutting tool is simply that of a wedge, which is forced into the material for the purpose of separating a portion of it from the main body. The thinner this wedge is the less is the power required to drive it in. The tool or material should be driven at the speed which is the most effective, so that the work will be accomplished in the shortest time. The speed is only limited by the heating and softening of the cutting edge, due to the friction. The heat which is generated at the point of the tool, when cutting, is eliminated by being conducted to the body of the tool, and from this to the surrounding air by radiation. The

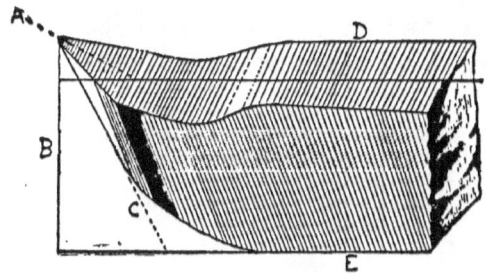

Fig. 120.

tool which is to be used for heavy cuts, such as a machinist would have to take, must have sufficient metal in it near the cutting edge to resist the heating and consequent softening, so that the heat may be carried away rapidly. When taking a heavy cut, a liquid of some kind is employed, usually either oil or water, to assist in carrying away this heat. The thinner edged tool cuts easiest, not because there is less friction, but because the metal is distorted less in its removal. Both the tool and the work must in all cases be as rigid as possible, so that there will be the least possible vibration. The edge of the tool must be made very keen to prevent it from slipping over the surface, this precaution being especially necessary when turning tempered steel.

Those tools which are used in the slide rest, may be subdivided into two classes, outside or external and inside or boring tools. They are still further designated, either from the nature of the work they perform or some characteristic of the tools themselves. Thus, a front tool is one that has its cutting edge in front; a side tool is one that cuts on the side; a cutting off tool one that is used for that purpose, etc.

When making a tool for any purpose it is necessary that it be left as strong as possible, yet sufficiently keen to make a smooth and clean cut. Fig. 120 shows a tool with the various angles. The angle the cutting face A makes to the perpendicular line B is called top rake, while the difference between the line B and C is called the clearance. D and E represent the top and bottom faces of the tool respectively.

In Fig. 122, which has excessive rake and small clear-

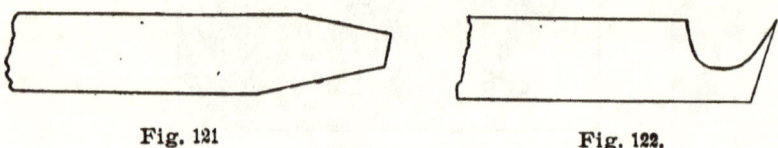

Fig. 121. Fig. 122.

ance, it is obvious that the shaving will not meet with the same resistance as it would in Fig. 120. A tool could be made so keen, as shown in Fig. 122, that a light shaving would come off almost straight, but such a tool would be very weak and soon become dull, because there is not metal enough to rapidly convey the heat from the cutting edge; but there are times when such a tool can be used to advantage, such as in cutting soft, tough metal that has a tendency to stick or weld itself to the edge of the tool, as do copper and aluminum. When turning, either of these metals, the tools may be supplied with a small amount of oil, or kept moist with water, to enable them to make a smooth cut. The strain upon the tool is downward and forward, so that if the body of the tool is slight, or it stands so far out from the tool post as to be unable to withstand the pressure due to the cut, without springing, it will spring into the cut, using the point of least resistance in the tool or the tool post as a fulcrum, but if the tool is so formed that the top of the cutting edge is below the top of the body of the tool, a pressure sufficient to spring the tool would cause it to leave the cut, which, of course, would reduce the depth of the cut. In all cases, the tool should not extend beyond the tool post more than is necessary to well clear the work, as it is thus subject to a less amount of spring.

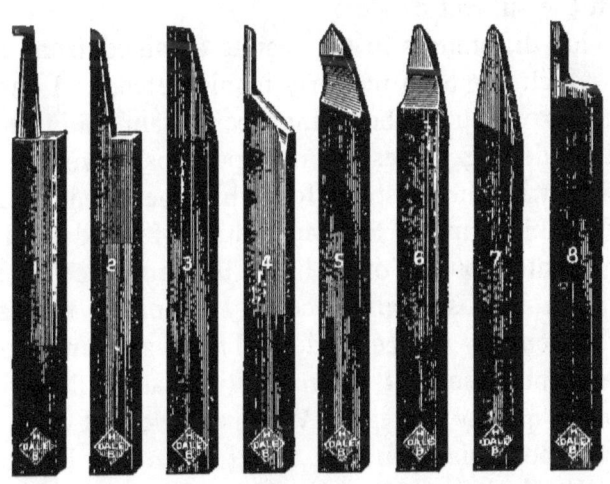

Fig. 123. Slide Rest Tools. No. 1, Boring Tool; No. 2, Centering Tool; No 3, Side Tool; No. 4, Smoothing Tool; No. 5, Turning Tool; No. 6, Round-Nosed Tool; No. 7, Thread Cutting Tool; No. 8, Parting or Cutting-off Tool.

Fig. 123 shows the usual shapes of cutting tools for use in the slide rest. These are the same as those usually employed for similar purposes in the machine shop, and the workman will find it convenient to have several sets of varying sizes and different angles of top rake and clearance so as to be prepared for cutting various grades of metal. These may be made of bar steel, either round or square section as desired, the only points of importance being the shapes of the cutting edges and that the body or shank of the tool contains metal enough to give the necessary stiffness, to avoid springing, while the metal itself should be of uniform texture and capable of being properly hardened, without subjecting it to heat enough to burn the thinner portions while tempering.

When one stops to consider the air of mystery which many persons endeavor to cast around the operations and processes in the various trades, it is not all surprising to note that the hardening and tempering of steel has indeed had its full share of attention from these wise men, if we may judge by the many recipes to be found in almost every book touching upon the subject of steel.

The wide differences in the results obtained from a piece of steel which has been properly manipulated, and one from the same bar which has been improperly handled in the heating and hardening processes, may, perhaps, have had something to do with the mystery, for, while there seems scarcely any reasonable limit to the capabilities of good steel when properly treated, on the other hand, the same steel, if heated higher than is absolutely necessary in order to insure a proper hardening, will be made so brittle and unfit to serve any useful purpose that we might just as well have used the poorest quality instead. While we do not wish to be classed as pessimistic in our views upon the subject, we do feel that it is our duty to cast aside this mystic robe and give the reader solid facts, which are in keeping with the advancement and enlightenment of the twentieth century. Steel differs principally from its basis (iron, which is an elementary substance) in the amount of carbon it contains.

The amount of carbon contained ranges from nothing in wrought or malleable iron up to one and one-half to two per cent in steel suitable for making cutting tools, and with five per cent of carbon we have a cast iron.

It is somewhat difficult to specify just where malleable iron leaves off and steel commences, for the best authorities differ on the subject. That variety which contains an insufficient amount of carbon to cause it to harden thoroughly, such as would be required for a drill or turning tool, is known among the trade as mild steel, and is of no use to the watchmaker, but might be used in making the larger clocks, especially tower clocks. Steel is produced by three separate methods, and is known as natural, shear and cast steel.

Natural steel is made from the iron as it comes from the smelter by putting the molten metal into a converter and forcing a quantity of air through it, by which means a portion of the carbon is burned away. In making shear steel, bar-iron is first roasted while in contact with carbon, in a cementing furnace, when it is known as blister steel. This steel is now taken, and after heating, is hammered and worked, and several bars are welded together. This bar is sometimes cut and again welded and hammered. Single shear and double shear show to what extent the process has been carried. The name shear steel is derived from its applicability to the manufacture of shearing or cutting tools. Cast steel is blister steel, which has been broken up, fused in a crucible, cast into ingots, and rolled or hammered. Tool steel is a special grade of cast steel, and should be well hammered, which makes it tougher and of finer grain than steel which is rolled. The more a bar of steel is hammered without crushing it and worked, the better it becomes. On a square bar of steel which has been hammered, the corners, being not so well supported as the center, will be found to be more compact, and, consequently, of better quality. The test of steel consists in an actual demonstration of its ability to retain the cutting edge in good condition for the greatest period of time.

All the care and skill exercised by the manufacturers of steel will be wasted if the workman is careless in the operation of heating. The true secret of hardening steel is the bringing it to a temperature at which it will harden thoroughly, and no higher, for, if the temperature is carried above this point to any great extent, the steel will be burnt. On the other hand, if the temperature is not brought sufficiently high the operation can be repeated without detriment to the material. When heating a large piece of steel, the heat should be applied gradually, until the temperature becomes uniform throughout the entire piece. If an intense heat is applied suddenly the result will be that the outer surface will reach the required temperature for hardening some time before the inner portion has had time to reach that stage, and the result will be similar to case hardening a piece of wrought iron, i. e., the outer shell will be hard while the inner portion will be soft, for it must be remembered that a temperature below that which is required to harden it, in reality anneals it, or leaves it softer than before heating. This fact is frequently taken advantage of by skillful tool makers; for example, in drill making, where the drill is large and long, so that the strains due to torsion in working would be likely to break the drill in the hole if it were not tough and elastic in its center while the edges must be hard enough to cut tough steel.

The ideal method of heating steel is by means of a muffle, as in this way the flame does not come into direct contact with the work, where gas is used, nor the burning fuel when coal or coke is used. In the case of heating directly by gas flame and a blow pipe, aside from the danger of overheating the steel, there are times when a coating is formed on the steel which prevents it from hardening thoroughly, and yet this same piece of steel, if heated in a muffle, would be found to harden satisfactorily. In using a muffle, the heat can be brought to the required temperature, and maintained there, and can be judged much better than in an open fire, as by means of a peep-hole in the muffle the work can be closely watched until the proper degree is reached.

When heating pivot drills and similar small articles, great care should be exercised to prevent overheating. For this purpose the melted lead or cyanide baths are sometimes used. These consist of either lead or cyanide, brought to the required temperature in a wrought iron pot or ladle.

Into this bath the article is plunged and allowed to remain until it assumes the same heat as the bath and is then quenched. In heating small pieces in this way, there is no danger of burning, as the smallest portions will only be brought to the temperature of the bath itself.

The room in which the steel is heated should be darkened, so that the heat may be judged by the color of the article. It is evident that we can more closely judge of a cherry red in a dark room than we can in front of a window in the sunshine. If the watchmaker is tempering at his bench, in a bright light, a sheet of cardboard, blotter or large book, placed on edge between the lamp and the light, so as to shut off the light, will enable him to see the blue flame of his lamp clearly and allow him to judge the color of his drill or tool much better than in a strong light. In tempering small objects, such as pivot drills, this is important, as the heat rises beyond the proper temperature very quickly after it starts to redden.

For the ordinary purpose of hardening, water is capable of giving results equal to those of any of the most elaborate formulas. The water should be about 70°. Considerable care should be exercised in the plunging, and this depends greatly upon the shape of the article. Tools which are comparatively long and narrow, such as slide rest tools, drills, etc., should be plunged vertically in order to prevent distortion. In heating an article which is to be subsequently brightened, it should be covered with soap or powdered borax, which prevents oxidization. When an article, such as a drill, is required to be extremely hard, it may be quenched in mercury, being very careful not to inhale the fumes arising from it, as they are very poisonous. A saturated solution of caustic potash or concentrated lye will make a still harder and tougher drill, and pivot drills have been made in this way, by skillful men, that would drill a piece of steel hardened in mercury. The main point in using hardening solutions is to get one which will conduct the heat quickly away from the piece to be hardened. Anything that will do this will serve the purpose. Pivot drills have been tempered by heating and thrusting into a raw potato.

Tempering is the act of withdrawing a portion of the extreme hardness from steel, in order to increase its elasticity, thus making it stronger and tougher. Steel is tempered according to the purposes for which it is intended, and this is determined largely by color. Color, however, is not an infallible guide to the hardness of steel, as much depends on the quality of the metal and its polish. When a piece of metal is whitened, after being hardened and then heated, the surface will gradually pass from a white to a light blue-green. This can best be exemplified by taking a piece of hard steel and heating it and observing the changes of color. It first assumes a very pale straw yellow, almost instantly followed by a darker yellow, these colors giving a temper desirable for metal cutting tools, as slide rest cutters, drills, etc. Then follows a dark straw yellow, tinged slightly with purple, suitable for punches, chisels and percussion tools. Then comes a purple and dark blue, suitable for springs, balance staffs and pinions, and finally, a pale blue, and blue tinted with green, which are too soft for any of the above purposes. These colors are not perceived by the workman unless he has had considerable practice in watching them, as they merge into each other in such a way that unless the man doing the work has a good eye for color and can recognize instantly the shade he wants it is likely to pass into the next shade before he recognizes it and withdraws the heat. If the hardened piece has been polished the colors will be much brighter and more distinct than if it is covered with scale from the hardening and a rough piece has varying shades owing to the light being reflected from the metal at various angles so that it seems to have an uneven color, and hence it takes practice to judge what the color really is. Now each kind of steel has a shade that will give better results than a degree of heat slightly above or below will impart.

Annealing, or the softening of steel, is accomplished in two ways, i. e., by heating and allowing it to cool slowly, and by heating to a less degree than that used for hardening, and then suddenly quenching in water. Some mechanics in annealing in the first mentioned manner, cover the heated article with hot ashes or some other non-conducting material; others put the article between two pine boards and allow it to burn its way in, thus encasing it in a charcoal bed, but for ordinary purposes it will be sufficient to heat the article and allow it to cool slowly in the open air. In the water annealing process, the article is first heated to a cherry red, and when the red color is just disappearing (when in a darkened room), the article is plunged in water.

If the watchmaker starts to make his tools of a known grade of steel it will undoubtedly be better for him to stick to that steel as long as he can obtain it, as he will then learn from experience just what shade of color to use in tempering after hardening, just how hot to make it before plunging in the hardening solution and numerous other little points concerning its use. Do not change your steel because someone had better results with another. Learn your steel; if you change you will only have to learn the new one. Leave the wonderful improvements to be studied by those who are using steel enough to make it a point of economy. You will use less than a pound of steel a year in your cutting tools so that economy in its purchase is not an object.

Economy of time in doing your work is the only economy you can practice, and this is best assured by having a full knowledge, gained from experience, as to the qualities a tool should have. Thirty or forty slide rest cutters, of varying sizes, rake and clearance, will last the average watch maker fifteen years; he loses, breaks and gives away more than he uses up by sharpening.

In the machine shop the cutting end of the tool is always hardened and compacted by heating to a low red and hammering after forging to shape. It is possible to overdo this hammering with a small tool by hammering hard enough to separate and crush the fibers of the metal instead of bringing them more closely together. When this is the case the tool will have brittle or soft, crumbling spots in it. When well hammered it will exhibit a close, even, dense structure, which will take a good edge and hold it if properly hardened. The machinist is also careful to leave the scale on the clearance angles of his tools, so that the side A C, fig. 120, is available for a large part of its depth, the tool being sharpened on top because it sharpens the end and sides with the removal of the smallest amount of metal and leaves the case hardened clearance sides with all their hard surfaces ready to be used as the cutting edge. In many shops a lathe hand is never allowed to remove this scale by grinding. All that is permissible is to smooth its edge on the oil stone after grinding on top, as the hardest part of a hardened piece of steel is always outside and hence the care that is taken to preserve this hard part for use in cutting.

The watch maker uses such small tools that he can buy the very best steels, which have been worked sufficiently before coming to him, and he may therefore merely cut a piece off the bar, file the end to shape, heat to a cherry red and plunge endwise in the hardening solution, taking care to keep the piece moving until the heat is gone, so that the heated portion, coming constantly in contact with cold water, has no opportunity of forming an envelope of steam and warm water about itself and thus cooling more slowly than if it were kept moving. The simplest way in which to accomplish this is to drop the piece, hot end downwards, into a bucketful of water, so that it will have time to cool by the time it reaches the bottom, or hold it under the cold water faucet, if supplied with water from city mains. Much poor hardening is done because the amount of water used is too small and too warm to be serviceable in cooling quickly. The blacksmith uses a half barrel and changes his water when it gets warm; or if he tempers in oil, he uses several gallons to temper a lathe tool or other object of similar size, and he keeps it moving until the redness is all gone, when it is dropped to the bottom of the trough and allowed to cool thoroughly. Of course, such small tools as the watch maker uses do not require anywhere near such quantities of liquid; the point we are making is that there must be enough liquid to cool the tool quickly and that the liquid should not be so warm as to defeat the object sought. Tempering a pivot drill in a pint cup is furnishing more liquid in proportion than the blacksmith uses in his half barrel with the larger tool.

The next point is the temperature. The hardening is accomplished by the difference in temperature possessed by the metal and that of the liquid when they are brought together. The different steels vary considerably in the amount of difference of temperature required to secure the best results, and this difference should never be exceeded. The objects sought are hardness, so that the steel will penetrate the metal to be worked, and toughness, so that the tool will stand the strains put upon it. These qualities are contradictory; the harder you make your steel the more brittle it becomes, so that a medium or compromise must be sought. The hardening liquids vary from about 40 to 80 degrees, being used at the temperature of the room. The steel varies from a dull red to a bright red. It should never be allowed to go beyond this into the whiter shades which accompany the higher degrees of heat, as it will be spoiled for use, because the expansion caused by the heat will spread the fibers of the metal, thus undoing all your work in compacting them with the hammer, and when plunged in the liquid the excessive contraction will destroy the fibers of the metal, making them crystalline and without strength. When this happens the steel is said to be "burned," and the best thing to do is to break off the burned portion and start over again.

Another point is that the workman seldom learns to watch the proper parts of his tool while heating, until a long series of more or less continuous failures enforces its importance upon his attention. You are trying to harden the cutting edges of your tool, not the whole tool; therefore, pay attention to these cutting edges and let the rest of the tool take care of itself. Plunge into the cooling liquid as soon as the cutting edges take the proper color and get the tool out of the flame into the liquid in something less than a second, if possible, as it is the difference in temperature when they meet that counts, not how hot the tool has been at some previous time. This is especially important with drills. Watch makers' drills are so small and weak that the heat is lost unless great speed is used in hardening and more drills are tempered in air than in the hardening liquid by the ordinary workman. Indeed, many use no liquid in tempering pivot drills, simply swinging them rapidly in the air until cold. We can not indorse this practice, as it is next to impossible to learn to heat the tool just right, for the ordinary man needs a long apprenticeship of the eye when it comes to distinguishing heat by varying shades of red which merge into each other rapidly, as is the case in heating such small tools.

The student may make most rapid progress by going into a machine shop and watching the blacksmith when he is making lathe tools, paying particular attention to the color of the tool just as it is being plunged into the oil or water. Then go home and try to get the same color on your tools. A few lessons will teach you not to burn your drills and other smaller tools, and that is the main point to be guarded against in your case.

That is the best tool which contains its hardest metal at the cutting edge and softer metal inside. This makes a tough tool. It is quite difficult to do this with tools so small as those we are considering, as they are apt to be hardened clear through and become weak in consequence. With larger tools it is accomplished habitually by many workmen.

If using anything besides water to harden with, such as cyanide, caustic potash, oil or other solutions, a wide mouthed bottle, known as a "salt mouth," with ground glass stopper makes perhaps the best vessel to keep your solution in. It should be kept full, so that small tools may be thrust in it readily with the tweezers. After hardening, stone off the working surface with oil on a rather coarse stone, so as to remove the scale formed during hardening, but not enough to remove the hardened surface of the tool. Having thus smoothed it up, polish the cutting edges with a fine oilstone, or if the tool be a drill or very small cutter, use a lap on the pivot polisher to produce the polished cutting edge, and then draw the temper with the alcohol lamp until the polished cutting edges are of the particular shade you want as given at the beginning of this chapter. Do not put your edges in the flame; put the shank in the flame and keep the edges out where you can watch them change color. Use a strong glass to watch the polished edges, if you are a novice or do not see well, as the desired color comes and goes again very quickly on such small tools as you will have occasion to use most frequently. The instant the proper shade—generally one of the shades of yellow—has been obtained, drop the tool in water—and be quick about it. This means that when making pivot drills, for instance, you must get your hardening liquid very close to your lamp flame. If you use a tilting lamp such as is very commonly used for cementing, you can bring your flame within an inch and directly over your water, so that the cooling is almost instantaneous after arriving at the proper color of heat. Older watch makers will remember the use of a raw potato for hardening pivot drills; the sole advantage was that the potato could be held close to the flame, so that less than one inch of movement would jab the drill into it when the proper heat was obtained. The blacksmith in the machine shop, making tools for engine lathes, will take his tool out of the fire, study its color for several seconds and drop it at just the right shade of red. With a pivot drill you must work just as fast as possible, as it is so small it cools almost instantly and there is no time to be leisurely; study your color in the flame.

Fig. 124.

Drills, as used to-day for general work, are of two principal kinds—namely: the twist drill and the diamond shaped, the latter so called because of the shape of the cutting edges. These two forms are shown in Figs. 124 and 125. The former is the twist, while the latter is the diamond point. Those drills which are used for other purposes than the drilling of holes, and which we might term special drills, are shown in Figs. 126 and 127. That shown at Fig. 126 is called a nib drill, and is used to flatten the bottom of holes, while that shown at Fig. 127 is a pin drill, so called from the pin or guide, and is used in recessing or counterboring for flat screw heads and such work, where it is necessary that the bottom be flat, or if formed as at A, it is used for countersinking. The cutting edges, of course, being ground to the desired angle the countersink is to be.

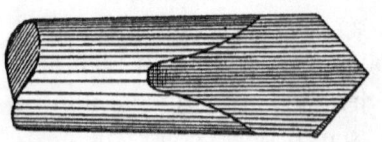 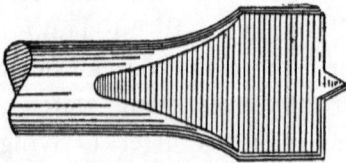

Fig. 125. Fig. 126.

Twist drills are now made in sizes small enough to be used in a great many of the operations connected with watches and clocks, and when it is possible to use them they are found to cut very fast; and on account of their form it will not be necessary to withdraw them to remove the cuttings, as is the case with flat drills when a hole of some depth is made. This is of considerable importance, especially in clock work, or when using larger sizes. The drill is not the same diameter, from end to end, but it slightly tapers towards the back, but this taper is so small as to be of no consequence in actual practice. It is quite sufficient, however, to prevent binding in the work. Neither are twist drills round, as is generally supposed, the diameter being eased away from a short distance beyond the advance edge of the flute. This is done to reduce the friction of the sides and also for clearance for the cutting edges.

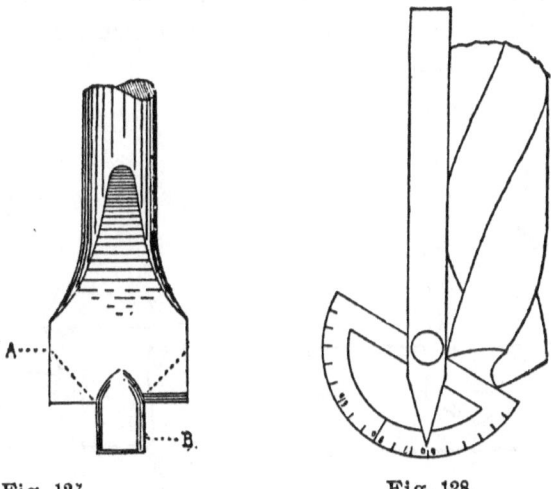

Fig. 127.   Fig. 128.

The grinding of the cutting edges must be done with great accuracy, and to do it properly by hand requires considerable experience, so that drill grinding machines are now generally found in all modern machine shops. The cutting edges are usually ground to an angle of 60 degrees to the center line of the drill, as shown at Fig. 128, and when it is to be used on brass this angle may be decreased slightly, and the cutting edge should be so ground as to give less rake and keenness. The result, if both cutting edges are not ground to the same angle, is that one edge is compelled to do all the work, consequently it will require twice as much time to do a given amount of cutting and will become dull much sooner. This is illustrated by Fig. 129. When the angles are unequal, the point of the drill may or may not coincide with the center of the drill. With the point central, the hole would be the same diameter as the drill, while if it is not central it will drill a hole larger than the drill by twice as much as the amount the point is out of center, as shown at Fig. 130. A very good guide to tell if each edge is doing its proper share of the work is to observe if the cuttings come from each flute equally, and if they do not, they will show which edge is faulty. The difficulty in grinding the twist drill, especially in the smaller sizes, or such as can

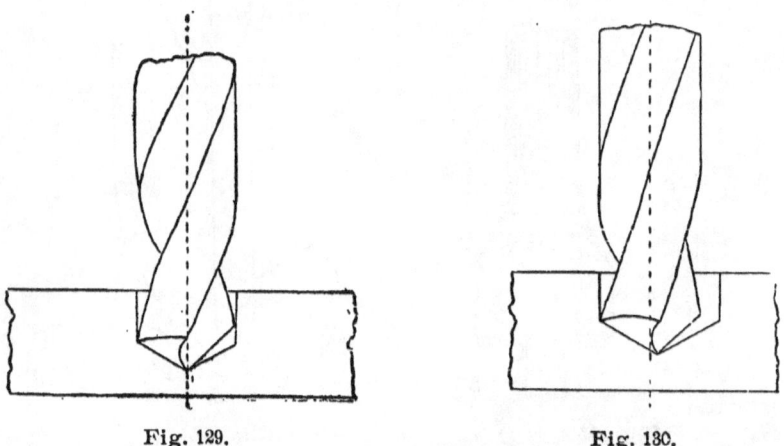

Fig. 129.   Fig. 130.

be used in watch work or small clock work, without the aid of some technical arrangement, is a serious drawback to their use, but if the workman has a pivot polisher they may be ground by setting it at the proper angle and using a lap on it, so that the two edges have the same angles exactly and the point will then be exactly in the center.

Place the drill in a chuck in the lathe-head in such a position that the proper amount of clearance will be given to the cutting edge; this amount must be determined by a trial, but, as it can be set at first with tolerable certainty, one trial should be sufficient. Now set the grinder so as to grind the desired angle on the cutting edge relative to the center of the drill, and grind the first edge. Then note the position of the pin in the index of the lathe-head, which should have been previously inserted, so as to hold the spindle from rotating and revolve the drill half way round by turning the lathe spindle. After fastening it with the index pin, proceed to grind the opposite edge, and if the drill has been properly set in the chuck it will cut correctly.

When using the twist drill, care should be exercised in the feed when the point is about to emerge from the opposite side, as there is a tendency to run through on account of the

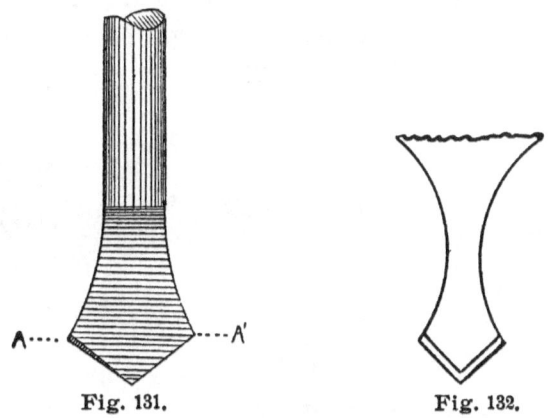

Fig. 131.   Fig. 132.

spiral or twist form of the drill. The best way to avoid any trouble is to put a piece of metal at the back into which the drill can run until the cutting edges are entirely through the work, which will finish the hole up true and smooth.

The flat, or diamond point, drill, as usually made in the smaller sizes, as shown in Fig. 131, in which the sides are relieved to such an extent that it is greatly weakened, and there is nothing but the points AA[1] left to support the sides, and every time such a drill is sharpened the size is reduced a considerable amount, so that after being sharpened a few times such a drill is unfit for the job intended, and a new one must be made. To obviate these faults, the drill should be made with an almost imperceptible taper towards the shank, as shown in Fig. 125. If, when drilling, the point of the drill, at Fig. 131 should strike a hard spot in the metal, or from any other cause which would tend to make it run to one side, it would be more affected than such a one as shown at Fig. 125, the sides of which would offer sufficient support, so that the hole would be very near straight at the worst. Drills, with the cutting edges, as shown in Fig. 132, are put upon the market by foreign concerns, and are intended to be used in the bow drill, but are unfit to be used in lathe work, where they revolve continually in one direction, as the angles of the cutting edges are so formed as to prevent the greatest efficiency of the cutting edges when it is in use, forming a V edge, which can only scrape the metal off.

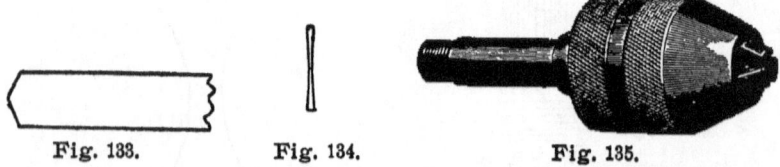

Fig. 133.   Fig. 134.   Fig. 135.

When using a flat drill it should be withdrawn every few revolutions, so as to prevent clogging, which would cause it to stick and bind, and break the drill, especially in the smaller sizes, such as the pivot drills, where great care and delicacy of touch are necessary to prevent breaking. When drilling steel or wrought iron, the drill should be supplied with oil, but in cast iron or brass this will not be necessary if the drill is properly made and in good condition; however, there is occasionally a case where oil might be used to advantage, as where the drill has a tendency to stick. It is just as important in the flat as in the twist drill, that each cutting edge be equal, and it might be added that it is the case in all drills of whatever kind or nature. To obtain this equality of the edges, it is necessary to use the lathe when making a drill. Turn a cone on the end of the rod or wire, as shown in Fig. 133, of the angle to the line of centers, that the cutting edges are to be.

The turning of the cone above mentioned, on the end of the rod or wire, is only necessary when the sides and cutting edges are formed by hand. When the sides and cutting edges are formed by means of a rotary grinder on the slide rest or a lap on the pivot polisher, it is not necessary, as the grinding will true them up if they are unequally roughed out by hand.

Then flatten the sides by filing or grinding, and lastly, giving the requisite amount of clearance to the cutting edges and then hardening; this method is easy enough in the larger sizes of drills, but is almost impossible when we get down to the small pivoting sizes. The following method will be found very accurate for these smaller drills: Having a piece of steel slightly larger than the finished drill is to be, harden it thoroughly, and draw the temper to a light straw color. To harden such a piece, after heating to a red heat, it should be dipped endwise so as to prevent its springing out of true. After the piece is tempered, put it in the lathe and grind it until true, with the parallel grinder or pivot polisher set so as to grind slightly tapering towards the back end of the drill, just sufficient so that the part back of the cutting edge will not bind in the hole. Usually one or two degrees will give clearance enough, as this clearance is on each side of the drill and the total taper towards the shank is therefore double the amount for which the pivot polisher is set.

When the blank is ground down to size, throw the lathe belt off and place the index stop at sixty, and in such a position that the lathe spindle may be revolved exactly half a revolution, and fix the lathe spindle so it can not move; then, with the grinding spindle of the pivot polisher set to the requisite angle and in the proper direction, proceed to grind the two side faces of the drill, leaving sufficient metal at the end so that the point of the drill is not too frail; now set the grinding spindle again to such a taper as will grind the cutting edges; then revolve the lath spindle so that the top will turn towards you; fix the index pin in the eighteenth hole from that in which it was when the sides of the drill were ground and flattened. When one side is done, turn the lathe spindle half a revolution and grind the other one, and you have as true a drill as can be made.

When we say the eighteenth hole, we refer to the modern American lathes, which have a head stock index of sixty holes. The idea is to revolve the spindle one-quarter way round and then add the three extra holes for clearance for the cutting edge.

By grinding the sides of the drill, as above, it leaves them concave, as shown in Fig. 134, which enables us to make the drill point thinner, while the drill as a whole is as strong as if the sides were perfectly flat. In this way a drill of five one-thousandths of an inch or smaller may be made with the same accuracy as any of the larger ones, and in no instance could one so small be made by hand accurately.

Drills may also be sharpened by the same method. For holding the drill in the lathe head when drilling, a special drill chuck should be purchased, so that the wire chucks may be preserved and shielded from the heavier and coarser work as much as possible. Fig. 135 shows a drill chuck which is small and accurate enough for jewelers' use when mounted on a shank which will fit the throat and the draw-in spindle. The advantage of such a chuck is two fold, for while it protects the wire chucks it at the same time permits the holding of drills of various sizes where such would necessitate the changing of a wire chuck every time a drill with a different sized shank was used. When the work is held in the lathe head and revolved, the drill, if very small, should be held in a drill chuck made for the purpose, and which fits in the tailstock spindle, but if no such chuck is at hand the drill may be clamped by any suitable device to prevent it from turning with the work while the shank end rests in a female center in the tailstock spindle.

A pivot drill if put in a pin vise and held in the hand is liable to be broken, as there will be more or less side pressure upon the drill, and for this reason the tailstock should always be used when drilling, that the pressure will only be in the direction necessary to perform the work. When making a pivot drill it should be as short as possible, which will reduce the spring and consequent breaking.

Fig. 136.

When it becomes necessary to drill tempered steel, the drill must be carefully sharpened and not allowed to become dull, for if it should it will act as a burnisher, and so form a surface so hard that it will be difficult to remove it.

The tit drill is seldom employed, and when such a one is needed it can be made in the same way as the pin drill, which is shown in Fig. 127, and is very useful in countersinking a hole which has already been drilled. The pin B fits the hole to be countersunk, so it is a good working fit, while the body is of such a size that it will cut the countersink of the required size. To make such a drill, the pin is first turned down to the required size; then flatten the sides and form the cutting edge. A combined countersink and mill may be made, as shown in Fig. 136, which has four cutting edges. A central hole is drilled in a rod of steel of, say the total diameter of the threaded portion of any screw it is desired to make, while the body is left as large as the head of a screw which is to be countersunk. Now, with a circular mill, cut away the metal so as to form the cutting edges, to which, of course, it will be necessary to give an angle sufficient for clearance. Cut off the rod and drill and tap the hole in the side for the set screw. Harden and temper to a straw. As described we have a mill that may be used for making screw blanks by fastening it so as to be held in the tailstock and advancing it endwise to the material for making screws.

To make all the screws of the same length, a stop may be put in the hole which will limit the length of the threaded portion, being held by a screw tapped through from the outside. When it is to be used as a countersink, all that is necessary is to make a pin which will fit the hole in the mill with some friction, while the portion of the pin extending beyond the cutting faces is made a working fit in the

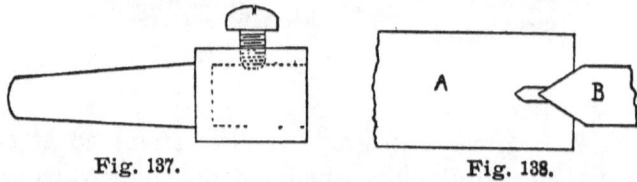

Fig. 137.   Fig. 138.

hole that is to be countersunk. For holding such a mill, a holder, as shown in Fig. 137, can be made, which may be used in the tailstock while the rod is held by the chuck in the lathe head. By using such a mill, a screw can be made in much less time than if turned out by hand, or even with the slide rest. Drills for centering and countersinking work, which is to be turned between centers, may be made by grinding a cone to the same angle as the lathe center, then flatten one side until a full half of its diameter is ground away. Before using the center drill, a small hole must be drilled somewhat deeper than the countersink is to be made, so that the point of the lathe center will not touch the bottom of the hole. This is made plain by Fig.

Fig. 139.

138, where A is the work and B is the drill. Sometimes the drill and countersink are made in one piece, as in Fig. 139, or a hole may be drilled, into which the drill is inserted and held by a screw.

It is important to have these cutters for tail stock centering perfectly true, so that the lathe centers may fit exactly in the holes which will be made by them, as the centers will then resist the wear better and so remain true longer. Before drilling the centers in the work, the ends of the work must be made tolerably flat and true with a graver, then, after the centering with this tool is done the work is swung on the lathe centers, and before starting to turn the work these ends which have just been centered are to be turned off true, so that the wear may be the same all the way around, which it would not be if the end was uneven. This has already been referred to on pages 82 and 83. After the center hole is drilled, the countersink is put in the tail-

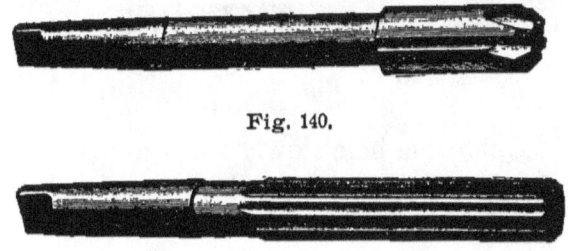

Fig. 140.

Fig. 141.

stock, while the dog is put on one end of the work and revolved on the center, bringing the tailstock spindle up until the center is sufficiently deep, then turn the work end for end and finish the other center. By centering the work, as above, we get the countersinks directly in line with the centers of the lathe, which gives a true bearing all around, which is necessary for accurate results.

When an accurate hole is required, the drill will be found unsatisfactory on account of its roughness and the fact that it may not be round and of the same size all the way through, or it may not be straight, if a long, deep hole, and after drilling the hole somewhat less than the size is to be when finished, the reamer is to be passed through, which will leave it very true and smooth. Fig. 140 and Fig. 141 show two styles of reamers, but for the greatest accuracy the one at 140, owing to its form, is the best, as the sides form a guide for the cutting edges which compels the tool to maintain a true hole. In making a reamer, great care is necessary that it be accurately formed, as the work will not be more accurate than this tool. The body of the tool, back of the cutting edges, should be just enough smaller that it will follow in the hole without undue friction when supplied with oil. The greatest accuracy is obtained by leaving the quantity of metal to be removed by the reamer the smallest amount that will true up to size properly, and the reamer

Fig. 142.

should be fed into the hole slowly so as to give the cutting edges ample time to cut away all of the metal and clear themselves.

Reamers are sometimes used for making taper holes; a fluted reamer is shown in Fig. 142, or another style may be made by grinding a piece of hardened steel to the required taper, then grinding away two sides until the cutting edge is formed. The fluted reamer is very well adapted for accurate tapers, but as each portion of the cutting edge forms a separate cutter, owing to the taper, it will be necessary to finish the cutting edges more carefully than in the cylindrical forms if we expect the surface to be left as smooth and perfect. When grinding or finishing the cutting edges of reamers, it should be done as explained for tool grinding.

When a disc or hole larger than can conveniently be drilled is to be made, it should be bored with a boring tool in the slide rest. The sizes and shapes of these tools are illustrated and described as slide rest cutters, Fig. 123.

CHAPTER X.

TURNING WITH THE GRAVER AND SLIDE REST.

In using the graver, it is probably more difficult to explain just how it is done, than in many other operations performed upon the lathe; but since the workman is known by his chips, this will perhaps form the best guide by which he can tell if the severing of the metal is accomplished under normal conditions. The graver must be well sharpened, so as to cut freely, and to test it for keenness, try the point on the thumb-nail; if sharp it should stick or cut into the nail, but if it is not sharp it will slide over the nail easily.

The T rest should have the top edge slightly below the line of the centers of the lathe, so that the cutting edge of the graver may be held on this line. The T rest should be smooth, having no notches or rough places in it, the temper being such that the graver will have a tendency to stay at the spot where it is placed and not slide away, yet not so soft that the graver will cut down into the metal. In setting the T rest, set it as close to the work as possible, yet at the same time so it will clear it nicely, with the height so that the cutting edge of the tool will strike the work near the center. By setting the rest close to the work, it gives the hand more leverage and at the same time a more delicate feed. When turning at night, or where the light is not sufficient to enable the work to be distinctly seen, it will be found a great aid if a piece of white paper be laid on the top of the T rest shoe, which will form a background against which the work will be plainly seen. When the graver is properly sharpened and presented to the work, the pressure necessary to make it cut will be very slight and the cutting will come off with a clean, lively appearance in the form of a spiral, leaving a smooth cut, more or less polished, according to the metal operated upon and the finish of the graver. Some workmen aver that it is necessary to learn to cut with the point of the graver, as it is the only possible way to learn to cut *true*, which *may* be so, but it is certainly not the way to turn smoothly, which is of quite as much importance and a necessary complement to truth. It is not to be understood that the point of the graver is never to be used to turn with, for there are places where the use of it is indispensable, such as turning out sharp corners, undercutting, etc., where a clean, sharp angle is to be left; but for accuracy and smoothness it certainly cannot be recommended.

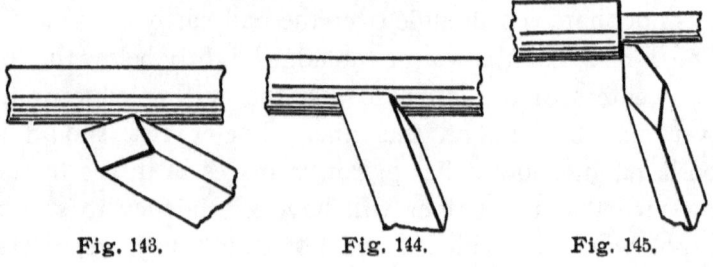

Fig. 143.　　　　Fig. 144.　　　　Fig. 145.

The length of time a point will remain in good cutting condition, even when used by an experienced hand, is so short that this alone is sufficient cause to limit its use to such occasions as are indispensably necessary.

The angle of the cutting edge of slide rest tools for general use is forty-five degrees, but in hand-tools the angle is not so imperative as in those which are rigidly held in position in the slide rest, since the hand may readily change the angle of presentation of the cutting edge to the work, so that all the conditions will be satisfied. The side of the graver is to be used and, presented to the work as indicated at Fig. 143, will give a spiral cut which will be a smooth and clean one. For turning brass, the graver is sometimes held as shown in Fig. 144. You can judge if the tool is cutting properly by the appearance of the cutting, which should be in the form of a spiral. By thus holding the graver, the necessary angle of negative rake to make a smooth cut on brass, may be readily had. The handle of the graver should be grasped with the right hand, while the left supports the tool on the T rest and holds it to the cut. The feed is accomplished by raising the handle of the graver at the beginning of the cut and gradually depressing it so as to change the point of contact of the tool with the work more towards the point of the graver, which will cause it to traverse the cut lengthwise of the work and towards the graver point, but the extent of this motion is small, so that if the portion to be turned is of considerable length, it will be necessary to advance the graver farther along the T rest; but when this is necessary, the graver may be grasped somewhat more firmly and moved along the top of the T rest, similar to a slide rest, which will expedite the work. When a quantity of metal is to be removed, without regard to accuracy or finish, the point of the graver is slightly rounded, just enough so that the delicate point is removed, by rounding the back angle of the graver and presenting it at a right angle to the work and feeding it by swinging the handle back and forth. In this way a heavy cut may be taken, until the work is approximately to size, then finish by holding the graver as before explained. In turning shoulders, the graver point may be formed as shown in Fig. 145; however, the width of the portion removed should be slight and the angle should be less than ninety degrees.

When beginning to learn to turn on the lathe, brass should be taken first, as it is easier to cut than steel. The beginner should not attempt any difficult or fancy turning at the outset, but should confine himself to turning a true cylinder, leaving the final cut so smooth as to appear as if it had been polished. At the same time the hand is being trained, the eye must not be neglected, as it should be able to detect any slight defect either in form or finish, and it is at this juncture that an accurate gauge is an absolute necessity to aid the eye and show where the inaccuracies are, but the gauge should only be used after the piece is turned and to the eye appears correct. A micrometer gauge should be used for measuring diameters, and a small straight edge for the straight portions, and for testing the shoulders, which may be attempted as soon as a smooth straight cylinder an inch in length can be made that will show no error greater than one or two thousandths of an inch. See that all portions, the sides of which are to be straight, are so, while all parts that are to be curved are uniformly so, this being the whole secret of turning out beautiful work. To be able to turn a nice true shoulder, is something but a few workmen can justly boast of, and it requires a great deal of patience and practice to be able to do it well, the greatest difficulty being to join the two planes, at the same time leaving the angle clear and sharp. The accuracy of the shoulder may be tested by placing the straight edge across it, when it will show if too much or not enough metal has been removed. In turning up to a shoulder, such for instance as in a straight pivot, it will be found that it is necessary to turn down the pivot next to the shoulder, until it really appears to be smaller than the outer end, in order to be of the same diameter from end to end. Various fancy forms may next be attempted, not so much from their utility in actual practice, as to train the hand and eye. After brass can be worked satisfactorily, annealed steel may be taken, following this with steel tempered to a blue. In cutting tempered steel, it is necessary to have the graver very sharp, so that it will cut as soon as it is applied to the work. Should the graver fail to cut cleanly, it must be examined and re-sharpened if necessary, but if it still refuses to cut, another graver should be tried, as the first one may have had the temper lowered too much; however, there should be no difficulty in turning steel tempered to a blue, or even a purplish blue. When turning tempered steel, the graver must be re-sharpened as soon as it is necessary to exert any extra pressure, in order to make it cut, as the extra pressure would cause the steel to burnish and become hard on the surface, so as to sometimes effectually resist all attempts to remove it, even with the best of gravers. The only way of removing such places, is to start at one side with the point of the graver, which must be kept sharp, and usually it will be sufficient to get the cut started beneath the hard skin, when the turning may be proceeded with in the ordinary method; but at times it will be necessary to continue using the point of the graver, and it may sometimes even be necessary to re-temper the piece before it will yield.

It is probably of as much, if not more importance, to be able to distinguish between work that is correct and that which is incorrect, as to know the methods by which it is accomplished, since the former is a matter of education, while in the latter case the natural talent will often come to the rescue, when the conditions to be satisfied are known. As previously pointed out, the work should be turned first as nearly as possible with the eye alone, then proven by using a gauge. Of course it is not possible to train the eye so as to turn out the work of the desired accuracy by its aid alone, but we should be able to judge very closely, leaving the final correction only to be done by the gauge, which will expedite the work. That the judgment may be matured, the quantity of metal removed from one measurement to another should be noted. When examining the work, it will be easier to detect any fault, if it is held so as to reflect the light to the eye, which is the most delicate test for accuracy and smoothness of finish. If the light is reflected uniformly, it shows an accurate surface.

When doing fine and delicate turning, such as pivots, it is best not to use any liquid to moisten the graver, as it would cause the chips to adhere to the work, and so interfere with the view of the cutting point, which it is at all times necessary to have in order to tell what is being accomplished, and besides, it is of questionable advantage to use anything in the lighter work.

The use of the graver can best be exemplified by following the various steps in the making of a balance staff, as in this operation the graver is used more than in any other and thoroughly covers the various forms of hand turning.

When making a balance staff, the method which follows is beyond reproach from the standpoint of accuracy, this, of course, being the main point, all others being secondary considerations. Take a piece of steel wire somewhat larger than the hub of the finished staff is to be. If the wire is not true turn it down for about an inch of its length, still leaving it a trifle longer than the finished staff is to be. After hardening the turned portion, draw the temper to between a purple and a blue. The color will be found to vary under different circumstances, but the steel should be left as hard as can be readily turned with a well-sharpened graver. The reason for this is, that the harder the steel is left the better the finish that can be put upon it, and it also resists wear much better, while a blow that would break it would be very apt to ruin a softer one.

Never use a piece of wire sticking out in front of the chuck further than is necessary to make the piece of work, as the centrifugal force will cause it to spring and run untrue, particularly when you start to turn down preparatory to cutting it off. Having the piece of wire tempered, select a properly fitted chuck and put it in the lathe, letting the wire extend out from the face of the chuck about one and a half times the length of the finished staff, and proceed to turn out the top end of the staff as follows:

When making a new staff the dimensions should be put down on a piece of paper, and, to get these accurately, only good measuring instruments should be used. If the old staff is at hand it may be utilized for getting the measurements for length if it is not too badly broken, for instance, one pivot broken off or bent. To get the length of the staff remove the end stones and place the parts in the position in which they belong, then with the douzieme gauge place on jaw on the outside of each hole jewel which should be left in its place, and we get the length of staff approximately. The reason why we cannot get the exact length of staff is that the setting of the jewel hole is sometimes left higher than the jewel, or that of the end stone may have been left the same way instead of being just flush, but if we notice how the jewels are set an allowance can be made which will need but very little correction.

For measuring diameters, a micrometer or a Grossmann gauge can be used, but if the former, it must be handled very carefully, as owing to its weight and the force of the

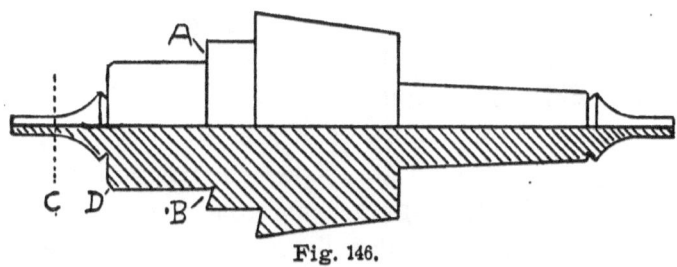

Fig. 146.

screw it would be very easy to bend a pivot with it, and of the two forms it is perhaps more accurate and besides costs much less. The advantage of the Grossman gauge is that the jaws are actuated by a spring which always gives a uniform tension on the work and can be handled quicker. Could we but have an accurate measuring tool with which we could measure the distance from the end of the staff to a shoulder, or the distance from one shoulder to the next, it would greatly facilitate the accuracy of the work, but as it is seldom that these measurements must as close as those of the diameter, it is not so imperative, however, such an instrument would be very advantageous.

A staff, in outline, is shown at Fig. 146, which we shall use as a pattern to work from. Bear in mind that the closer you can get the work to the chuck the better, as there will be less liability to error.

Stone off the end of your wire to a flat. We have now arrived at the point where it is necessary to know the lengths and measurements of the various parts; the length of the staff from end to end of the pivot; from end of lower pivot to roller shoulder; the location of the balance shoulder and collet, with their diameters, etc. In most instances these may be secured from the old staff, which is to be removed from the balance by cutting away the riveting, so that the balance may be driven off without in any way distorting or injuring it. Always examine the old staff by trying it in its place in the watch to see if the shoulders were properly located, and if not, they may then be corrected in the new one, whereas if this is not done at first we may copy mistakes in the old staff and have to make a second one after we have found out our mistake.

To facilitate the handling for measurement, insert the old staff in a pin vise. Put the T rest in position ready for turning and with your graver make a mark on the new wire about where you judge the upper end of the collet shoulder will come. Now compare this with the old staff and see if the distance is the same, and if not, correct it by holding the old staff up to the one in the lathe. This method is applicable in all cases when transferring measurements from one shoulder to another, whether in staffs, pinions or other work having shoulders.

Having located the collet shoulder, we proceed to rough out the top pivot. In the same way we now locate the collet seat, as shown at *A*, Fig. 146, and turn this down approximately to size. We are now ready to fit the balance on its seat. The balance should fit snugly on the staff. We now proceed to turn down the collet shoulder to size (leaving sufficient material for the final finish), and undercut for the balance riveting, as indicated at *B*, Fig. 146. The bearing for the collet should not be made tapering, but should be cylindrical throughout; but rather than have the lower end smaller than the upper, it would be better to have a very slight taper. If, however, we can turn it perfectly cylindrical, it is better, because the staff is to be held in the chuck by this portion when it is reversed for turning the lower end, and if perfectly cylindrical the chuck will hold it more accurately than if it had ever so slight a taper.

Up to this point we have used only the two gravers shown at Fig. 145 and Fig. 147. These two gravers are ground to a 30° cutting face and were originally identical, both being lozenge shaped, but it will be noted that the graver shown at Fig. 145 differs only from Fig. 147 in having the point broken or ground off to a trifle less than 90°, as shown in the diagram. Some writers aver that this angle should be 90° exactly, their reason being that they can turn with two cutting edges at one time, leaving a square shoulder. This theory we wish to condemn, as there are but very few shoulders, in actual practice, that require to be exactly square; in fact, all shoulders should be undercut very slightly, as those that require to be very sharp and clean can only be made so by the final polish of the revolving lap. The shoulders for the roller and balance should be slightly undercut, so that the bearing points will be at the outer edge of the shoulders on the staff, which will bring the roller and balance up true in the flat when they are staked on the staff. Should the roller or balance be slightly out of the flat, or thicker at the center, they will then still be truly seated on the staff, which would not be the case were the shoulder on the staff left square.

The T rest should be moved as closely to the work as possible, the balance seat being turned with the graver held in the ordinary manner. In turning the seat for the collet, the graver is held so as to allow its point to undercut for the riveting of the balance to its seat at the same time the corner is squared. Ordinarily, among watchmakers, the sides of the collet shoulder are left straight and cylindrical, but if the cut shown at *B,* Fig. 146, is made, it will be found to materially improve the appearance of the staff after the riveting is done. To make this cut, take a graver with a long and keen point.

Now proceed to turn down the pivot to size, allowing, say, 1-1000 of an inch for the final polishing. This is done with a graver similar to Fig. 147, but with the back angle or point slightly rounded, so as to give a round cutting edge. We now come to one of the difficult propositions,

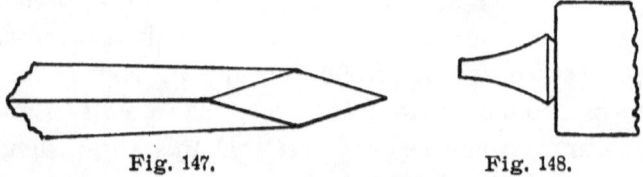

Fig. 147.   Fig. 148.

that of turning a perfect conical pivot. The majority of watchmakers, when making a conical pivot, taper it from the point of the pivot to the crest of the oil stop, as shown in Fig. 148.

This form is decidedly unmechanical, non-theoretical and bad in practice, for it has a tendency to wedge the pivot in the jewel, and the bearing is constantly changing, owing to the necessary end shake for freedom. The pivot should be made cylindrical from the end up to the dotted line *C* in Fig. 146, and from this point on the cone should rise in a uniform curve to the crest of the oil stop.

To turn this pivot, the graver should be rested on the T rest and gradually moved forward until the cylindrical portion has been cut, and then, without removing the graver, swing the handle around from you, towards the right, which will throw the point of the graver slightly towards you and to the left, and this movement will cut the cone at the base of the pivot.

The pivot must be made neither too long nor too short; if made too long, the pivot is unduly weak and liable to break, and if too short, it is liable to rest in the jewel on the conical portion, and the resistance of the oil will be greater, especially if the oil sink in the jewel should be filled with oil. The length will depend, in a considerable degree, on the thickness of the jewel; if the jewel is thin, the pivot may be correspondingly shorter. An average proportion for the cylindrical portion of the pivot would be to make it three times as long as the jewel is thick. By the thickness of the jewel we mean the bearing proper in the hole jewel—that portion on which the pivot rests.

The oil stop is turned out in two ways; one is to undercut, and the other to turn the shoulder back of it square and polish flat. This latter method we think is preferable, as it leaves a nicer finish. Chamfer off the corner of the collet

Fig. 149.   Fig. 150.

shoulder, as shown at *D*, Fig. 146. This should never be neglected, for if you do you are liable to have trouble when you come to put the balance spring on.

Now rough out the lower end of the staff, from the hub to the bottom of the pivot, being careful that the graver does not catch and that the metal is removed in very light cuts, to avoid springing the upper end. This work is performed with what is known as a cutting-off tool, which is illustrated at Fig. 149. This portion of the staff, although only roughed out, should be turned perfectly smooth, to afford a smooth bearing for truing up, when we reverse our staff in the chuck, as the work on the lower half of the staff will be done while the staff is held in the chuck by the portion *DB*, Fig. 146, and this is so short that it is trued up in the chuck by spinning, the same as is done with cement, before the chuck is finally tightened.

We now proceed to finish off and polish the upper end of the staff, as will be described in the chapter on pivot polishers, or we may polish it by hand if we have no pivot polisher. This we proceed to do by dressing down, first, with oil stone powder and oil applied by means of a bell metal or soft iron slip, formed as shown at Fig. 150. One side of this slip is left with a sharp corner, while the opposite side is slightly rounded. The sharp corner is for square shoulders, while the rounded side is for the conical portion of the pivot. The slip should be cross filed and made perfectly flat with a No. 3 file, in order to hold the powder. Charge the slip with a very small quantity of the oil stone powder, and resting it on the end of the fingers of your left hand, place it lightly under the pivot, and as you push the slip forward move your hand from right to left, so as to give a circular motion to the slip, which will cause the lines to cross and recross each other, thus leaving the pivot smooth by grinding out all graver marks. This motion is to be given when grinding all portions except close up to the square shoulders, where the slip is to be moved back and forth, at right angles, so as to leave the surfaces smooth. The oil stop is finished with the sharp edge of the slip.

Clean the work thoroughly with pith and alcohol, leaving no trace of the grinding material. Now, with a slip of the same form, but made of zinc, proceed to polish with diamantine. The end of the pivot is to be slightly rounded, rather than to be left flat. The best way to accomplish this is to use a stone slip cut from a fine, close grained stone, like jasper. The surface of this stone is to be ground down until it has a polished surface, and is yet rough enough to slightly cut the metal, which still leaves the metal with a polished surface. A person who once tries such a stone slip will not willingly be without it afterwards.

We are now ready to cut off the staff from the end of our stock, leaving it sufficiently long to allow for the final stoning for length. The cutting off is best effected with a sharp-pointed graver. Select a chuck which will fit the collet shoulder, bearing in mind what has been said about the use of half sizes where accurate work is desired, Fig. 33, Chapter III, and putting the work in the lathe, proceed to stone it off with an Arkansas stone slip, to the required length. Next loosen the chuck a little, true up your work in the chuck by means of a piece of pegwood, shaped to use conveniently, resting it on the T rest. If the staff does not run true at first, change its position in the chuck until the outer end of the pegwood shows little or no vibration.

When this has been accomplished, tighten the chuck again and proceed to turn down and finish the lower end, being careful that no unnecessary force is used which might spring the staff or throw it out of true. Proceed with the final turning down, grinding and polishing, as described in making the upper end.

CHAPTER XI.

GRINDING, POLISHING, SNAILING, DAMASCENING.

The pivot polisher is an outgrowth of the desire to save time by securing a continuous and rapid motion of the lap in the reverse direction from that in which the work is revolved. So far as we are able to ascertain the first form of polisher was adapted to be used in the tool post of the lathe, and was invented by C. Hopkins Van Norman of the Waltham Watch Tool Co. about 1872. This polisher was run with the spindle in the upright position, as shown in

Fig. 151. The Original Hopkins Pivot Polisher of 1872.

Fig. 151, and the flat face of the lap was brought up to the under side of the pivot. It was simple in construction and worked nicely although it was soon found advisable to depart from the method described. Polishing from the under side of the work was universally practiced at that time with hand polishers or bell metal slips, sapphire files, etc., as it was the easiest method of allowing the watchmaker to see what he was doing while working, and the new device naturally met with less opposition by following the accepted methods. Its capabilities were soon perceived, and in 1882 the much more elaborate device shown in Fig. 152 succeeded it.

This consists of a separate shoe, carrying a turn-table, graduated in degrees, on which is mounted a yoke pivoted at the bottom and carrying an accurately ground traverse spindle, with stops to regulate the amount of oscillation of the yoke. The end of the spindle was taper ground, inside and out, so as to carry laps, cutters, fraises, etc., and idler

Fig. 152. Hopkins Pivot Polisher.

pulleys allowed a considerable movement of the traverse spindle without interfering materially with the tension of the driving belt. This design has remained practically unchanged to the present day. The idle pulleys have been de-

No. 153. Moseley Pivot Polisher.

tached and carried further up so as to permit of swinging the spindle further from the line of centers of the lathe; micrometer attachments have been added to the spindle, so as to give a definite feed and thus permit of grinding to exact size. Some manufacturers have mounted it on the slide rest; others have retained the shoe. It has steadily grown stronger in construction as its manifold capabilities as a drill, milling machine and grinder have caused it to be subjected to harder work than polishing pivots, but its general design has been unchanged.

The spindle and its bearings are the important parts to be looked after, and in the best makes these are made of tool steel, hardened and tempered; then after being ground between dead centers with a parallel grinder, they should be ground again by what is known as lead grinding, if the

Fig. 151. Moseley Parallel Grinder, which can also be used as a Pivot Polisher held in Tool Post of Slide Rest.

greatest accuracy is desired. The bearings for such a spindle should be of hardened steel and fit the spindle accurately. The inside and outside tapers at the end of the spindle should be finally ground while the spindle revolves in its own bearings, thus securing the greatest possible accuracy in them. For driving, a small, round belt, smooth and pliable, is used, and may run direct from the speed wheel on the counter shaft to the small pulley on the polisher spindle. A better way, however, is to use an idler fixture, running the belt up over the pulleys and down to the spindle, as by this method of belting we can move the spindle to a greater extent without appreciably changing the tension of the belt. The piece which supports the spindle is jointed to the base piece so as to permit of its being vibrated to and fro, thus smoothing the work, and by means of a stop the extent of this vibration may be limited, while at the same time it gives us the means of a delicate feed, which is necessary when feeding to the spindle. A delicate spring is so arranged as to hold the lap away from the work and give a pressure in a direction opposite to that of a pressure by the hand upon the small finger piece which is used to bring the lap into contact with the work.

One very important factor which seems to have been overlooked by some of the makers is a stop, by means of which the traverse of the spindle may be limited, as the needs of the work require. This stop, in some form or other, is absolutely indispensable, if we desire the greatest

Fig. 155. Rivett Pivot Polisher, to be held in Graduated Tool Post of Rivett Slide Rest.

possible accuracy in the work, which is one of the principal points recommending the use of this attachment. Imagine a person, however steady his hand, holding such a spindle to its work, with no solid stop, so as to give no error greater than 1-10000 of an inch, yet with a properly made tool this is easily accomplished; in fact, this should be about the limit of error permitted in fine work. An adjustment must be provided by which the center of the polisher spindle may be placed above or below that of the center of the lathe spindle. In some makes, which fasten on the slide-rest, there is no adjustment provided, but it may be raised the necessary amount by placing rings of different thicknesses under it. A good assortment of laps is necessary to secure the best results and all should be made of the same diameter to avoid the necessity of moving the fixture after it is once set, when using more than one lap.

In using the polisher, see that it fits the shoe of your lathe and that the shoe is in position and has no dirt under it. This precaution brings the spindle parallel with the line of centers of the lathe when the index on the graduated circle is at O. In this position it may be used to grind parallel if desired or you have the correct starting point from which to set the machine to grind a known angle.

In grinding, the position of the spindle with reference to the line of centers depends upon the shape of the laps which

Fig. 156. Rivett Pivot Polisher and Grinder Mounted in Slide Rest.

you are using. Some men prefer to turn cylindrical laps and then to finish the ends to such a curve that they will form perfectly coned pivots when held parallel to the pivot. If charged with perfectly graded diamond powder, by rolling between two pieces of hard steel, such a lap will do good work for a surprisingly long time. If the laps are dished or coned so as to grind only on the end of the lap the spindle must be turned at right angles to the line of centers and the end of the lap will grind the straight part of the pivot while the edge of the lap grinds the cone. In such a case the cone is made longer or shorter by altering the height of the polisher spindle. To make the cone longer, raise the spindle; to make it shorter, lower it.

In grinding a taper it is necessary always to set the center of the lap at the same height as the lathe center.

If the turning has been skillfully done, so that it is smooth and within .03 MM. of the required size a fine brass or soft bell metal lap, used with diamantine and oil, will grind and polish at the same time, making the use of other laps unnecessary. Originally it was thought necessary to use a steel lap charged with oilstone powder for grinding; this was followed by a bell metal lap and coarse crocus; and then by either a tin lap with rouge and oil, or one of boxwood and Vienna lime with oil. Many still use one or more of these and they are all good.

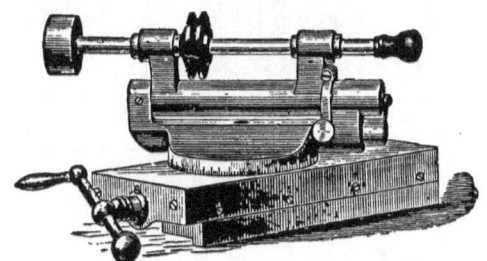

Fig. 157. Webster Whitcomb Pivot Polisher.

In using any of them care should be taken to keep the laps constantly moving forward and back in order to avoid the formation of grooves and ridges. The operator should be careful also not to let the work get dry or a black scum will fill up the surface of the metal, spoiling its appearance. This is especially important in snailing or damascening, as here the appearance of the work is the only reason for undertaking it at all, and if a bright and lively play of light is not secured on the finished work it had better be left plain. Use a lap charged with evenly graded diamond powder on such work and keep it well flooded with oil, washing off the black with fresh oil as fast as it forms, and success is certain.

For the snailing we would advise a special set of five laps, made of brass, fitted to the taper hole of the spindle. These laps are smaller than the regular, but cupped in the same manner and charged with either diamond powder, or a different grade of emery for each lap. These laps should be used for this purpose only. To do the snailing, select the lap to be used, put in the spindle, release the thumb nut under the bed, raise up the shoe and stick an ordinary pin

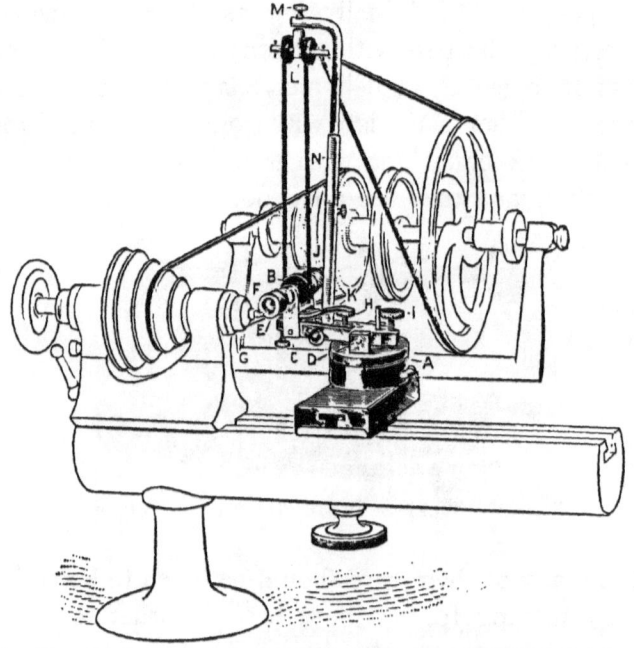

Fig. 158. Hardinge Pivot Polisher, Showing Correct Position for Grinding and Polishing.

under it and then re-fasten the nut. This tips the spindle so that only the edge of the lap strikes the wheel. The lathe must then be put on its slowest speed. The lap must run in the opposite direction that the lathe spindle does. The lap should run fast and the work slow. A little practice is all that is necessary to do good work. The style of the work may be changed almost without limit, by changing the shapes of laps, and by making a wheel part polished and part snailed, and by changing the spindle by setting it at different angles.

Laps are made of various materials—soft steel, cast iron, bell metal, zinc, tin, ivory and box wood, the first four being sufficient for any job, however fine, and as they hold their form better than the other it will not be so difficult to keep them in shape.

When using the pivot polisher every precaution must be taken to prevent any particle of the grinding or polishing material getting into the bearings, which would soon cause

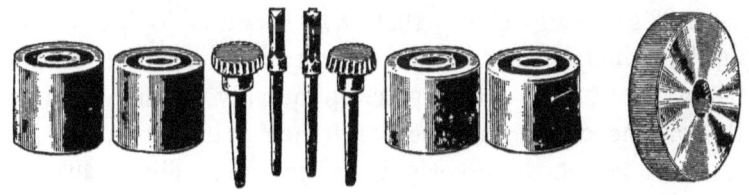

Fig. 159. Group of Laps, Cutters and Stones for Use in Pivot Polisher.

them to wear and become unreliable for accurate work. If an emery or carborundum wheel is used, it should be a light one, and revolved in such a direction as to throw the particles downward; and to still further protect the bearings, when it can be done a cover should be made for them of some light cloth. Many of these particles are so small as to remain suspended in the air for some time, yet more or less of them will find their way into the bearings, even if we are as careful as we can be. Every precaution should be taken to keep the pivot polishing fixture in as good condition as possible and it is better if none of the grinding wheels are used on it, but there are very few workmen who have a parallel grinder, so that it is very convenient to use the pivot polisher instead at times for truing up lathe centers, grinding and polishing the sides of wheels, barrels, winding squares, and a thousand other things. The liability of the particles to fly may be lessened by laying an oiled cloth beneath the grinding wheel to catch the cuttings, which will protect the lathe bed as well. In all operations of grinding or polishing, the two surfaces in contact must always revolve in opposite directions, which will give an effective velocity equal to the sum of the two while if they revolved in the same direction it would only be equal to the difference. Laps of all kinds should be relieved, and must never be allowed to remain cylindrical throughout their entire length.

By relieving the laps as stated, it also makes the truing up quicker and easier, which must be done as soon as they become untrue. The lap truing chuck is to be used for truing up the laps in the lathe and may also be used to true any grinding wheels that may be fitted to the polisher spindle, which is sometimes very convenient for grinding various tools. To true up a lap quickly mount it in the lathe on the chuck as stated and then grind or lap it with a stone or lap on the pivot polisher spindle. This is the only practical way to true a heavily charged diamond lap, although laps charged only with rouge, crocus or diamantine may be turned off and then ground to get the necessary truth and accuracy which counts for so much in using this tool.

The pivot polisher is also an excellent milling tool, for milling out odd places in a plate or bridges, either for stem wind wheels or springs, where the part of a circle only is wanted to be removed. This is done by small milling tools fitting the hole in the spindle, with ratchet shaped teeth cut on their sides and ends, the sizes and shapes being made to suit the occasion, driven at high speed by the countershaft. They cut not only quickly but smoothly. Wheels may also be crossed out by these same tools. It is also a good tool for eccentric drilling, drilling index holes, etc.

Never have the belt tighter than is necessary to prevent slipping.

The best kind of oil to use for oiling the lathe or pivot polisher is pure sperm oil.

Always wash the pivot polisher off in gasoline after

using, and oil with sperm oil before using again. The work never wears out a tool, but dirt or foreign matter in the spindle invariably does. When a spindle is properly cared for the oil keeps clear and we can see through it while running.

While the pivot polisher fixture is all that can be desired for turning out new work, it is at the same time unsuitable for repolishing old and worn pivots unless we have some way by which we can mount our work so that the part to be refinished will run dead true, since unless it does run perfectly true all parts of the work will not be concentric with each other after being refinished. If the work was originally made by a skillful hand and has not been in the hands of the botch it will not be a difficult matter to mount it in the lathe with a true and properly fitting split chuck. It will not suffice to have the work almost true for the reason given above. From the fact that much of the work coming in for repairs is not of a class where we may expect to find work where all parts are concentric one with the other, it is not a rare thing to find that try as we may, we cannot chuck it so that it will run true, yet at the same time it is not bad enough to throw away, for this is a class of work where it is to be expected that we will not find fine or accurate work, and besides in this same class of work it is very seldom we can get the customer to pay for the repairs which are actually necessary to make the work reasonably satisfactory, not to mention work which, while not absolutely necessary it would at the same time be advantageous to have done. In the above class of work it is of course, out of the question to use the pivot polisher fixture, so that the only resource left us is to do the work of repolishing by hand. By doing this work by hand, the polishing slip is able to follow the inaccuracy of the work more or less perfectly and thus a job which will be reasonably satisfactory may be done. First of all the work should be mounted in the lathe and centered as perfectly as it is possible to have it. If the pivot is badly cut so that rings are formed around it, it will be necessary to use a bell metal or soft steel slip with oil stone powder until the surface is perfectly smooth. The corners of the slip should be square or rounded according as the pivot has a square or conical shoulder. The oil stone powder should have been decanted so as to free it from all the coarse particles, of which very many will be found in it, as usually sold. The decanted powder is mixed with oil until it forms a thick paste after which it is ready to use. The surface of the slip should be freshly sharpened by filing and a very small amount of the oil stone powder should be applied at a time, just an amount that is perceptible and renewing it again if necessary. Preparatory to using the polishing material the oil stone slip should be partially cleaned so that there remains but a slight trace of the grinding material, which leaves a surface that is all but polished.

The work should revolve as rapidly as convenient and the to and fro motion of the slips should be somewhat slower so that the work may make several revolutions to each movement of the slip, which will avoid the forming of flat places on the pivot. The slips must not be drawn back and forth at a right angle to the center of the work but should cross and recross constantly at various angles to make the surface smooth. A jasper slip is far superior to that made of metal for smoothing pivots. It is formed in the same shape as that made of metal and should have two surfaces of varying grades for each style of pivot. They are made by grinding both of the surfaces perfectly flat and smooth, one being stopped just short of a polish while the other one is left somewhat coarser.

Diamond being the hardest known substance, it may be used as an abrasive when others would fail. It is used in the form of powders of various grades of fineness, by allowing the crushed pieces to settle after being suspended in oil. As the larger and heavier particles will settle first we have in this method a means of separating the coarser from the finer particles by allowing them to stand a greater or less length of time. The powder is made from small diamonds, chips and such pieces as have no great commercial value, and pulverizing the pieces in a mortar made up specially for the purpose. The principal use of the diamond is to charge discs of various substances called laps, which carry the particles of powder imbedded on their surface. When the lap is to be used for grinding away a quantity of metal it is usually made of copper, although any other soft and tough metal may be used; but if it is for polishing it is made of ivory, boxwood, tortoise shell, or celluloid, and the powder is the very finest. To make a diamond lap, turn out the lap to the required form and charge it with the diamond powder by forcing the particles into it with a piece of steel as hard as it is possible to make it. When charging such a lap a hammer or roller may be used to imbed the diamond powder, but whatever method is adopted, it should be carefully done, so that the particles will remain permanently imbedded. A well-charged diamond lap will retain its size longer than any other form of cutter, and can be used in many places where any other material would fail. But the appearance of the work done by such a lap is entirely dependent upon having the powder with which it is charged entirely even in size. Any coarser particles imbedded in a lap will make scratches on the work.

Carborundum is a product of the electric furnace, and is so hard that it has, to a considerable extent, taken the place of diamond powder. When carborundum is used in the form of a powder it must be mixed with oil and applied to the lap in small amounts. It may be purchased from the material dealers in various grades of fineness, up to the thirty minute powder, which is very fine. It must never be used to finish any of the wearing surfaces, as owing to its extreme hardness small particles are liable to be left imbedded even in the hardest steel. Even the finest carborundum powder will not leave a perfect polish on steel, but it makes a beautifully grained appearing surface on tempered steel which contrasts nicely with a dead black polish.

Corundum and emery are natural products of the earth, but as they are inferior to carborundum they are now but little used by watchmakers.

Oil stone powder is used in the same manner as carborundum, and wearing surfaces may be finished with it so as to be almost polished. It is about the only abrasive that should be used in finishing bearings.

Diamantine. For polishing steel work this polishing agent answers all the requirements for producing a fine dead black polish. It is put up in two grades No. 1 and 2.

No. 2 is the finer, and will take the place of No. 1 in watch work. It is mixed with watch oil to form a stiff paste, on either an iron or a glass plate, with a knife blade or a piece of steel, and the plate must be provided with a suitable, close fitting cover to exclude all dust or foreign substances. The cover should not be removed except when actually necessary to use the diamantine. When beginning to mix it with the oil but a very small amount is necessary, for as the mixing nears completion it becomes thinner, so that what at the start would appear too small an amount of oil will be found sufficient when finished. A lap of bell metal will be sufficient in ordinary work, but if the finest polish is desired a zinc or tin lap should be used.

Vienna lime is a pure anhydrous lime, obtained, as its name indicates, from Vienna. It is extensively used in the watch factories for the final polishing of steel, but while in such cases it is very satisfactory, as there is no difficulty in keeping it fresh owing to the quantity used, such is not the case where a bottle, if the entire contents could be utilized, would be sufficient to last for a considerable time. Simple abrasion does not seem to be the only effect produced, for unless the lime is used while it is slacking the results are not satisfactory. It should therefore be kept in an

THE AMERICAN LATHE.

air-tight place away from the light, taking out only enough for immediate use. Take a hard, solid lump that can not be mashed in the fingers, the harder it is the better the polish, and with a knife cut down as much as is necessary for the job; moisten it with alcohol to form a thin paste and apply to the work on a piece of peg wood or box wood. But a few strokes are necessary and the polishing should be stopped before the lime is entirely dry and the work wiped off with pith.

CHAPTER XII.

MULTIPLE EDGED TOOLS FOR CONTINUOUS CUTTING.

The chief advantage of the American lathe over its fiddle-bow predecessor is its gain in the time necessary to do work; ease of operation, truth, accuracy, solidity, etc., all being time-saving accomplishments merely, where the standard of work remains the same. Probably many watchmakers have never looked at the matter in just this light, but after all is said it simmers down to just that. Accurate work was and is done on the fiddle-bow lathe; the ease of operation of the modern methods simply saves the strength and nervous energy of the operator, in order that he may have them available for more work in a given time; the certainty with which an angle is obtained when desired merely obviates a series of tests for truth which the older methods required. Time is the only gain—time and the consequently greater earning power of the watchmaker who has a full outfit of tools and thoroughly understands their use.

So, too, with the tools which we are about to describe the chief gain is in time; a properly formed counterbore with eight cutting edges will do the work in one-fourth of the time taken by the older tool with two edges, will stay central and make a cleaner, rounder hole; the milling cutter is a better tool than the fly cutter, for the same reason, provided that it is properly made and kept sharp. Another important consideration is that the tool will maintain its size and shape as much longer as it has more cutting edges. Where a tool is of such a size and character that it may become standard, this is an important consideration, especially in cutters for wheels and pinions, as a fly cutter unless made and kept sharp by an expert, changes its size (and often changes its shape also) every time it is ground. These are the considerations which have led to the discarding of the fly cutter in the machine shop and which are now putting the planer and shaper out of business, in favor of the milling machine in many shops. The gain of time involved should be equally important to the watchmaker; if he does not think so, let him, if on salary, go upon piece work and then see what time means to him. It means just as much to the man who hires him on a salary and his salary is fixed by the amount of time he takes on the succession of jobs which make up a day's work.

There are certain characteristics which are common to all cutters, fixed or rotary; these are clearance, rake and shape of the cutting edge. If the reader will turn to Chapter IX and read what is there said as to rake, clearance, etc., he will see that a milling cutter is simply a collection of such tools arranged about a common center. The tool is sharpened upon its top, for the same reason that the top A, Fig. 120, is ground. The rake is measured from the radial line passing from the center of the cutter to the point of the tooth. In circular cutters this rake should be very slightly negative to prevent the teeth from digging in and causing chattering or gouging. Cutters when purchased usually have no rake, this angle being 90 degrees; if it digs, stoning or grinding off one degree, making the angle 89 degrees, will usually give a very smooth-running cutter for steel. This negative rake should be increased for brass.

The clearance angle, B A C, Fig. 120, is also duplicated in the milling cutter, but is subject to some modifications. If there is space enough between the teeth of the cutter to allow the chips to curl out freely, as shown in Fig. 119, the clearance (called backing off) of the teeth in such a cutter may be very little, possibly two degrees, generally not more than five degrees for steel, or ten for brass. If, however, the teeth are so close as to follow one another like a saw, they must have a greater clearance angle (from forty to sixty degrees), because we are now combining the clearance and the space for chips and it must be large enough to accommodate the chips or they will interfere with the cutting edge of the succeeding tooth. When this happens the cutter is said to be choked and it will spring away from the work, or spring the work.

Having now found our rake and clearance angles in any revolving cutter, just as in the single cutter, we will next consider the shape of the cutting edge. Either the single tool or the milling teeth may be made to cut on more than one side and in curved or straight lines. The single tool is filed or ground to shape. The other is turned in the lathe to give the desired shape of cutting edge before the planes of top rake and clearance are cut, otherwise they are similar.

The cutters are hardened in the same way and drawn to the same color. They may be most effectively sharpened with a thin, flat, soft iron or copper diamond lap whose edge is turned or ground to fit the angle formed by the rake and clearance planes of the tooth and the lap charged only on the side next the rake of the teeth, as that is the side to be ground. If the cutters are large enough to admit the entrance of an oil stone or fine carborundum wheel between the teeth, either will be found effective, but the smaller ones are most effectively sharpened with the diamond lap. Either stone or lap may be mounted on the arbor of the wheel cutter and the necessary care taken to preserve the angles of rake and clearance of the cutters as originally made. This can be readily done by proper adjustment of the graduated turn table and the index pin of the divided head on the pulley of the lathe. Unless the cutters are constantly used, they will not require sharpening more than once in six months, perhaps not over once a year, so that the trouble taken to mount the wheel cutting attachment for sharpening is not so great as it seems, particularly as a number of cutters may be sharpened while the lap or stone is mounted and ready for operation. In this way the shape of the cutter and its working qualities are preserved. Cutters too small to be sharpened successfully are used like files, i. e., thrown away when worn out, and new ones made.

Having thus briefly surveyed the multiple edged tools, we will now turn our attention to the single edged revolving cutter, or fly cutter. This is a most important tool for the reason that it is quickly and cheaply made and is sufficient to do a large amount of work; it is therefore the form which is usually selected when only one wheel or pinion is to be made. It gives a greater freedom for chips than any other cutter and is therefore largely used for working brass, copper and other metals of a tough and fibrous nature, so that the chips roll up and curl around the tool and the edges of the work; speed and clearance are the prime necessities in such metal and the fly cutter is therefore the best adapted for such work.

The first requisite in making up fly cutters is to determine upon a standard size of shank, as the watchmaker will need many of them and they should all fit the holes in the cutter arbor and thus allow of the use of one holder for many cutters. This being determined, turn out four flat discs of steel, for collars, thick enough so that there will be plenty of metal left after drilling and of such a diameter that the tool may be firmly held between their outer circumference and the hole for the cutter arbor. See Fig. 160. Make the center hole so as to be a snug fit on the arbor of the wheel cutter, and relieve the edges of the hole. Then take an arbor chuck, (See Figs. 90 to 92), and make an arbor on it of the same size as that of the wheel cutter, so that the collars will fit it exactly as they do on the cutter arbor. Place two of these collars on the arbor and bolt them up firmly. Set the index pin at zero in the lathe head. Place a drill in the pivot polisher and drill a hole through the two collars half way between the center and circumference. Turn the index to

180 and repeat the operation; do the same with the other pair of collars. These holes are for steady pins and the pins should be made to fit tightly in one collar and loosely in the other of each pair, so that the collars will go together

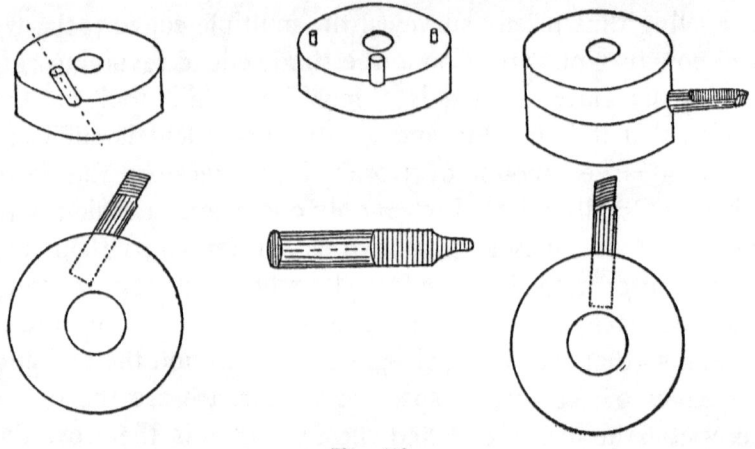

Fig. 160.

readily but will not turn after getting in position. Now place one set of collars on the chuck with a piece of paper between them and set the index pin to stop the lathe head. Place in the pivot polisher spindle a drill of the same size as the stock for your fly cutters; center this drill accurately and then turn the pivot polisher spindle to 90 degrees and drill a hole exactly between the two collars, so that when they are separated half the hole will be in each collar, as shown in Fig. 160. Make it deep enough to hold the fly cutter firmly. Separate the collars and throw away the paper. This pair of collars is for the cutter arbor and they will hold the cutters firmly in any position. Mount the other pair of collars on the chuck with paper between them and lower the pivot polisher so that the hole will be below the center and will therefore make an angle with a radius drawn from the center; have the hole the same size and depth as in the other pair. These collars are to be used on the chuck for turning up fly cutters.

To make a fly cutter take a piece of round wire, place it in the hole and clamp the collars firmly. Turn off a flat side on the wire, longer than the length of the cutting edge and a little wider. This flat side is to be the front of the cutter. Loosen the collars; turn the wire a little more than 90 degrees, so as to give the necessary clearance, clamp it tightly again, and turn up one-half the shape of the tooth, including the end of the tooth; turn the wire again so as to give the same clearance on the other side of the tooth and make that side of the cutter. Harden and draw to a straw color. Such a cutter will retain its size and shape (if ground only on the flat side) until it is ground too thin to be of further service All cutters made from the same size of wire will fit the collars on the cutter arbor and they may be readily changed without loss of time in adjusting when roughing and finishing cutters are to follow each other. The amount of material is practically nothing, simply a bit of round wire, and the time taken is the least possible. If the wire is of generous size the cutter will be thick enough to do rapid work for years without springing. The amount of backing off, or clearance angle, of the tooth depends upon the angle formed with the center in drilling the collars for the chuck, and as all curves are formed by turning, their shapes and relative distances remain practically the same, if the cutter is ground on the front only. It will get shorter as it wears back, but the shape of the tooth will be unchanged.

Such fly cutters are extremely useful in making up rotary cutting tools, such as are shown in enlarged form in these pages, and they have the advantage that they may be kept as master tools on such patterns as are used sufficiently to wear out quickly, thus enabling a worn cutter to be replaced without loss of time. This is particularly important on cutters which are too small to sharpen them successfully, such as the burrs, which are thrown away as soon as they become dull.

To make a cheap and effective cutter for wheels and

pinions in watch and clock repairing perhaps the method devised by D. H. Church, of the Waltham Watch Company, is more readily available to the average watchmaker than any other which could well be devised. In this cutter the backing off, or angle of clearance of the teeth, is produced by making a number of saw cuts tangent to the circumference and extending well towards the center, as shown in Figs. 161 to 165. The teeth are then bent back until the sawed slot is closed at its rear end and thus furnishes a support for the back of the tooth. This is accomplished between collars, to keep the teeth in line and prevent their springing sidewise. The amount of clearance is governed by the thickness of the sawed slots and is uniform if properly done. If the cutter is thin it may have the teeth closed in a vise and any portions which are bruised or marred may be cut off in making the spaces for chips. It is then hardened between washers, to prevent the teeth from springing in hardening, after which the collars are removed and the rake of the teeth ground as desired. Very heavy cutters have their backs cut away to form a step or bearing, as shown in our illustration of a heavy cutter, Fig. 161, and a pair of spring tongs is adjusted in the vise so that their jaws bear on these steps, thus bending the teeth far enough to close the slots without marring the teeth.

The center holes of milling-cutters should fit the arbor closely at their center but should never be a snug fit at the outsides of the hole. All such holes are curved outward from the center on each side, as is shown in the sections of Figs. 161 to 164, so that the cutter may adjust itself flat and true with the collar on the center arbor, which it might not do if a snugly fitting center hole was not perpendicular to the sides; such a cutter would wabble.

Very thin leaves of pinions on accurate work are often cut "straddle"; that is with the cutter placed exactly over the tooth and cutting the shape of the tooth and half the space on each side of it as shown in section at Fig. 162. The

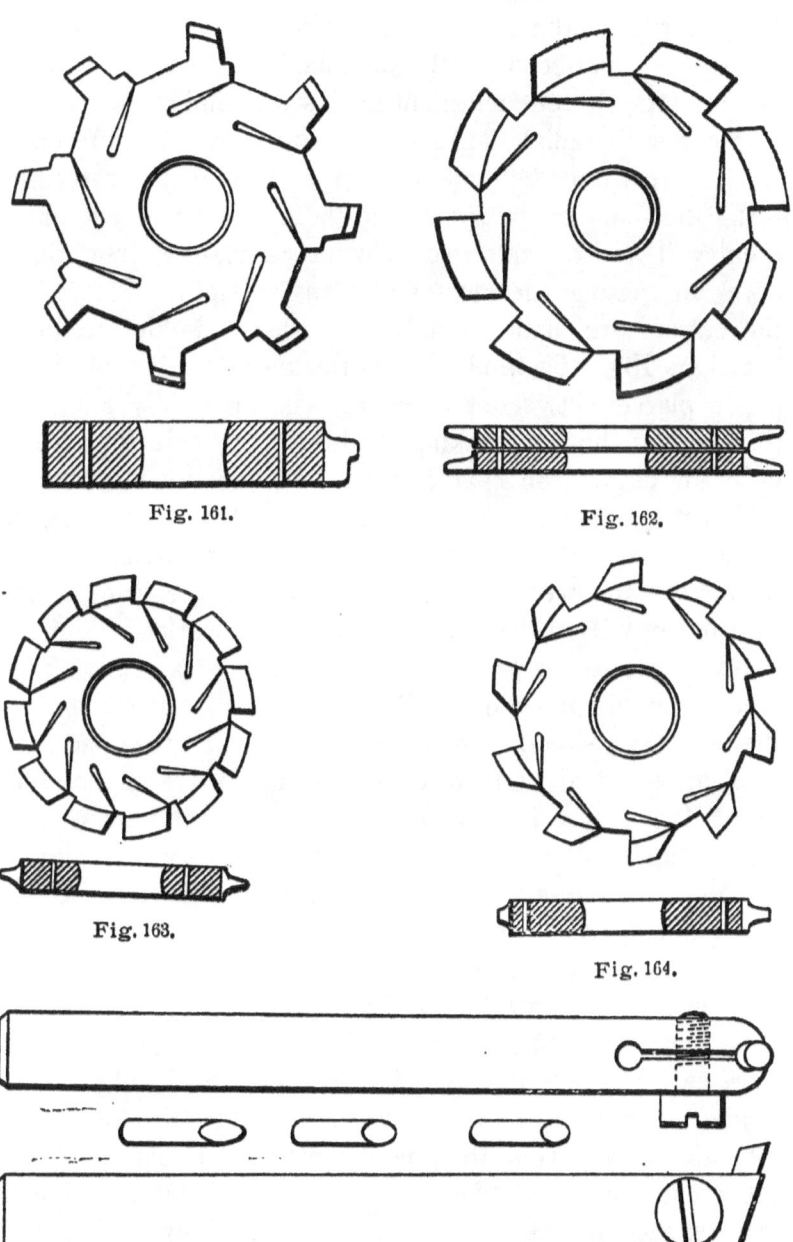

Fig. 161.

Fig. 162.

Fig. 163.

Fig. 164.

Fig. 165.

advantage here is that there is no side strain to spring a thin leaf, as all of the pressure is downward. Such pinions, however, cannot be cut with radial flanks. We show a pinion at Fig. 166 with one tooth cut in this way and those on each side cut with radial flanks in order to show the difference. Such cutters must be made the shape of the tooth, instead of being the shape of the space, and those who attempt to make them will find an enlarged drawing to scale a great time-saver in getting the curves and angles right. Sometimes the cutters are made in halves, as shown in the sectional drawing, Fig. 162, and then a thickness or two of tissue paper placed between the halves will materially alter the thickness of the leaf, making the cutter available for several different pinions on coarse work. We do not recommend this method, but merely note the fact that it is done, as we are not discussing the shapes and proportions of gear teeth here and we take it for granted that the student will inform himself on that subject from other works.

Reference to the greatly enlarged view of a section of a wheel and pinion (Fig. 166) will show that if we follow the ordinary method of making the cutter suit the space, we shall have a straight front edge, a straight flare to the pitch line, a long curve from thence outward for the wheel and a much shorter curve (nearly a half circle) for the pinion. Properly cut, these are epicycloid curves; practically we can approximate very closely to these curves by grinding a round wire, previously hardened, and cutting it off at a greater or less angle to serve as a cutting tool in forming these curves, as shown in Fig. 165. This hardened steel wire cutter is held in a tool holder, as shown, and the tool holder is bolted firmly in the tool post of the slide rest, with all slides set square to the line of centers of the lathe. Having previously turned the cutter smooth on both sides, bored and relieved the center and obtained the desired diameter, the special tool (Fig. 165) is placed at the proper distance from the center of the cutter and run in until the curve on

THE AMERICAN LATHE.   211

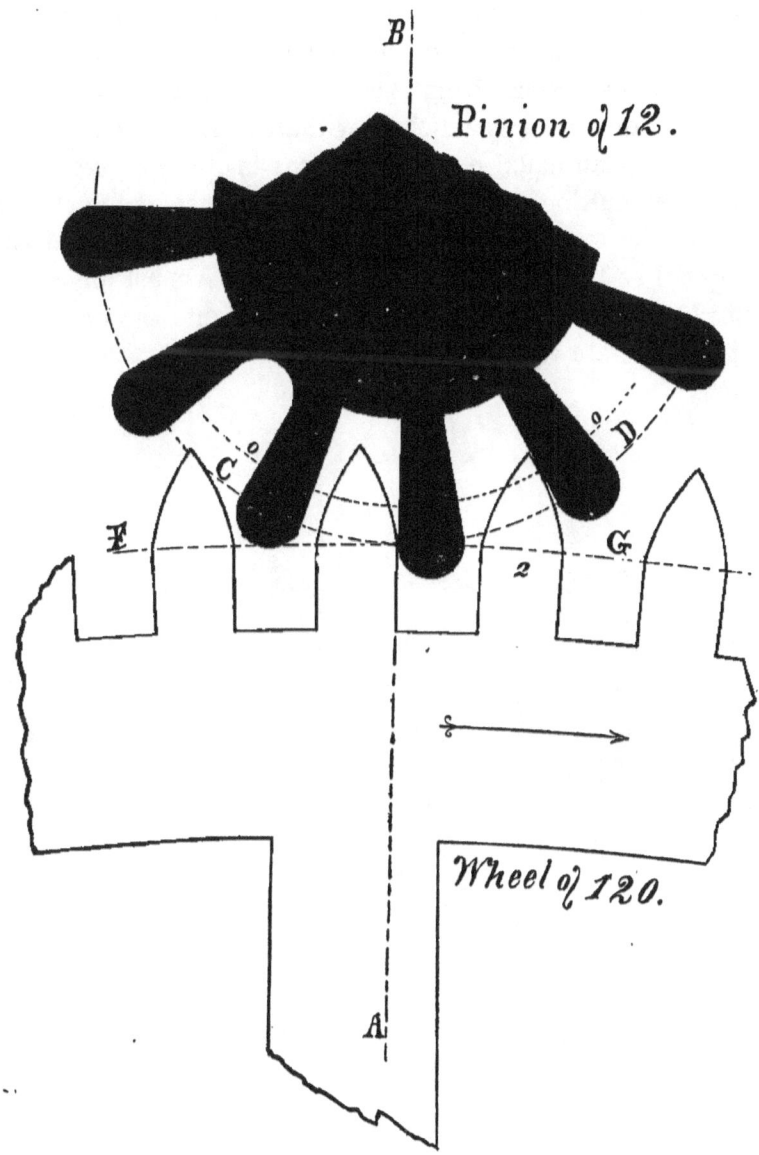

Fig. 166. A B Line of Centers; F. G., Pitch line of wheel; C D, Pitch line of Pinion. It will be noticed that one tooth of pinion is drawn with round bottom.

one side is formed. It is then run out sufficiently to clear the disc, moved a sufficient distance to the left and run in again to form the curve on the other side. The curves are made equally distant from the center by counting the turns of the slide rest screw when withdrawing the cutter and then giving an equal number of turns in the opposite direction when cutting the other side. The curves of the cutting edge of the wire will be alike if the wire is well ground and mounted so that the flat portion is level. Almost any curve may be closely approximated in this way, and the process is rapid, accurate and cheap.

THE AMERICAN LATHE.   213

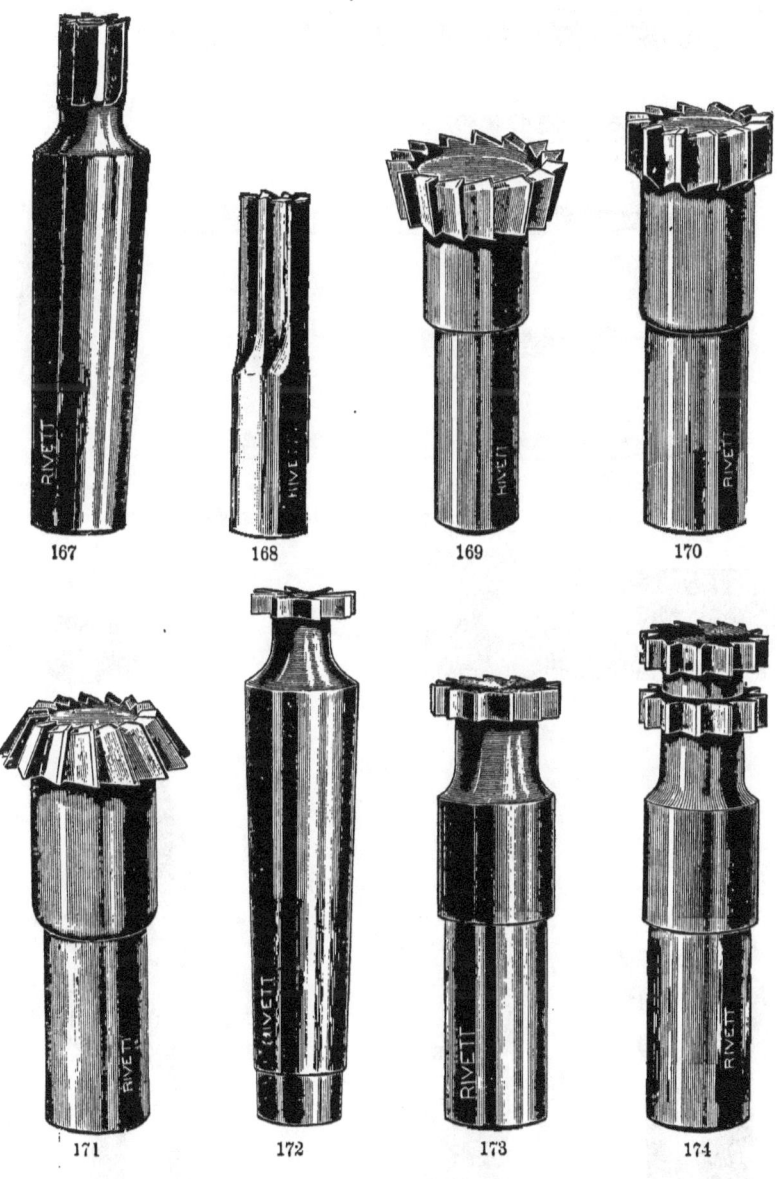

Figs. 167 to 174. Group of end and side cutting mills of shapes suitable for the watchmaker, enlarged to show construction. In cutting sinks, channels, crossing out wheels, etc., the work is held in the face plate, or on a cement brass and swung by hand to feed against the mill when cutting arcs of circles. Straight lines are cut by moving the pivot polisher spindle with the work held by the index pin of the lathe.

214　　　　　THE AMERICAN LATHE.

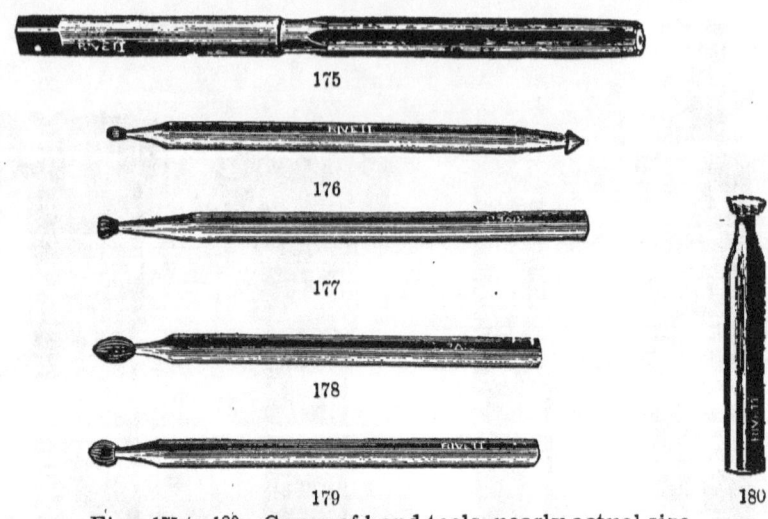

Figs. 175 to 180. Group of hand tools, nearly actual size.

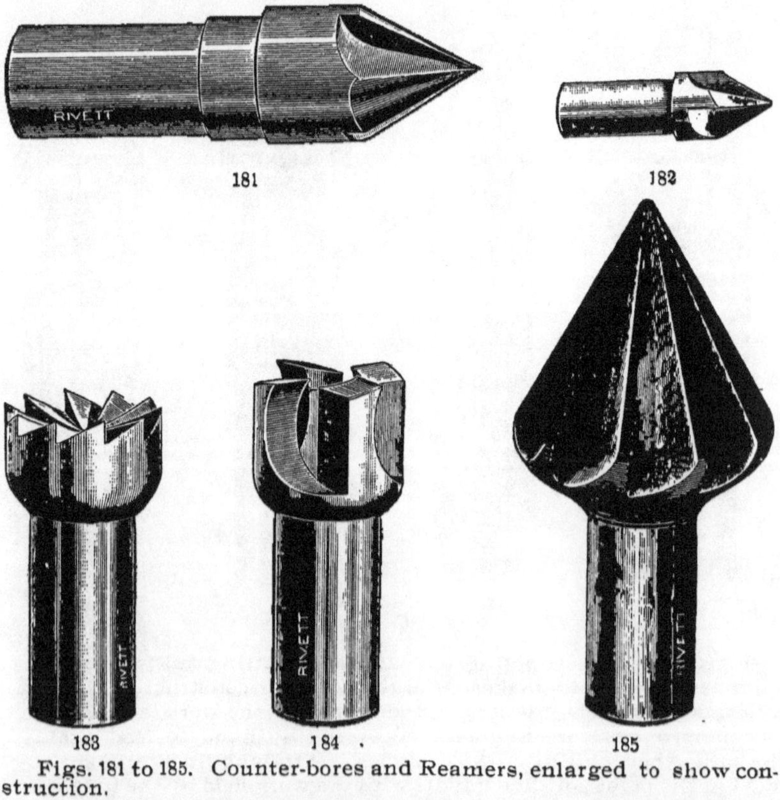

Figs. 181 to 185. Counter-bores and Reamers, enlarged to show construction.

THE AMERICAN LATHE. 215

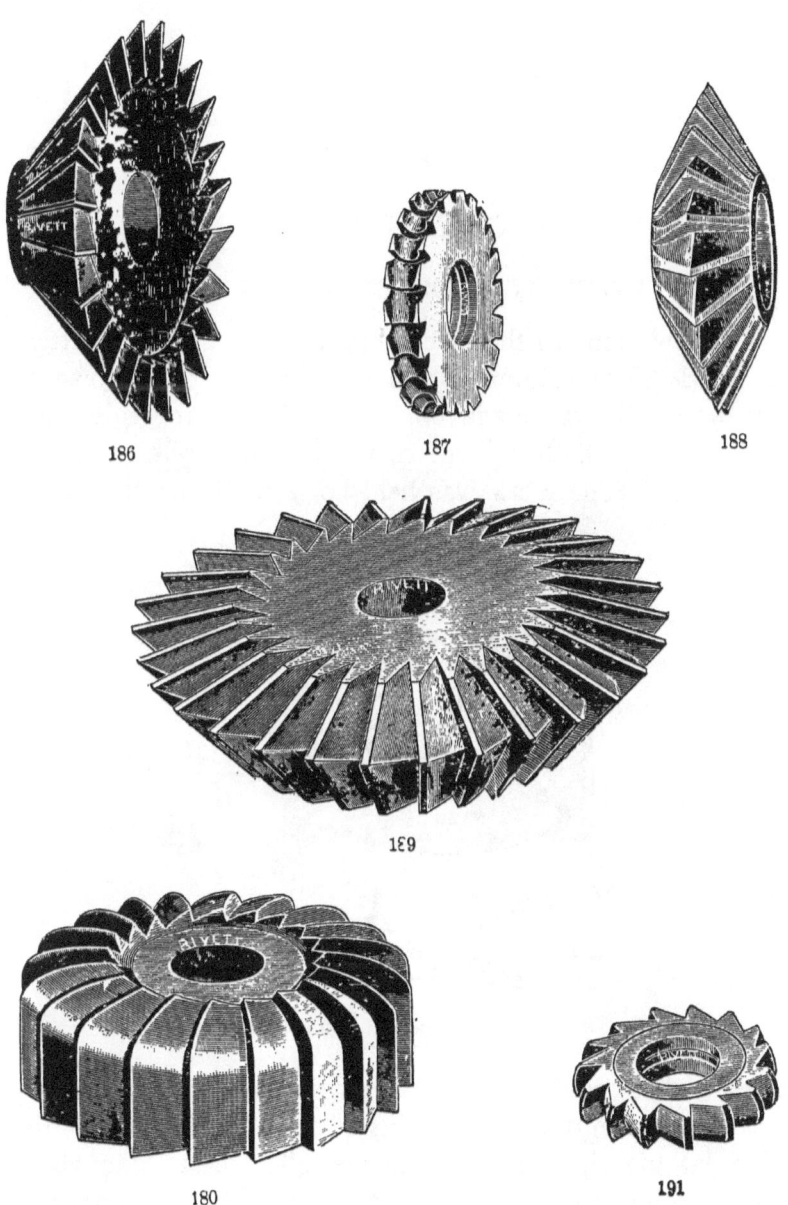

Figs. 186 to 191. Enlarged views of milling cutters for use on wheel cutter, making tools shown in Figs. 160 to 191; cutting ratchet wheels and other purposes.

CHAPTER XIII.

WHEEL CUTTING ATTACHMENTS FOR THE WATCHMAKER.

We now come to the machinery with which these cutters are used. The original wheel cutting engine is shown in Fig. 192. It was made of brass, with narrow gibs and slides and the cutters were carried on mandrels supported on centers. The work was held horizontally on the center

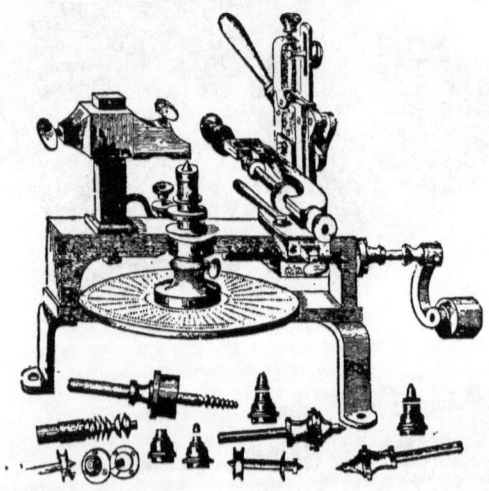

Fig. 192. The original wheel cutting engine.

of the index spindle by a clamp carried on a square upright post and the cutters were adjusted and fed by moving the slides at the right of the machine. The best thing about this machine was the large index plate. The sliding carriage was too light in all its parts and wear and lost motion soon resulted if the machine had steady use. Heavy cuts would spring the tool carriage, and altogether it left much to be desired. Many of these tools have been imported from Europe, but are nearly all discarded in favor of the modern attachments to the lathe.

The early wheel cutting attachments to the American lathe carried the cutters on a vertical mandrel running between centers, as shown in Fig. 193, and the yoke for the mandrel was bolted to the lathe slide rest. This gave larger bearing

Fig. 193. Early wheel cutting attachment with cutter on a mandrel running on centers.

surfaces and firmer support to the mandrel, and hence was an improvement, but it still left much to be desired in the way of adjustability, and was therefore superseded by the modern, closely fitted, well supported steel arbor, which is adjustable to all angles.

With the modern Moseley, Webster-Whitcomb and Hopkins wheel cutting attachments, the work to be cut is held in the chuck in the lathe spindle, while the cutters are mounted on an arbor carried on an adjustable knee which is bolted to the slide rest. Figs. 194 and 196 illustrate the various adaptations of the common principle. Either a large index with holes or smaller ones with notched edges is mounted on the lathe spindle at its rear end, the index being prevented from shifting on the spindle by a pin in the spindle which fits a slot in the center hole of the index and acts like a key and key way on an ordinary wheel and shaft. It is

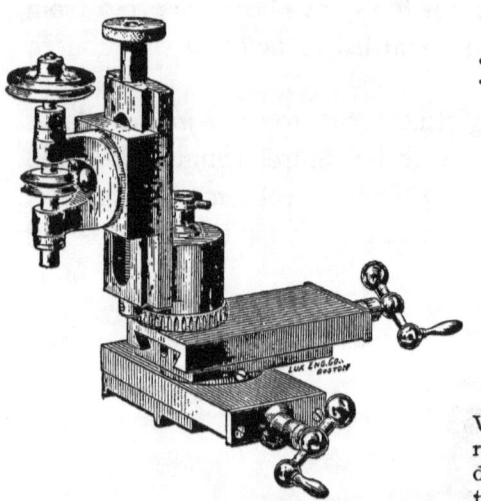

Fig. 194. Hopkins Wheel Cutter bolted to Slide Rest.

Fig. 195. Moseley 3-Spindle Wheel Cutter to bolt on slide rest; also made with one spindle; the pump center shown at the rear is used to align the cutters with each other and with the lathe center.

Fig. 196. Webster Whitcomb Wheel Cutter mounted on slide rest in place of the top slide, which is removed, when desiring to use the wheel cutter.

important that a close fit be secured here, as any looseness would result in angular motion between the spindle and index, and thus cause irregular spacing of the teeth on the wheel that is being cut. The index is kept from turning by a latch (Fig. 197), which is inserted either in a hole on the underside of the lathe bed or in the T slot and adjusted so that the point of the latch will enter the slots or holes of the index. All these parts are shown in position at Fig. 198.

Fig. 197. Latch for Index Plate.

The Rivett lathe uses a different system, in which the work is held in a quill in the slide rest, which is turned vertically by means of an adjustable graduated knee carrying a shoe to fit the slide rest. (Fig. 199 to Fig. 201.)

The wheel cutting attachment consists of the revolvable tailstock, quill and twelve index plates with spaces of the following numbers, 22, 26, 34, 48, 50, 54, 56, 60, 64, 72, 80 and 84. The quill fits into the top of the slide rest in place of the tool holder, and has a spindle to take the same chucks as the head spindle. The index plate is kept in place by two lugs milled from the solid spindle, which makes it very firm. The revolvable tailstock fits the bed of the lathe and is secured to it with the same firmness as the headstock. The upper part is made to fit the slide rest. The upright is so graduated that it can be set at any angle required, and there is also a slide with lateral feed for very fine adjustment. When the slide rest is to be used with the wheel cutting attachment the handle of the bottom slide is changed to the opposite

Fig. 198. Webster-Whitcomb ready for work, showing large index plate, lathe, countershaft, idler pulleys, etc. The spindle of the wheel cutting attachment is shown horizontal for the purpose of cutting spiral stem winding wheels, the spiral being secured by swivelling the slide rest, the cutter acting upon the work on the upper side. When the cutter spindle stands vertically, for the purpose of cutting ordinary wheels and pinions, the belt would run direct from the countershaft to the spindle, and not over the idler.

end before mounting it on the revolvable tailstock. No extra belting, pulleys or countershafts are needed.

Index plates of the numbers needed for the average watch or clock may be purchased cheaply of any material dealer; if not ordered at the time the wheel cutter is purchased, the size and make of lathe on which they are to be used should always be given. These index plates, with notches, are far more convenient than the large index plate, as mistakes in wheel cutting are frequent with a large plate where the operator must count a number of holes in the plate every

Fig. 199. Quill to go in Rivett slide rest, with index, latch and draw-in spindle for wheel cutting.

Fig. 200. Graduated and adjustable knee to hold Slide Rest vertical for wheel cutting.

Fig. 200.

time he shifts the work for another cut, and such mistakes are very expensive to the man who is paying for the time of the workman who makes such a blunder. A notched index of the right number of teeth is merely turned until the latch enters the next notch, making the liability to error much less.

When very accurate index plates are needed these notches are made with one side radial and the other slanting about 20 degrees, as shown in the index plate on the testing machine (Fig. 202). This style of slot assures the greatest possible accuracy, because when the index finger enters a notch the radial side of a slot stands vertical, thus not easily permitting any chips to lie on it, while the other side, being at an angle, has a tendency to force the radial side tight

Fig. 201. Rivett lathe arranged for wheel cutting.

against the index finger. Should a chip get between the angular side and the index finger it would not impair the accuracy of the divisions. This form of slot has another great advantage in that the wear is confined to the slanting side of the notch where it does not impair the accuracy of the work. Moreover, the accuracy being determined entirely by the radial side, the precision work is confined to that side. The inserted pieces shown are fitted very carefully and screwed in so that they may be hardened and easily removed if a mistake be made and too much removed from a piece in the final correction and testing. The lever shown in Fig. 202 has a proportion of forty to one.

Pinhole index plates are made by polishing the surface, cutting a hair line circle on which to center the drilled holes, and laying them out with a pair of strong dividers (having hardened needle points) and a strong glass. Corrections are made by drilling out the hole, plugging it and drilling a new hole.

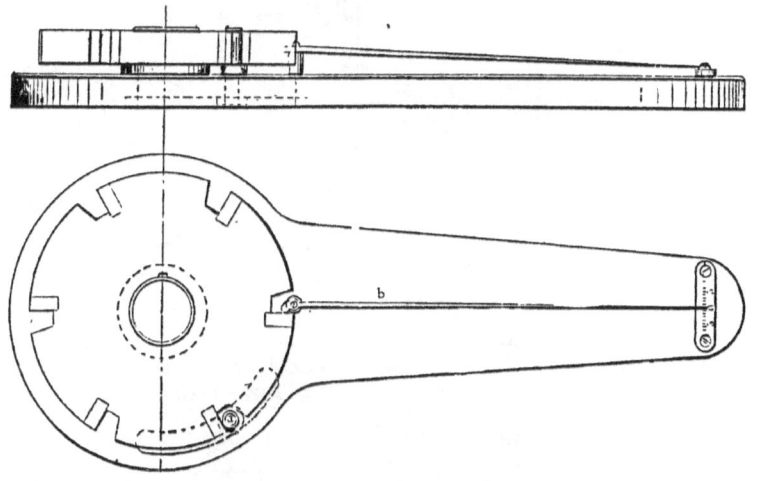

Fig. 202.

The 60-hole index on the pulley of the lathe spindle may also be used in cutting a number of index plates for use with the wheel cutter, as follows: 2, 3, 4, 5, 6, 10, 12, 15, 20, 30, 60.

These methods are given for the sake of completeness, as it may happen that the watchmaker is thousands of miles away from a lathe manufacturer or material dealer, and where communications are irregular or badly interrupted, so that he must help himself out by making what he needs. Where this is not the case the workman will find it much better to buy his index plates from the manufacturers of the lathe he is using, as index cutting is about the most difficult job a machinist can attempt unless he is already supplied with costly and accurate machinery for the purpose, when, of course, it becomes a simple matter.

To make a dividing head get a piece of hard brass or soft steel ¼ inch thick by 3⅛ long and 2 inches wide, as shown at A, Fig. 203. Next make the slot XX and rivet in a piece

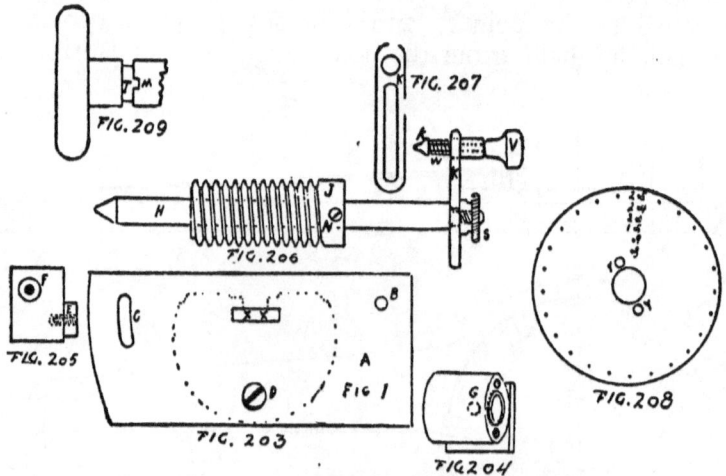

Fig. 205 to 209 Details of worm, worm wheel and index for dividing head to attach to a watchmakers lathe.

about 1½ inches long that will fit the T slot in the lathe bed, as shown by dotted line in Fig. 203; then drill the hole B, and with the dividers at this point draw the arcs that make the sides of the slot C. Now make the hole for the screw F which is screwed into the lathe bed; then make the block G, Fig. 204, which is held to the plate A, Fig. 203, by a knurled screw through the hole B. The block G is made of a piece of brass ¾ inch in diameter and ⅝ inch long with a piece of plate brass ⅛ inch thick brazed to it as shown in cut.

The block, Fig. 205, is made of brass or steel, ¾x⅜ inch, with projection E made to fit the curved slot C, Fig. 203, and held in place by a knurled screw from the back side of the plate in the same way as the block G. Now it will be seen that these two blocks, when in position, hold the arbor H, Fig. 206, the block, Fig. 205, being bored out at F to fit the end of arbor H, which is turned at 60 degrees taper. The arbor is ¼ inch in diameter and the hole in block G is reamed to fit. The piece shown at K, Fig. 206, is of steel 1⅜ inches long by ⅜ inch wide, and is held in position by the knurled nut S. It is shown in place at Fig. 210, the arbor H being flattened on two sides to fit the slot in piece K. The hole in the end of K is for the tube that holds an index pointer R.

The index plate, Fig. 208, is held on the block G by two screws going through the holes YY in the plate and screwing into the block G, which is turned off on the end so as to leave a ring 1-16 inch high around the hole in the center to fit the index plate to. Now with the index on we can bring our index pointer, R, in the right position for any circle on the plate by loosening the knurled nut S and moving piece K. The worm J, Fig. 206, is held against the block G by the set screw N. The worm can be procured of any large hardware house or machine shop, also a gear, 32 pitch, 120 teeth; then ream it out, to fit the drawing-in spindle of the lathe at T, Fig. 209; then file the notch M in the end of the lathe spindle and fit a piece of steel into the gear that will fit the notch M in the lathe spindle. This notch will not hurt the spindle in the least, but should anyone desire they might use a brass or fiber washer between the spindle and the drawing-in spindle when not using the gear. In Fig. 210 we give a photograph of the whole machine erected in working order. When in use the worm must be held tight to the gear and great care must be taken in boring out the gear to fit the spindle, or in turning down if made solid, for if it is out of true it will be a serious error. The index pointer R is held on the plate by the spiral spring at W. If we have no indexes to begin with we can put on a plate with only one hole in it and with this plate we can make five indexes, Nos. 4, 5, 8, 12 and 15, and with these numbers others can be made, using a perfectly centered drill in the pivot polisher to drill the index plate with while the plate is held by a taper in the lathe. All parts of the machine must be very nicely fitted to avoid error.

INDICES AND NUMBERS OF TURNS FOR GEAR CUTTING WITH WORM AND WORM GEAR OF 120 TEETH.

Numbers that are not divisible and numbers that cannot be divided so as to have an index less than 100 are omitted.

Number Wanted	Circle on Index	Turns	Holes	Number Wanted	Circle on Index	Turns	Holes	Number Wanted	Circle on Index	Turns	Holes	Number Wanted	Circle on Index	Turns	Holes
4	Any	30	0	86	43	1	17	165	11	0	8	255	17	0	8
5	"	24	0	87	29	1	11	166	83	0	60	256	32	0	15
6	"	20	0	88	11	1	4	168	7	0	5	258	43	0	20
8	"	15	0	90	3	1	1	170	17	0	12	260	13	0	6
9	3	13	1	92	23	1	7	171	57	0	40	261	87	0	40
10	Any	12	0	93	31	1	9	172	43	0	30	264	11	0	5
12	"	10	0	94	47	1	13	174	29	0	20	267	89	0	40
14	7	8	4	95	19	1	5	175	35	0	24	268	67	0	30
15	Any	8	0	96	4	1	1	176	22	0	15	270	9	0	4
16	4	7	2	98	49	1	11	177	59	0	40	272	34	0	15
18	3	6	2	99	33	1	7	178	89	0	60	273	91	0	40
20	Any	6	0	100	5	1	1	180	9	0	6	275	55	0	24
21	7	5	5	102	17	1	3	182	91	0	60	276	23	0	10
22	11	5	5	104	13	1	2	183	61	0	40	279	93	0	40
24	Any	5	0	105	7	1	1	184	23	0	15	280	7	0	3
25	5	4	4	106	53	1	7	185	37	0	24	282	47	0	20
26	13	4	8	108	9	1	1	186	31	0	20	284	71	0	30
27	9	4	4	110	11	1	1	188	47	0	30	285	19	0	8
28	7	4	2	111	37	1	3	189	63	0	40	288	12	0	5
30	Any	4	0	112	14	1	1	190	19	0	12	290	29	0	12
32	4	3	3	114	19	1	1	192	16	0	10	291	97	0	40
33	11	3	7	115	23	1	1	194	97	0	60	292	73	0	30
34	17	3	9	116	29	1	1	195	13	0	8	294	49	0	20
35	7	3	3	117	39	1	1	196	49	0	30	295	59	0	24
36	3	3	1	118	59	1	1	198	33	0	20	296	37	0	15
38	19	3	3	120	Any	1	0	200	5	0	3	297	99	0	40
39	13	3	1	122	61	0	60	201	67	0	40	300	5	0	2
40	Any	3	0	123	41	0	40	204	17	0	10	304	38	0	15
42	7	2	6	124	31	0	30	205	41	0	24	305	61	0	24
44	11	2	8	125	25	0	24	207	69	0	40	306	51	0	20
45	9	2	6	126	21	0	20	208	26	0	15	308	77	0	30
46	23	2	14	128	16	0	15	210	7	0	4	310	15	0	6
48	4	2	2	129	43	0	40	212	53	0	30	312	13	0	5
50	5	2	2	130	13	0	12	213	71	0	40	315	21	0	8
51	17	2	6	132	11	0	10	215	43	0	24	316	79	0	30
52	13	2	4	134	67	0	60	216	9	0	5	318	53	0	20
54	9	2	2	135	9	0	8	219	73	0	40	320	8	0	3
55	11	2	2	136	17	0	15	220	11	0	6	324	27	0	10
56	7	2	1	138	23	0	20	222	37	0	20	325	65	0	24
58	29	2	2	140	7	0	6	224	28	0	15	328	41	0	15
60	Any	2	0	141	47	0	40	225	15	0	8	330	11	0	4
62	31	1	29	142	71	0	60	228	19	0	10	332	83	0	30
63	21	1	19	144	6	0	5	230	23	0	12	335	67	0	24
64	8	1	7	145	29	0	24	231	77	0	40	336	14	0	5
65	13	1	11	146	74	0	60	232	29	0	15	340	17	0	6
66	11	1	9	147	49	0	40	234	39	0	20	342	13	0	5
68	17	1	13	148	16	0	15	235	47	0	24	344	43	0	15
69	23	1	17	150	5	0	4	236	59	0	30	345	23	0	8
70	7	1	5	152	19	0	15	237	79	0	40	348	29	0	10
72	3	1	2	153	51	0	40	240	4	0	2	350	35	0	12
74	37	1	23	154	77	0	60	243	87	0	40	352	44	0	15
75	5	1	3	155	31	0	24	244	61	0	30	354	59	0	20
76	19	1	11	156	13	0	10	245	49	0	24	355	71	0	24
78	13	1	7	158	79	0	60	246	41	0	20	356	89	0	30
80	4	1	2	159	53	0	40	248	31	0	15	360	3	0	1
81	27	1	13	160	16	0	12	249	83	0	40	364	91	0	30
82	41	1	19	162	27	0	20	250	25	0	12	365	73	0	24
84	7	1	3	164	41	0	30	252	21	0	10				
85	17	1	7												

The method of attaching the wheel cutting fixture to the lathe will be readily seen by referring to Fig. 198. Particular care should be taken to have the piece which is being cut firmly secured upon an arbor or cemented or soldered to a chuck. When secured on an arbor with a nut or screw washers as large as can be used without being in the way

Fig. 210.

of the cutter should be put between the nut and the wheel, to be cut so that no unnecessary strain may come upon the teeth. The more firmly the work is secured the more positive will be the truth of the cutting. Escape wheels for clocks will usually have to be cut with the "fly" or single-toothed cutter. The French clock "visible escapement" and chronometer escape wheels, and those like it are best cut by two or more cuts. The first being a plain slot of the width and depth wanted; the other being to cut the curve of the back of the tooth, which is done with a cutter shaped to correspond with the desired curve. Ratchet-pointed escape teeth are cut with one cut, always turning the blanks backward that the tooth being cut may have the support of the uncut metal until the last one is reached, the pressure of the cutter being strongest in the sloping side of the tooth. Transmission ratchets having teeth cut both on the end and circumference should have the ratchet teeth cut first. Transmission ratchets with spiral teeth on the edge are cut thus: Turn the cutting spindle one-quarter round, so that it is horizontal. Turn the top slide of slide rest to the right 15 degrees, set the cutter exactly over the center of the blank; the idler pulley stand must be used. See Fig. 198. Winding pinions are straight, or of 12 or 15 degree tapers. Cut with a ratchet cutter. Crown wheels are usually soft soldered to a brass cement chuck for cutting. If the teeth are highest towards the center (as the wheel is in the watch) turn both slides so that the handles are together. Then turn the top slide to the right 15 degrees and fasten it. Set the cutter as nearly right as possible and cut one tooth. If not deep enough turn the screw to the lower slide so to draw it toward you. All wheels with teeth highest in the center must be cut with the cutter on the further side of the lathe; all others may be cut in front or over the blank. All ratchet teeth (steel wheels) have the knife edge of the cutter set in line with the center of the lathe spindle. *In cutting steel wheels keep the cutter well oiled.* Grooved ratchets are cut in the ordinary wire chucks, first at one end and then at the other, the groove for the yoke spring being turned the last thing before tempering. Watch escape wheel blanks should be at least three times as thick as the finished wheel is to be (in order to stand the cutting) and soft soldered to a brass cement chuck, care being taken not to anneal the blank. In cutting a tooth that inclines drop the cutting spindle below the center of the lathe, or raise it above the center, using the front of the cutter as a guide.

Sometimes wheels are cut with the cutter in the lathe chuck and the work staked on its pinions and held in the rounding-up tool. The rounding-up tool consists of a yoke adapted to bolt on the slide rest, having closely fitted male and female centers, the lower one of which works in the center of a snail-shaped table, or rest. Fig. 211 shows the

Fig. 211. Rounding-up Tool Bolted on Slide Rest.

attachment in position and Fig. 212 shows the attachment with a wheel on its pinion, resting on the table, with the table turned so that its edge supports the web of the wheel ready for work. The shape of the snail provides for supporting wheels of various sizes by turning it so that the cutter comes the right distance from the center. Wheels cut by this method are not recommended, as the spacing must be done by the eye and hand and only a workman of great skill can make them at all presentable. Wheels may, however, be duplicated in this way by laying the old wheel on top of the blank and using it as a guide.

The proper use of the attachment is as a rounding-up tool, the chuck and cutter for this purpose being shown at Fig. 93. The cutters are cheap and it is best to buy them, but they may be made by turning up a soft steel blank to fit the teeth and then making a number of file cuts on the working surface with a diamond pointed graver and then hardening.

A very good way to avoid this work and get through speedily is to turn up a soft blank to fit the space and then charge it with diamantine and oil or fine diamond powder, the latter making a very smooth and fast cutting tool for this purpose. If properly made it is superior to the regular cutters in speed and smoothness of work. It is particularly advantageous on thin wheels, which are easily sprung when using the regular cutters, as the grinding by the lap throws less strain on the teeth and leaves a smoother surface.

It is frequently observed that young watchmakers, and regretfully be it said that some of the older and more ex-

Fig. 212. Rounding-up Tool, showing wheel and pinion in position for work on them.

perienced ones, are rather careless when fitting wheels on pinions. In many cases the wheel is simply held in the fingers and the hole opened with a broach, and in doing this no special care is taken to keep the hole truly central and of correct size to fit the pinion snugly, and should it be opened a little too large it is riveted on the pinion whether concentric or not. Many suppose the rounding-up tool will then make it correct without further trouble and without sufficient thought of the irregularities ensuing when using the tool.

We will presume that in the drawing, Fig. 213, the wheel, as shown by the dotted lines, had originally been cut with its center at m, but through careless fitting it had been placed on the pinion at o, and consequently is very much out of round when tested in the calipers, and to correct this defect it is put in the rounding-up tool. The cutter commences to remove the metal from tooth 7, it being the highest, next the neighboring teeth 6 and 8, then 5 and 9, and so on until tooth 1 comes in contact with the cutter. The wheel is now round. But how about the size of the teeth and the pitch? The result of the action of the cutter is

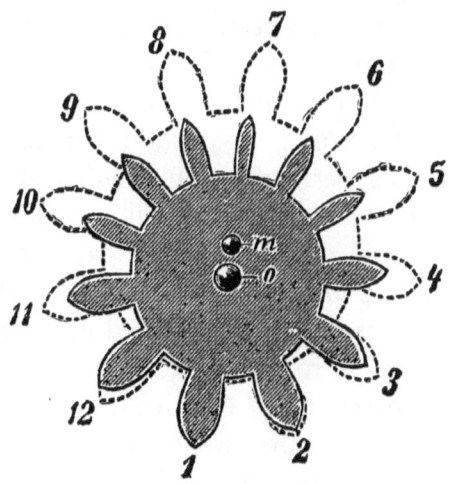

Fig. 213. Shows how a badly centered wheel is left by the rounding-up cutters.

shown by the sectionally lined wheel. Many will ask how such a result is possible, as the cutter has acted equally upon all the teeth. Nevertheless, a little study of the action of the rounding-up cutter will soon make it plain why such faults arise. Naturally the spaces between the teeth through the action of the cutter will be equal, but as the cutter is compelled to remove considerable metal from the point of greatest eccentricity, i. e. at tooth 7 and the adjoining teeth to make the wheel round, and the pitch circle being smaller the teeth become thinner, as the space between the teeth remains the same. At tooth 1 no metal was removed, consequently it remains in its original condition. The pitch from each side of tooth 1 becomes less and less to tooth 7, and the teeth thinner, and the thickest tooth is always found opposite the thinnest.

In the case of a wheel having a large number of teeth and the eccentricity of which is small, such faults as described cannot be readily seen from the fact that there are many teeth and the slight change in each is so gradual that the only way to detect the difference is by comparing opposite teeth. And this eccentricity becomes a serious matter when there are but few teeth, as before explained, especially when reducing an escape wheel. The only proper course to pursue is to cement the wheel on a chuck, or putting it in a step chuck or in any suitable manner so that it can be trued by its periphery and then opening the hole truly. This method is followed by all expert workmen.

A closer examination of the drawing teaches us that an eccentric wheel with pointed teeth—as cycloidal teeth are mostly left in this condition when placed in the rounding-up tool, will not be made round, because when the cutter has just pointed the correct tooth (tooth No. 1 in the drawing) it will necessarily shorten the thinner teeth, Nos. 6, 7, 8, i. e., the pitch circle will be smaller in diameter. We can therefore understand why the rounding-up tool does not make the wheel round.

As we have before observed, when rounding-up an ecentrically riveted wheel, the thinnest tooth is always opposite the thickest, but with a wheel which has been stretched the case is somewhat different. Most wheels when stretched become angular, as the arcs between the arms move outward in a greater or less degree, which can be improved to some extent by carefully hammering the wheel near the arms, but some inequalities will still remain. In stretching a wheel with five arms we therefore have five high and as many depressed parts on its periphery. If this wheel is now rounded up the five high parts will contain thinner teeth than the depressed portions. Notwithstanding that the stretching of wheels is objectionable and is often unavoidable on account of the low price of repairs, it certainly ought not to be overdone. Before placing the wheel in the rounding-up tool it should be tested in the calipers and the low places carefully stretched so that the wheel is as nearly round as can be made before the cutter acts upon it.

It is hardly necessary to mention that the rounding-up tool will not equalize the teeth of a badly-cut wheel, and further should there be a burr on some of the teeth which has not been removed, the action of the guide and cutter in entering a space will not move the wheel the same distance at each tooth, thus producing thick and thin teeth. From what has been said it would be wrong to conclude that the rounding-up tool is a useless one, on the contrary, it is a practical and indispensable tool, but to render good service it must be correctly used.

In the use of the rounding-up tool the following rules are to be observed:

1. In a new wheel enlarge the hole after truing the wheel from the outside and stake it concentrically on its pinion.

2. In a riveted but untrue wheel, stretch the deeper portions until it runs true, then reduce it in the rounding-up tool. The better method is to remove the wheel from its pinion, bush the hole, open concentrically with the outside and rivet, as previously mentioned in a preceding paragraph. But if the old riveting cannot be turned so that it can be used again it is best to turn it entirely away, making the pinion shaft conical towards the pivot, and after having bushed the wheel, drill a hole the proper size and drive it on the pinion. The wheel will be then just as secure as when riveted, as in doing the latter the wheel is often distorted. With a very thin wheel allow the bush to project somewhat

so that it has a secure hold on the pinion shaft and cannot work loose.

3. Should there be a feather edge on the teeth, this should be removed with a scratch brush before rounding it up, but if for some reason this cannot well be done, then place the wheel upon the rest with the feather edge nearest the latter, so that the cutter does not come immediately in contact with it. If the feather edge is only on one side of the tooth, which is often the case, place the wheel in the tool, so that the guide will turn it from the opposite side of the tooth; the guide will now move the wheel the correct distance for the cutter to act uniformly. Of course, in every case the guide, cutter and wheel must be in correct position to insure good work.

4. To obtain a smooth surface on the face of the teeth a high cutter speed is required, and for this reason it is advantageous to drive the cutter spindle by a foot wheel.

Fig. 214 shows a rounding-up tool adapted to be mounted in the T-rest where a workman has no slide rest. While we do not advise the watchmaker to try to get along without a slide rest, still if a man has no money he must makeshift as best he can and such a man will find the attachment shown above of considerable service to him.

There is one use of this tool, which does not seem to be generally known in the trade. That is its use in grinding the faces of pallets, pallet stones, etc., when they have become cut or it is desirable to change the angle. By mounting a thin lap in the lathe chuck and holding the staff between the centers of the rounding-up tool these faces may be nicely polished or by a little manipulation they may be slightly rounded if desired. The work is done easily, quickly and in the proper plane if due care is taken in setting the lap and rounding-up tool.

Escape wheels may have a circular lift given to their teeth in this way and with care all the teeth may be given a uniform lift of just the desired curve.

THE AMERICAN LATHE.

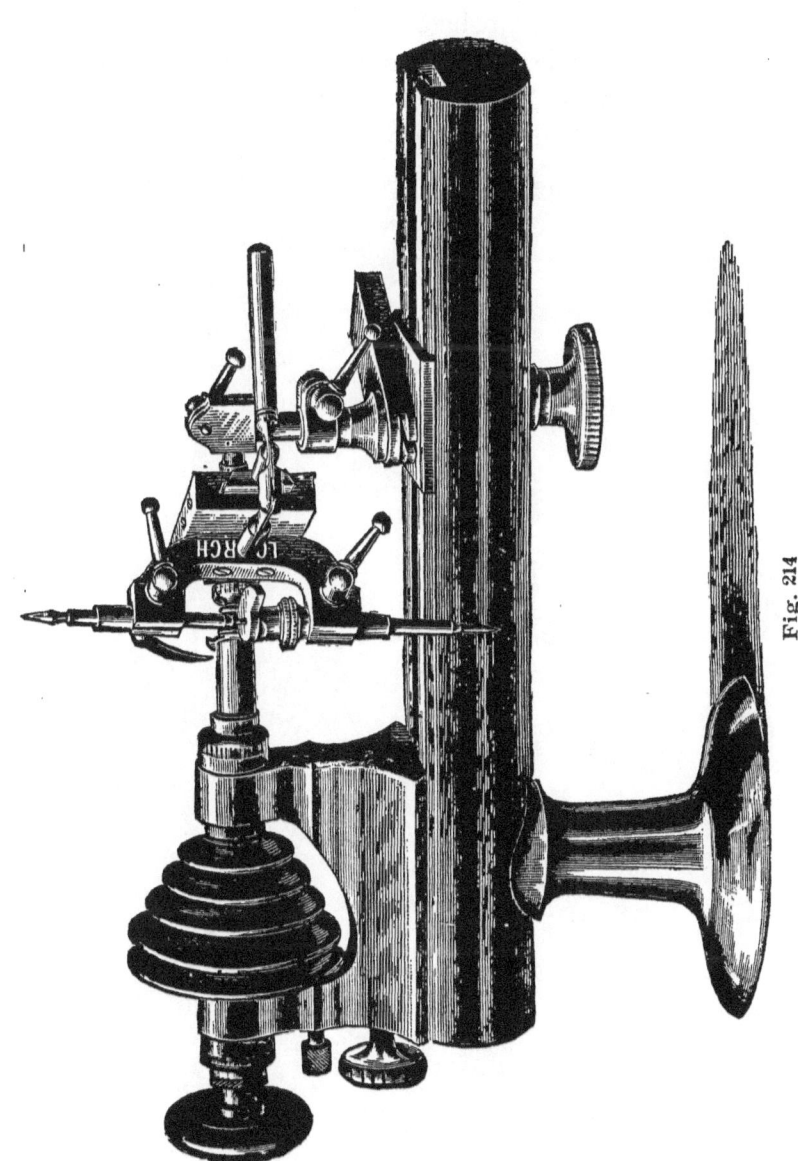

Fig. 214

Very thin laps should be used so that each end of the anchor may be swung against the lap without resetting the attachments. If the pallets are stone the lap should be charged with diamond powder and they may be polished without change of lap if the diamond powder be uniform and sufficiently fine.

CHAPTER XIV.

TURNING AND PIVOTING LONG, THIN WORK WITH THE STEADY REST.

There are several methods of doing the pivots on clock work, music boxes, etc., either of which will give good results. One is to have a number of female tapers of varying sizes of holes with the upper halves ground away. These are fitted to the spindle of the tailstock and form a support for the end of the pivot when polishing pivots of such staffs, the work being done on the upper side of the pivot, which projects above that portion of the center which has been cut away. This necessitates having a number of such centers with varying sizes of holes to take different sized pivots. The work is held and rotated by an ordinary split chuck in the headstock spindle.

Another method is an adaptation of the old method used in the Dracip Lathe, see Fig. 9, in which a wing projects from a stud held in the T-rest and the outer end of the work is supported by a hole drilled of the proper diameter in the wing. This leaves the end of the pivot free, but uses the rest, which we need to turn with, unless we buy another rest. We also need a number of such wings to accommodate the great number of holes we shall need from time to time.

To do away with both of these objections and retain the freedom of working on clock pivots and other work of a similar nature the machinist's follow rest has been adapted to the watchmaker's lathe. The follow rest of the machine shop, however, is carried on the side rest, so as to remain close to the tool and prevent springing. The steady rest is clamped to the bed of the lathe and supports the work on the points of the three jaws. Such work is generally centered by adjusting the jaws to the circumference of the arbor while the pivot rests in a female center in the tail stock and after trying it for truth the tail stock is removed and the free end is then available for any work that may be desired

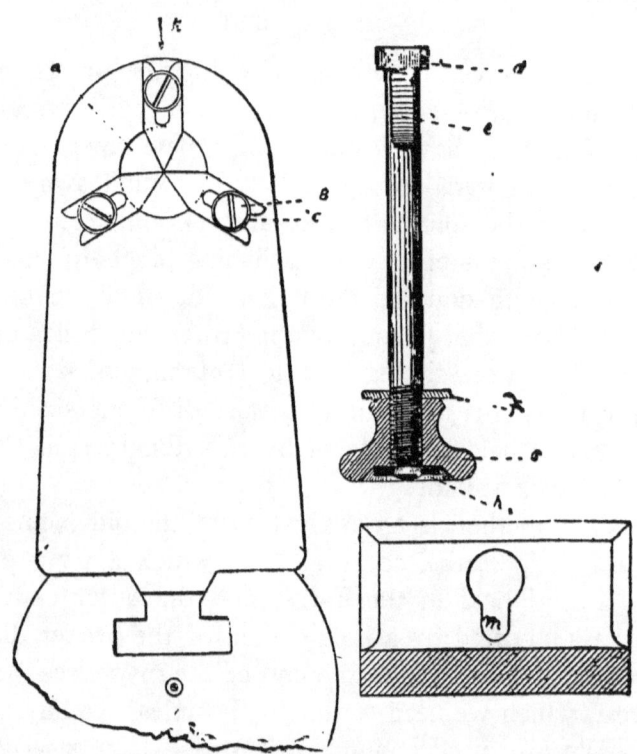

Fig. 215. Design for steady rest, to be made by the watchmaker.

to be performed on it. Pivots may then be turned up with the graver and T-rest, or they may be ground and polished with the pivot polisher, and when done they will be concentric with the arbor if the jaws of the steady rest were properly adjusted.

The steady rest should be set up with the projection of the base toward the headstock and the jaws nearest the end of the work to be done. This brings the jaws to the extreme end of the work, furnishes the best support and also allows the T-rest to be brought up close, where it will properly support the graver. The jaws should not be more than one-eighth of an inch in thickness, and thinner ones are frequently desirable. They are generally made up of hard brass, German silver or nickel; steel would scratch the work where they bear upon it in revolving. The standard may be made of iron or brass and should not be thicker than a quarter of an inch. Fig. 215 shows such a rest drawn full size with 1-32d taken off in finishing the stock, which was a quarter of an inch at the start. Ways should be filed for the jaws to slide in, to prevent them from turning when being fastened and the jaws should fit these ways, to keep the points radial to the center. The key-hole slot in the base allows the bolt to be readily slipped in; or the slot may be extended through the outer edge as a plain slot. The screws for fastening the jaws should have washers under them. To facilitate the adjustment of the jaws I put wings on the set screws by slotting the heads and brazing in a piece of thin stock.

Fig. 216 shows a self-centering back rest. The jaws are worked by an independent ring which is accurately made by special tools and which fits the body of the back rest very closely. This ring is operated by the handle, A, which fits the holes, B, in the ring. Everything is taken care of in this tool to make it first class. The jaws can be turned end for end, which gives it all the range desired, and they are locked by the thumb screw shown at the right. It is made to fit all standard lathes.

A good lathe hand will never attempt to use a steady rest until he has the job turned perfectly round where the jaws will bear on it, because the jaws do not have full contact with the shaft, and any irregularity at this point will appear when the other and adjacent parts of it are turned up. To do a good job with a steady rest it is best to have the jaws fit a considerable portion of the circumference of the shaft, as the tool leaves it, but not necessarily the finished size, unless the arbor is finished at one cut. When this is done and ordinary care is used in keeping the jaws in contact satisfactory work will be turned out regularly, and it will also be a source of surprise to find how often the pivots of a French

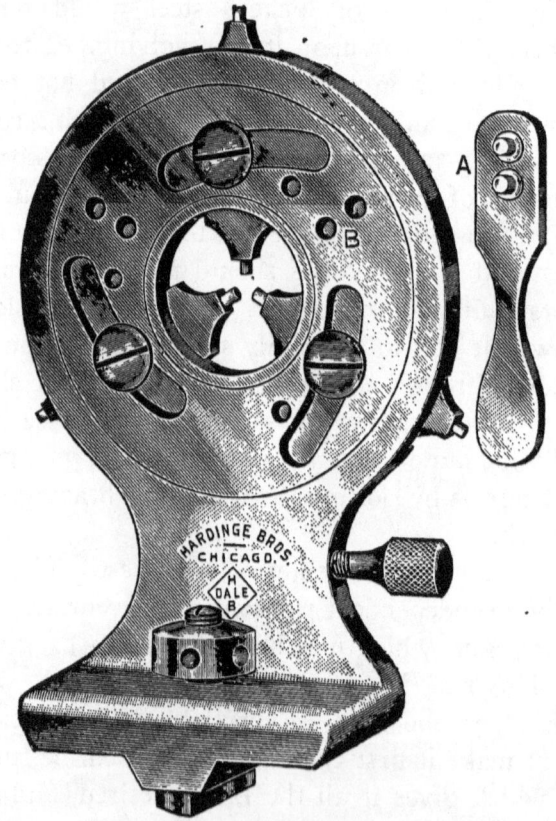

Fig 216. Self centering back rest for the watchmaker's lathe.

clock you are repairing will be discovered to be badly out of center when tested by revolving the work with steady rest jaws closely fitting the arbor. It is frequently the case that the trains of such clocks are untrue in several ways, and the pivots will sometimes offset errors in the wheels and pinions and sometimes double them, according to how they are staked on. Many a fine looking clock has been cured of mysterious stoppages by the discovery that the pivots, which had been made in the manner shown in Fig. 9, were out of center. Wheels, pinions and pivots should all be tested in such clock trains, as with the wheel on one end of the arbor and the pinion on the other their relation to each other and to a common center cannot be readily ascertained, except by revolving the arbor by its circumference in the manner indicated above. Drilling and pivoting clock arbors while they are held in the steady rest is readily done, but in the case of the French clocks spoken of it should not be done without first testing the truth of both wheel and pinion, as if errors offset each other, it is wiser not to correct them in such work as this.

CHAPTER XV.

IDLER PULLEYS, BELTS, COUNTER SHAFTS AND FOOT WHEELS.

Our study of the lathe and its operation would be incomplete without paying close attention to the methods of driving not only the lathe, but also the various attachments. This subject is much more important than it seems, for much of the ease and facility of operation will be lost if the lathe, and especially the attachments, are driven improperly, whereas with suitable methods of driving everything will work easily and without undue fatigue and its consequent deterioration of the skill of the operator.

Idler pulleys must be used in certain positions in which we wish to place the wheel cutters, and also when polishing, grinding and damascening, and milling or drilling with the pivot polisher. Idler pulleys were at first mounted on the carriage of the pivot polisher and all the older forms of attachments have them in this way, as it was supposed that the time gained by being able to set up pulleys and attachment at one operation more than counterbalanced the disadvantages. The chief drawback to this was the lack of range of the adjustment; any considerable movement changed the tension of the belt and therefore the movements of the spindle, interfering with its nicety of operation and making it harder to drive. It was also difficult to obtain belts having the necessary elasticity. For these reasons the use of idler pulleys on the various attachments has been generally discarded in favor of a separate idler pulley with adjustable standard, which may be slipped into a socket screwed to the bench near the headstock of the lathe, as shown in Fig.

198. This allows of a longer belt being used and permits greater freedom of movement of the tool, while, because of its greater length the belt may be looser and will then hug the small pulley better on its slack side and thus give greater driving power. A belt braided from silk sewing "twist," with the joint spliced so as to make a long and imperceptible joint, makes an ideal belt for the pivot polisher. It should be braided in four strands, which will give a round belt, using from two to four threads in each strand according to the thickness of belt desired. This makes a very strong and smooth running belt, if the splice is made long enough to be invisible. Use a needle in making the splice, fastening each thread separately. In braiding belts a small weight tied on each strand about eighteen inches from the point where the strands pass into the braid will give a facility in handling the strands, as they are then always under tension and are readily controlled by the fingers while braiding.

The idler pulleys should be large, say from two to two and a half inches in diameter and with long hubs and thin webs, as such pulleys run slower and take less power to drive than smaller ones. Hard rubber with brass hubs makes the lightest pulleys, though they may be made of indurated fiber or of metal. The long hub prevents the wheel from wabbling under side strain of the belt and thus prevents binding of the pulley on the stud, which would absorb power and slow the cutter or lap spindle. The stud on which the idle pulleys travel should be ground of uniform size throughout and be an easy fit to the hubs of the pulleys, so that they will move freely with the change of position of the cutter spindle.

Heavier belts for wheel cutting, etc., are made of round or twisted raw hide, braided cotton, etc. The principal thing to look to in these belts is to see that they are sufficiently flexible and that the joint is such that the cutter spindle will not "jump" when the joint of the belt is passing over that pulley. Careful workmen sew these joints with silk or linen, much as a machinist laces a belt; others use a thin, short hook because the belt may be readily unhooked and taken off when through using the attachment. If the spindle has a very small pulley an S-hook should be used as it gives greater freedom for the belt in passing the pulley. If one is using a speed pulley outside the pillar of the countershaft as in Fig. 217, the spliced endless belts will be found much the best on account of their greater smoothness of working. Endless belts should be put on the spindle of the attachment before the joint is spliced; forgetting this point has frequently caused trouble and annoyance.

A good countershaft with speed pulley is absolutely necessary with every complete lathe outfit, in using milling tools, wheel cutters, etc. The advantages of a countershaft are many. By its use you carry the belt to the back of your bench, where it is out of the way, and you obviate the necessity of having holes in your bench on each side of the lathe, that small tools and articles are so apt to fall through, and last, but not least, you can change the speed of your lathe readily by shifting the belt from one step of the cones to the other, which, owing to the difference in the sizes of the pulleys, causes the lathe to run faster or slower with the same motion of the foot than it would if belted directly to the lathe. Experience shows that no watchmaker who ever used the countershaft has been willing to give up its use.

In selecting countershafts, as in lathes, special attention should be paid to the quality of material and workmanship, rather than design, but one should be selected with a rather large and long shaft, so that the speed pulley may be readily changed back and forth to line up with the special attachment in use. This will require a shaft of at least eight inches in length or longer, depending upon the length of lathe bed.

Fig. 217 shows a speed countershaft with rigid base and Fig. 218 one with all its parts adjustable. The advantage claimed is that the countershaft may be moved about to take up slack in all belts, but we think that this advantage is more theoretical than real. A twisted raw hide belt from the cone pulleys on the lathe to those of the shaft is readily adjusted by twisting or untwisting to regulate the tension. The idler pulleys should take care of the tension of belts on attachments, etc. This leaves only the vertical adjustment to take care of the stretch of the belt to the foot wheel. Against this there is the tendency of all adjustable tools to

Fig. 217.

give way when they should be rigid. The countershaft in Fig. 218 runs on centers, while that in Fig. 217 runs in boxes. The pulleys in Fig. 218 have extension split sleeves which are compressed by thumb nuts, thus clamping them to the shaft in any desired position.

As a matter of fact, we think, only the speed wheel on a countershaft should be adjustable, and the greater the rigidity of the rest of the apparatus the better. Once properly lined up, it should stay where it is put. The tension of a flat belt on a foot wheel is easily taken care of by proper lacing and that of a round belt by twisting, and we therefore consider all this adjustability a detriment. The speed pulleys on countershafts vary from 4½ to 5½ inches in diameter, the larger diameter being preferred by many on account of the increased speed given to the spindles of attachments by its use. Provision is generally made for moving it about three inches on the countershaft by watchmakers who do clock and other work, while those who do

Fig. 218.

watch work only need no adjustment in this respect, having a more than sufficient movement allowed by the stud on the idler pulleys for any movement of the cutter or polisher spindles on work that is so short. In use the countershaft, and especially the speed pulley, must be kept true, or chattering of the cutters, etc., on the work is sure to follow. Many an attachment has been condemned because the jump of the belts from an untrue shaft and pulleys made its proper working impossible.

The importance of complete control over the driving power of the lathe, and hence its motion, was early recognized, and its development has proceeded slowly, but surely, along experimental lines. The variation of speed demanded is great and the fluctuations are sudden. Wheel cutting, jeweling, polishing, grinding pallet jewels, etc., demand high speed and considerable power. Staff making and ordinary turning require speed and frequent stoppages for measurements. Opening wheels and jewel holes, uprighting, etc., require slow speed and frequently a backward motion; this is also true in tapping screw holes. Perhaps the slowest speeds needed are when the operator is pivoting a hard staff, or drilling out a cannon pinion, for great care must be used to avoid breaking the drill, as if this were done, it might be difficult to extract the broken portion of the drill, which must, of course, be done before the work can be proceeded with. Therefore a perfect control of speed is a necessity.

Perhaps the ideal power is a small motor with six speeds, four forward and two backward, all to be operated by a switch actuated by the foot; but such motors are expensive and can only be operated in buildings provided with electric light; the motor must be kept off the bench, to avoid danger of magnetism, and this makes a separate countershaft necessary, so that the foot wheel will in all probability never be displaced with the majority of watchmakers.

The necessity of perfect control has caused the retention of the hand wheel on the lathe in Europe to such an extent that it is very generally in use to-day. Fig. 219 shows a modern German lathe which is having extensive sale all over Europe, and it well illustrates the methods of driving by hand. The reader will notice a crank on each side, to permit the use of either hand in driving. This allows but one hand at the lathe and we think the American watchmaker would find it a difficult proposition to do much work with such a machine. Still, good work is done on them—with a greater expenditure of time. We show it here because we have made frequent reference to the European watchmaker having to learn the lathe over again when he

Fig. 219. Modern German Lathe driven by Hand Wheel.

comes to America, and it well illustrates the European habit of working to the right instead of to the left.

The origin of the use of the foot wheel with the lathe is unknown. It came in from Europe with the Bottum and Swiss wax lathes (see Fig. 226.) It had a rocking treadle, connected with a small, light wheel, much like the sewing machine treadles of to-day, except that it was narrow and designed for one foot. The diameter and weight of the wheel were soon increased, to slow the foot motion and steady the power when using lathe attachments, but there was little further development until 1877 or 1878. Fig. 220 shows one of these later wheels with a rockshaft through the base so as to get the connecting rod on the opposite side of the wheel, in order that the oil should not soil the clothing when using the wheel.

In 1877, J. H. Purdy, then at 178 State street, Chicago, made a swing treadle wheel, but stopped short when he

Fig. 220.

discovered that the motion of the treadle was much faster when the crank was in the upper half of its revolution than in the lower. This wheel was sold to a Mr. Johnson of Eau Claire, Wis., and is the original of the common swing treadle foot wheel of to-day.

The next attempt was by C. Hopkins, of the Waltham Watch Tool Company, who made a swing treadle with an arm at right angles to the top of the treadle and the connecting rod attached to the crank and the outer end of this arm. This partly remedied the unevenness of motion, but did not entirely correct it. This wheel is shown in Fig. 221. It was patented about 1879-80, one of the claims being the

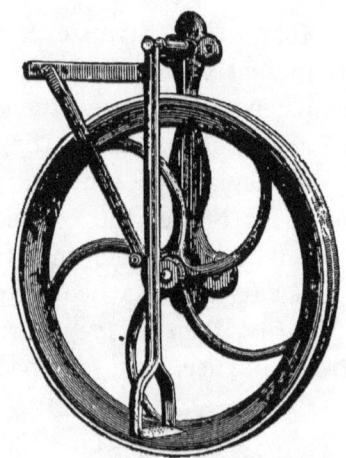

Fig. 221. Hopkins Foot Wheel.

stirrup on the treadle, which prevented the foot from slipping off and gave better control when stopping or starting the wheel. It was also supported by a bracket bolted to the

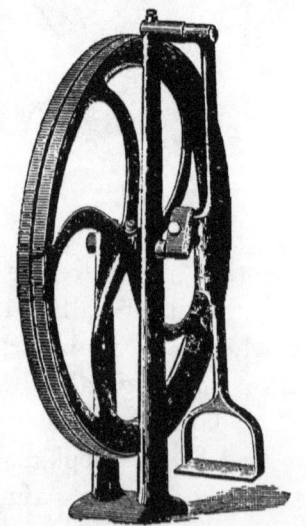

Fig. 222. Webster Foot Wheel.

end of the bench, instead of standing on the floor. Watchmakers' benches at that time had no bottoms, and this arrangement allowed the foot wheel to be moved with the bench and gave increased convenience in sweeping and cleaning under the wheel. The bolts held the wheel securely, while those attached to the floor by screws were constantly getting loose. This wheel was considered a great improvement, and it is still selling.

About 1888 Ambrose Webster re-invented the swing pendulum, which Mr. Purdy had discarded, and not being

Fig. 223. Oliver Foot Wheel with Double Race and Ball Bearings.

so exacting in regard to the evenness of motion he marketed the wheel, which immediately became a great favorite with the trade, Fig. 222, and has been liberally copied.

W. W. Oliver, of Buffalo, N. Y., next obtained patents on a double roller and race, which could be adjusted for wear, made the wheel silent, during rapid motion, and also avoided jerking and back lash at the end of each stroke, Fig. 223.

Hugo Schmidt, predecessor of the Chicago Watch Tool Co., was the first to apply ball bearings to the foot wheel, but made the mistake of selecting a 60-pound wheel for his experiment. He exhibited the new wheel to the trade, and it met with the objection that it "ran too easily, so that it could not be stopped properly." He, therefore, discarded the bearings as worthless. Other manufacturers took up the idea, applied it to 30-pound and 40-pound wheels, and it proved a grand success, so that it is now generally made on all the better wheels.

Fig. 224. Purdy Wheel with Double Pendulum.

About 1898, Frederick Purdy invented a swing treadle foot wheel, with bicycle spokes (to get all the weight in the rim) and two pendulums, carrying the crank race between them. This kept the race perpendicular and gave the swing treadle an even motion, but the wheel was too expensive on account of its bicycle spokes. It is now made with iron spokes and ball bearings and is selling well as a high-class wheel, Fig. 224.

Various modifications have also been made in the pedals, but the accepted usage of the majority has finally declared for a ball bearing, swing pendulum, 40-pound wheel, with stirrup or step and drilled so that it may be bolted to the bottom of the bench. In doing this care should be taken to

Fig. 225. Chicago Watch Tool Co., Wheel with single standard and Crank Pin in Wheel.

use bolts long enough to use check nuts on them, so that the wheel may be removed readily, if necessary, without its getting loose when in action; the practice of bruising the threads on the bolts after getting the nuts in place leads to awkward results when it is desired to remove the wheel, and for this reason it is strongly condemned.

CHAPTER XVI.

THE DEVELOPMENT OF THE WATCHMAKER'S BENCH.

From the "watchmaker's board," as shown in Fig. 219, or even the English bench of to-day, as shown in Fig. 226, to the modern American bench is a far cry. Previous to 1870 the form of bench shown in Fig. 226 had many examples in this country. Thence forward they became more elaborate; but up to 1881 there were no factory-made benches in the United States. It was customary for the watchmaker to go to a cabinetmaker of his acquaintance and order a bench which was then made by hand from drawings and measurements given by the purchaser and modified by the cabinetmaker according to his skill and the price to be paid. Sometimes these benches were very elaborately made from solid, fine woods, paneled all over and French polished; as they had no bottoms, the ends and tops were heavy, and the drawers were generally paneled fronts. More frequently the cabinetmaker was called into a store where a watchmaker's bench was already located and told to "make one like that." He generally tried to improve on it and sometimes succeeded.

In 1882, Hans Jessen and John Rosberg had established a wood-working factory under the name of Jessen & Rosberg, in Chicago, and J. H. Purdy gave them an order for benches; these had no bottoms, but were full paneled, with moulded drawer fronts, chalk box and aprons; they were well made and sold readily, as it was a great convenience to be able to buy a bench when you bought your lathe, and the firm soon did a large business in them. The bottom was soon added, as the bench could then be made stronger and lighter, and it was more convenient to have the foot wheel attached to the bench, Fig. 227.

In 1885, E. Schwarz, then a watchmaker for J. H. Purdy, complained of the constant loss of his tools, and asked Mr.

Fig. 226. English Lathe and Bench.

Purdy if a roll-top bench could not be made, so that it could be readily locked up when leaving work. Mr. Jessen was called in and given the problem, which he soon solved satisfactorily, and thus originated the modern roll-top bench in use to-day. The first roll-top bench had the foot wheel enclosed, which still further strengthened the construction at that end, and thoroughly protected the clothing of the operator. It also rendered it easier to keep clean, as there was no necessity of brushing behind the foot wheel every day when sweeping and dusting the shop. It was afterwards found necessary to increase the height of the curtain ends when closed, so as to fully clear the countershaft with speed wheel and also the lathe without moving either. Fig. 228 shows one of these benches with the form of foot wheel in use at that time.

Fig. 227. Flat Top Bench with Bottom.

As the foundation is to the superstructure of a building, so is the bench to a complete watchmaking outfit. With a first-class lathe and foot wheel, and a poor, shaky, vibrating bench, no first-class work can be performed. For this reason we believe that too much care cannot be bestowed on the choice of a bench. In selecting a bench, be sure to purchase from some large and reliable concern, where you are apt to get one which has been thoroughly seasoned. See that it is well put together and built from heavy substantial lumber. The panels should be glued up from crossed veneers, so that they will stay straight and not shrink and swell with changes of weather. As to the kind of wood, we prefer a bench with the top made from birch or maple, as the grain of the wood is close and the color finished is light, so that it is easier to distinguish small screws and parts than if the top were made of dark wood.

The arrangement of drawers, the boxing in of the foot wheel, the curtain top and other details must be left to the individual taste of the workman, but our choice would be a bench without a curtain top and one having many shallow drawers rather than one which has a few deep ones. Our reason for this choice is that we should not pile tools or attachments one upon another, as in so doing they will more or less mar or damage each other, which must be guarded against, and all the fine tools and attachments must be handled with the same care and consideration that we would give to the finest watch.

While the curtain topped bench, when new, has a tidy and neat appearance, it has its drawbacks as well as its advantages. As the bench grows old the curtain does not always work freely, and the curtain also acts as a receptacle for dirt and dust, so that in a short time you find that every time you close the top, dust is sifted down upon your work on the bench. When this happens the curtain should be taken out and thoroughly cleaned. This ought not to be necessary more than four times a year, unless working in an exceedingly dusty place. In many of these benches the countershaft and some of the lathe attachments have to be removed or folded down before closing the bench for the night, and this point should be carefully looked to before buying the bench, as makers will frequently try to reduce the size of the curtain top in order to reduce the cost and secure a lower selling price. With a flat topped bench the watchmaker acquires the habit of cleaning away his work each evening, but with the curtain top he is inclined to leave everything just where he dropped it and therefore his bench top is liable to be the receptacle for all kinds of odds and ends. Your bench top should be kept free from all tools and attachments except those in actual use on the job you are working on, or excepting, perhaps, the modern staking tool and alcohol lamp and cup.

Fig. 228. Roll Top Bench, closed.

When a job of lathe work is completed, always clean off any turnings, filings or dirt, so it will not get into the watch; also put away all tools and attachments in their respective places, and then, should you need any of them again it will be much easier to get them from their proper place than to look over a lot of tools left on the bench. Have a place for everything and see that everything is in its place.

Cultivate this habit at the start and it will be a source of considerable satisfaction to you to put your hands on a tool, attachment or article the minute you want it.

The watchmaker who cultivates the habit of order and neatness will always be pointed out and selected in preference to one who is careless and untidy. Those who are lacking in this respect should begin its cultivation at once and apply it to every detail of both the tools and work.

The drawers should be partitioned off lengthwise and crosswise into small compartments for the reception of the various small tools, sufficiently large that they will not lie one on top of another, keeping your tweezers in one compartment, broaches in another, small files in another, screw drivers, drills, taps, dies and the various other tools each in their respective divisions. Chuck blocks should be made to fit the drawers of the bench, having a hole drilled clear through the block for each chuck. They may be of soft wood, and soaked in oil, then dried. They should fit loosely, so that they may be lifted out and the drawers cleaned readily. In this way any dirt falling into the holes for the chucks will drop through into the drawer bottom and not foul the chuck.

The bench should be at least 40 inches high; from 40 to 44 inches long, and from 20 to 24 inches wide. A stool should be selected which is adjustable for height, and should be so adjusted that the workman does not bend over the bench. Always select a bench having a bottom securely fastened to it. Some makers, in order to cheapen their benches, make them without bottoms and they rest solely upon the back and side partitions. This is a faulty construction, and such benches are liable to tremble and shake when the speed is considerable and the foot wheel heavy. Many watchmakers prefer casters on their benches so that they may be readily removed when sweeping. Our choice is a bench without casters, carefully leveled, and then fastened to the floor with two or three strong screws. With such a bench you will avoid the nuisance of small objects rolling under it when dropped upon the floor, and as no dirt can get under it, there is no necessity of moving it when sweeping.

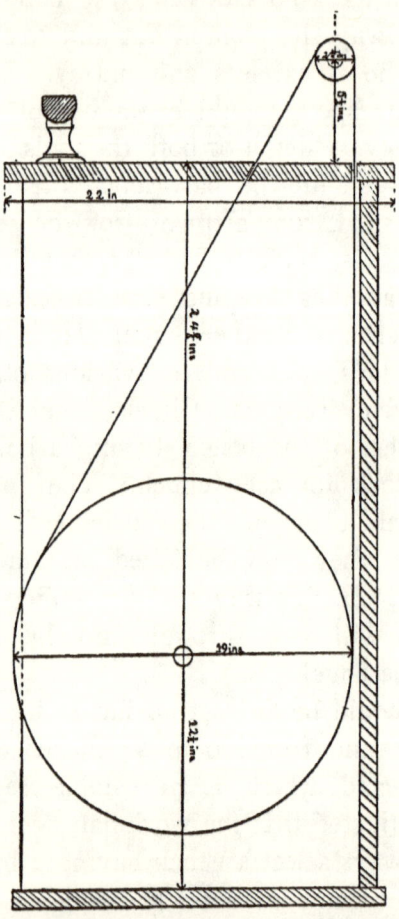

Fig. 229. Section of Bench showing proper arangement of Belt.

To prevent articles from falling off the bench, a strip extending one and one-half inches above the top, should be placed around the ends and back, while along the front edge a strip with rounded edges should be fastened so as to project above the top three-sixteenths of an inch, leaving an opening at one end through which to brush the dirt.

In selecting a bench avoid those whose tops are varnished or finished with shellac, but rather select one with an oil finish top, as alcohol will ruin the appearance of varnish whenever it comes in contact with it. With an oil top bench you can clean up often with soap and water without impairing its finish in the slightest degree.

In setting up a new bench and lathe before you bore any holes in the bench, place your foot wheel and countershaft in their relative positions which you expect them to occupy. If your foot wheel is twenty inches in diameter and your bench is twenty-four inches deep, bring the front edge of your foot wheel to within two inches of the front of your bench. Place your countershaft at the back of your bench so that the pulley will allow the belt to pass through the top one-half inch from the back of the bench. Now draw a diagram, like Fig. 229, on a scale of one inch to the foot, measuring carefully the height and width of your bench, the diameter of your foot wheel, height of your countershaft from top of bench, and the diameter of pulley on the countershaft. Transfer these measurements, carefully reduced, to your drawing. Draw lines representing the belt passing around the wheel and pulley. This will show you where to bore the holes in the top of the bench and also their angle.

See if this line would cut through the base of the countershaft, should it have one. If it does, shift the position of your foot wheel toward the back, until the belt will clear the base of the countershaft. Let the front edge of the bench be the base from which all measurements are made. When you have carefully corrected your drawing, so that the belt clears the base of the countershaft, transfer your measurements in feet and inches to the top of your bench, locating the position of your belt holes and countershaft. Mark these carefully with your pencil. Also locate the exact position of your foot wheel, by marking the screw holes. Never depend upon screws to hold your foot wheel in place, as they will almost invariably work loose, causing great annoyance. Select bolts long enough to pass through the bottom of the bench and base of foot wheel, countersinking for the bolts, so the heads do not protrude on the bottom.

Place the foot wheel in position, bolting it firmly to the bottom. Now make the holes for the belt, fastening the countershaft in such a position that the belt runs free.

In completing this study of the lathe and its accessories we desire to say that no credit is claimed for originality of the contents of this volume. From the circumstances of the case it had of necessity to be merely a compilation, as lathe practice is a growth, one man contributing an idea here, another there, and a third, still another. Under such circumstances all that could be done was to select the vital portions of that generally distributed knowledge and arrange them in such order that, when studied consecutively, they should contribute to a clear understanding of the limitations and capabilities of the American watchmaker's lathe. This knowledge and the ideas advanced have come from so many sources as to make proper credit to individuals impossible, and all that can be done, therefore, is to state that this volume is merely an attempt to record in serviceable form the general understanding of matters pertaining to the tools of the trade. For this reason it has been deemed better to confine the attention solely to the tools, rather than to give the individual methods of the writer in handling them, trusting that if the student understands the proper limitations of his instruments he will quickly develop the right methods of use, according to his surroundings and the work to be done. Study and practice will produce skill; skill and speed make proficiency.

INDEX.

A

Angle of Clearance . . . . .
. . 145, 149, 168, 203, 205. 208
" Cutting Edge . 149, 176
Annealing 159
Approximation of Cycloid
Curves 210
Arbor Chuck 106
Auxilliary Chucks 74

B

Back Rest 237
Balance Chuck 100, 101
Ball Bearing Lathes . . 46. 47
Ballou, Geo. F. 21, 22
" Whitcomb & Co., . . 22
Bearings Ball 46, 47
" Spindle . . . . . .
34, 35, 37, 41, 42, 44, 47, 49
Belts 243
" to Arrange, ... 260
Bench Flat Top 256
" English 255
" Roll Top 258
Bezel Chuck Snyder 85
Boiling-Out Pan 97
Brasses, Cement 90
Buff Chuck 105

C

Caliper, Jewelling 137
Carborundum 199
Cementing 88, 97
" Brasses 90
" Watchmakers' . . 89
Center Female 82
" Fitting of 83, 129
" Male 82
" Pump 78
" Square Back 131

Centering on Face Plate . 79, 80
Center Holes of Milling
Cutters 208
Chicago Watch Tool Co., . . 253
Chuck, Arbor 106
" Auxilliary 74
" Balance 100, 101
" Bezel 85
" Buff 105
" Cement . . 90, 91, 93
" Conoidal 60
" Construction of . 51, 87
" Crown 73, 86
" Cylinder 101
" Early vs. Modern . . 67
" European vs. American
. . , . . 38, 39. 40
" Flat Faced 58
" Four-Jawed 84
" Gem 86
" Jewelling . . . 74, 102
" Johanson 87
" Jumbo 100
" Lines of Force in . . 52
" Manufacture of . . 60
" Origin of 18, 55
" Pivot Drill . . . , 132
" Proper Fitting of 38, 40
" Scholer 87
" Screw 90
" Screw Finishing . . 102
" Sizes of 64
" Snyder 85
" Springing of . . 53, 57
" Step . . . . . , . . 72
" Stone Setting . . . 105
" Taper 103
" Testing of 68
" Threads of 40
" Wheel 75
" Wood 104
Construction of Chucks . 51, 87

263

C

Construction of Jewelling Tail Stock 139
" of Lathe . . 25, 50
Control of Power 247
Counterbores ... 171, 172, 214
Countershafts 244
Cutters, Clearance of . 145, 203
" Fly 205
" Hardening 154
" Making 147
" Milling 208
" Rake of 151, 203
" Slide Rest 151
" Tempering 161
" Shapes of Milling 213, 215
" Tool for Forming . 210
" Wheels, to make . . 208
Cutting Pinions with Straddle Mills 209
" Wheels 227
Cylinder Chuck 101

D

Dead Center Lathe 13
Diamantine 200
Diamond Powder ... 198
Dividing Head, to make . . 224
Dog Face Plate 82
Dracip Lathe 16, 17, 18
Drill Chucks, Pivot 132
Drilling Rest 131
" with Tail Stock 131, 133
Drills, Making 147, 164
" Pivot 168
" Sharpening ..., 165
" Socket 130, 172
Duplicate Spindles for Tail Stock 128

E

Egyptian Lathe 9
English Lathe, Early ... 10
" Mandrel 27

F

Face Plate, Dog 82
" Jaws of 78
" Universal ... 78
Fiddle Bow Lathe 12

Fitting of Centers ... 83, 129
" of Milling Cutters . 208
" of Shoe ..... , . 111
" of Slide Rest ... 115
" of Tail Stock Spindle 128
" of Tapers 83, 129
Fly Cutters 205
" to make ... 205
Foot Wheels 248, 253
Force, Lines of, in Chuck . 51

G

Gem Chuck 86
Grinding 107
" Faces of Pallets . 234
" with Pivot Polisher 195

H

Half Open Tail Stock ... 135
Hand Rest 109
Hardening of Steel 154
Hardinge Lathe 46
" Pivot Polisher . 194
Head Stock, Section of 35, 45, 46, 47
" Universal 77
Hollow Spindle, Origin of . 18
Hopkins, C. 249
" Pivot Polisher . . 189
" Slide Rest 120
" Watch Tool Co . 22
Howard, E. 137

I

Idle Pulleys 242
Index Plates 217
" " Testing ... 222
Indices Table of 226

J

Jacot Lathe 14
Jessen, Hans 254
" & Rosberg 254
Jewelling Caliper 137
" Chucks ... 74, 102
Johanson's Crown Chucks . 87

K

Kidder & Adams 20, 21

L

Laps 102, 108, 193, 199
Lapping Pallets 234
Latch for Index Plates . 219, 221
Lathe Ball Bearing . . . 46, 47
" Construction of . 25, 37, 50
" Dead Center 13
" Dracip . . . 16, 17, 18
" Early English 10
" Egyptian 9
" Engine 25, 26, 27
" Fiddle Bow 12
" Geneva 29, 32, 33
" Hardinge 44
" Jacot 14
" Kidder & Adams . 20, 21
" Modern German . . . 248
" Names of Parts 24
" Original Moseley 19, 20, 22, 24
" Prehistoric 8
" Rivett 44
" Section of . 31, 33, 44, 46, 47
" Sizes of 24, 43
" Spindles 34, 35,
   36, 37, 40, 41, 42, 44, 46, 47, 49
" Stark 21
" Universal 15
" Webster, Original . 20, 21
" Wax 89
" Webster-Whitcomb 22, 31

M

Making Cutters and Drills . 147
Mandrel, English 27
Milling Cutters 208
"   Fitting of . . 208
"   Shapes of 213, 215
Milling with Pivot Polisher 196
Moseley, Chas. S. . . . 18, 55, 80
"   Pivot Polisher . . 189
"   Slide Rest 116

O

Oil Stop, to Turn 185
Oliver, W. W. . . . . , 251

P

Pallets, to grind 234
Pan, Boiling Out 97
Parts of Lathe, Names of . 24
Pinion Cutters 209
Pivot Drills 169

Pivot Polisher 188
"   Hardinge . . 194
"   Hopkins . . 189
"   Moseley . . . 189
"   Rivett . . . 191
"   Webster-Whitcomb . . 193
"   Grinding with 196
"   Limitations of 197
"   Milling with 196
Polishing Pivots 186, 192
Power, Control of 247
Prehistoric Lathe 8
Pulleys, Idle 242
Purdy, Frederick 252
"   J. H. 249, 254

Q

Quill 125

R

Reamers 173
Rest, Drilling 131
"   Hand 109
"   Slide 132
"   T 109
Rivett Lathe 44
"   Pivot Polisher . . . 191
"   Slide Rest . . . 122, 124
Rosberg, John 254
Rounding-up Tool 229
"   "   to Use . 231, 235

S

Section of Engine Lathe . . 26
"   "   Watchmakers' Lathe 31, 33
"   "   Headstocks 24, 45, 46, 47
"   "   Slide Rest 118, 120, 122, 123
Schmidt, Hugo 251
Scholer Chuck 87
Screw Finishing Chuck . . 102
"   Tailstock 135
Sizes of Chucks 64, 76
Sharpening Drills 168
Sherwood 137
Shoe, Fitting of 107
Slide Rest 132
"   Fitting of 115
"   Hopkins . . 120, 121
"   Moseley 116

S

Slice Rest, Rivett	122, 124
" Sections of	118, 120, 122, 123
" Springing of	113
" Webster · Whitcomb	117
Socket, Drill	130, 172
Softening Steel	159
Spindle Bearings	34, 35, 37, 41, 42, 44, 46, 47, 49
" Hollow, Origin of	18
" Push	127
Spindles, Duplicate	129
Springing of Slide Rest	113
" " Spindles	36, 40, 41
Square Back Center	131
Stark, John	21
Steady Rest	237
Steel, Hardening of	154
Step Chucks	72, 74, 76
Stepping Device	72
Stone-Setting Chuck	105
Straddle Milling	209
Swing Tailstock	137
" " Clement	143
" " Hopkins	142
" " Moseley	141

T

Table of Indices	226
Tail Stocks	126
" " Push Spindle	127
Tail Stock as stop or Gauge	133
" " Half Open	135
" " Screw	134
" " Swing	137
" " " Clement	143
" " " Hopkins	142
" " " Moseley	141
" " Use of	144
" " Traverse Spindle	136
Taper Chuck	103
Tapers, see Centers	
" Fitting of	129
Tempering Cutters	161
" Steel	161
Testing Chucks	68
" Index Plates	223
Threads of Chucks	39, 40

Tool for Forming Cutters	210
" Jacot	14
Tools Angle of Cutting Edge	176
Traverse Spindle Tail Stock	136
T Rest	109
Triangle of Forces Applied to Lathe	28
Turning Balance Staffs	180
" Thin Work	237
" Oil Stops	185
" With Graver and Slide Rest	175
Turns	13

U

Universal Lathe	15
" Face Plate	78
" Head	77

V

Vienna Lime	200

W

Watchmakers' Cement	89
" Lathe Wax	89
Webster, Ambrose	20, 80, 251
" Whitcomb Pivot Polisher	193
" Slide Rest	117, 119
Wheel Chucks	75
" Cutter, Method of Attaching	227
" Cutting	216
" " Attachment, Early	217
" " Attachment, Hopkins	218
" " Attachment, Moseley	218
" " Attachment, Rivett	222
" " Attachment, Webster-Whitcomb	220
" " Engine	216
Wheels, Foot	248, 253
" to Cut	227
Whitcomb, John E.	21
Wood, Chuck	104

www.ingramcontent.com/pod-product-compliance
Lightning Source LLC
Chambersburg PA
CBHW032107220426
43664CB00008B/1160